SETH STEWART

From the stages of Broadway to the depths of the jungle

FOLLOW YOUR VISION
LIVE YOUR TRUTH

A seeker's journey to make sense of life and find oneness with the universe.

COPYRIGHT

Follow Your Vision, Live Your Truth

Copyright ©2025 Seth Stewart

All rights reserved. No part of this book may be reproduced, distributed, or transmitted in any form or by any electronic or mechanical means, including photocopying, recording, or by any information storage and retrieval system, without prior written permission from the author or editor.

Book design by:

Daniel Eyenegho

(@twenty4hrdesign)

ISBN: 979-8-9994774-0-8

Table of Contents

COPYRIGHT .... *II*
DEDICATION .... *IV*
INTRODUCTION *1*
MY STORY *5*
- Childhood *5*
- Meditation and Reese's *13*
- Who Am I? *15*
- Madonna *21*
- Broadway *24*
- Wake Up *27*
- In the Heights *28*
- Entrepreneurship *30*

THE CALLING *33*
- The First Call *33*
- Earth Mother, Talk to Me *34*
- Energetic Baseline *37*
- The Second Call *39*
- Tracker *40*

REINTEGRATION *45*
- Returning to Society *45*
- Grandpa Speaks Through Me *47*
- New Beginnings *50*
- First Ayahuasca Ceremony *51*
- Reintegration *54*

- What Comes Next *55*
- Hamilton *56*
- Broadway — One Last Time *58*
- Let's Go to the Woods *62*

DOWNLOADS *67*
- Finding My Tribe *67*
- The Return... *74*
- Downloads... *75*
- Return to Mama Aya... *76*
- I Became A Tiger *79*
- Sirius B *83*
- The Tree of Life *84*
- Light At The End of The Tunnel............................... *85*
- My Exit *88*

GOD IN DIMENSIONALITY... *93*
- Dimensions... *93*
- Viewing Dimensions Like a Radio............................. *96*
- Viewing Dimensions Like Spheres *96*
- Gatekeepers *96*
- Viewing Timelines *97*
- God as a Mandala.. *98*
- Fractals *99*
- The Trinity Head *100*

FINDING HOME *103*
- Finding Home *103*
- Power Animals *105*

- The Land 106
- Between Two Worlds 109
- Working Hard 111
- Mother Bear 113
- My Team 115

GALACTIC MEMORY 119
- ET Ant Visit 119
- Sedona 120
- Remembering Egypt 121
- Egypt Infiltrated 124
- Galactic Memory 126
- Remembering Lemuria 127
- Galactic History 131
- Spiritual War 135
- Inverted Matrix 136
- Energy As A Food Source 138
- See? The War 141

HIGHER SELF UPGRADES 143
- Upgrades 143
- Higher Realms 144
- Higher Selves Transmission 148
- I'm a Dragon 155
- More Dragons 157
- The Great Transit 157

CHRISTOS COLLECTIVE 159
- Angel Work 159

- My Friend on the Other Side 160
- Mission 162
- Meeting a Council — Mission Debrief 166
- We Are Angels 167
- Christos Energy 170
- Behold, I Am Within You 172
- Show People What We Are 173

THE SHIFT 177
- The Pandemic 177
- Void of Light 178
- Darkness 179
- Programming / False Matrix 182
- Darkness Sentinels 184
- AI 185
- AI Vision 188
- Organic Source Matrix 191
- Grounding 192
- Ayahuasca — Lost Mind 193
- Healing 199
- Shaman / False Healers 201
- Return to the Land 204
- Fairies? For Real? 206
- Freedom Codes 209
- I Wasn't Supposed to Be Here 211
- Spectrum 217
- Choice 218
- Shift 222
- Soul Braiding 228

WORKING SPIRITUAL TOOLS 229
- Working with Patients 229
- Demons 232
- Demon of Distraction 234
- Angels 236
- Getting Grounded 237
- Reprogram / Clearing Old Imprints 237
- Awareness Tools 240
- Critical Edge Exercise 241
- Threshold Exercise 242
- Discerning Outside Energies 243
- Working with Light 244
- Entity Removal 246
- Time to Sit Down 247
- Deeper Still — Personal Healing 251
- Pick Up The Pieces 252
- Return to Society For Real This Time 255
- Breathe Reset 256
- New Landtopia 258

HEALING THE MASCULINE 261
- Peace Be the Journey 261
- Healing the Masculine 265
- Accomplishments = Affection 266
- Fear of Commitment 266
- Love Patterns 267
- Survival Mode 270

- How Do We Heal This? *272*
- Relationships *273*
- Masculine / Feminine Separation *275*
- Her *279*
- Heirogamic Union *282*

MISSION WORK *287*
- Remember *287*
- Spiritual Team *288*
- Angel Christ Michael *289*
- Angel Christ Michael Protections *289*
- True Kings *293*

WHERE DO WE GO FROM HERE *297*
- Returning to the True Self *297*
- Steps to Remembering *298*
- Steps to Healing *300*
- Where Do We Go From Here *305*
- What Have I Learned on This Earth? *307*
- Empowering the Future *308*
- Exercise *309*

DEDICATION

This book is dedicated to all the believers; the believers of magic, the believers of the sacred, and the believers who believe in themselves. This book is also dedicated to my family, who have always supported me: my mother, father, sister, uncles, aunties, all my cousins, my soul tribe, teachers, mentors, and friends. You know who you are. I'd also like to thank God, my ancestors, and all the ancients who came before me, laid the path, and left behind tools of wisdom. I vow to do my part.

Hello, God. Do you remember yourself? Do you see yourself? Are you expressing yourself? Are you loving yourself? You are the beginning and the end. You are YOUR expression of God. And the Highest of the High, God Almighty, is trying to learn through you. So, what have you learned? What are you learning, God?

INTRODUCTION

What if I told you all of this is real? That magic is real and all you have to do is believe?

I am Seth Stewart, an eternal being in the human flesh for a limited time only. Jam! I am one of one hundred-plus billion humans to have existed on planet Earth. I'm here to share my story along with spiritual experiences that are a mere sneak peek of a much larger and unfolding picture. I was going to write this book anonymously as I was worried about being judged by family, friends, peers, and even others who haven't met me. It took me many years to move past those fears. And I pray that sharing my story will allow others to be open to new possibilities and be at peace with their own experiences.

This book is about getting back to nature, finding the true self, and staying on the spiritual path no matter what it takes. I will explain the journey of the heart, the alchemy of self, and other experiences I've had so far. To me, life is about understanding ourselves, this universe, God, and all forms of existence. It's about oneness; living in a natural state of *being-ness* to feel *oneness* with all things. The journey back to oneness takes surrender, consistency, and patience. The journey back to oneness within ourselves also involves letting go of parts of the ego to transmute old and dense energies which allows us to remember who we are as humans, where we came from, and why we are here on this planet at this time, in order to evolve into the highest version of ourselves.

I truly believe life on this planet is meant to be amazing! And at the same time, I know it can be "hard to human." Life gets weird, then it gets really weird, then amazing again, and awkward, and continues to be a rollercoaster as it is for all of us on this human journey. But this life is a chance to learn, grow, and evolve as individuals, as a collective, and as a planet. And finding peace in all things is the key to having a more balanced and enjoyable journey. Even though this is my personal journey of trusting my instincts and following my heart, it is a journey I'm sure many takes. I truly believe most people have always had a yearning to understand themselves and life itself.

Since I was eighteen, maybe even younger, life didn't make sense to me. I had a hard time believing in this reality. "What's going on? Why was it so hard to be happy? Why was it so hard to feel free? Why was there so much hate, jealousy, and greed? Why was there so much war? Why does it cost so much just to live as a human on this planet?"

These are some of the questions I'm sure many people have asked themselves at least once in their life. But what is it about humanity that we have yet to evolve to our fullest potential where we can live the lives we choose and, at the same time, live in harmony with each other, with nature, and the cosmos? What are we becoming and how do we want to meet our future? These questions were the catalyst to my search for answers.

I personally always found myself searching for "something," unsure of what that something was. I am an explorer. I need to discover what is "out there," but also within me. It's funny to even say a person has to "find themselves." Where were they?

Why were they lost in the first place? In the past twenty-plus years of searching for that something I couldn't put my finger on but knew it was there, I'd get confirmations. I've always been aware of things outside the five senses. Things would appear and disappear, sometimes with no one else around to validate. But many times, throughout the years, these experiences also happened with others, sometimes my friends, sometimes in larger groups as a whole. Eventually, I found what I didn't know I was looking for.

That something was remembrance of who I am and why I am here. I believe we as humanity are here on planet Earth to remember our true origins, not just on this planet, but also within the larger universal construct. If we were to remember that we are special beings from the stars, blessed with gifts from God, I think our world and the worlds we're connected to would evolve into the beauty and peace that most people could only begin to imagine.

As a seeker of truth and mystery, I can share the truth of these statements without question... "Seek and you shall find. Ask and you shall receive." Magic is found in nature and in the heart.

Finding purpose, truth, meaning, and all things one seeks on their spiritual search come over time with consistency. But a seeker *must* have patience and use their discernment, as the rabbit hole of information, history, and mystery never ends. "Finding yourself" is a "waking up" process. Even if there is a spontaneous awakening, the realization that a person was stuck in a dream or illusion and waking up to the multitude of realities still takes many years to process. Then, each person must decide if they want to follow their spiritual path. **I've realized most people misinterpret a spiritual awakening as an "arrival." I feel as though the spiritual path in life is a continuous spiral of evolution; moments of darkness, surrender, breakthroughs,**

awakening, and even ecstasy. But the journey is not always about "doing." Trust, surrender, and chill is also necessary in evolution. And it's important to remember to always come back to love. For that is where home is. That is where God resides.

This life has been a blessing, one I am truly grateful for. A life in which I try to be fully led by God and lead with a fascination for our beautiful Earth Mother. If I had one wish, it would be that everyone truly had love in their hearts. I believe if we loved ourselves, we could at least respect each other and love the Earth in the highest forms possible. I pray for peace in this world. I pray for love and respect in this world. I pray for you. For you are me, and I am you. We are all connected to each other, the planet, and the cosmos. I love you, my friend. I pray this story connects to your heart.

With that, take what you will and discard the rest. And welcome to the wild and wonderful story that has been my journey so far. Now, let's get weird.

MY STORY

Childhood

Let's take it back, way back. Back into time. One of my earliest memories was a spiritual memory. Around three years old, there was a big thunderstorm that lasted all night. I remember looking at the ceiling lying in bed when all of a sudden, about twenty nails came six inches down through our roof. I screamed and yelled for my mom. She ran downstairs and all I could do was point to the ceiling. She looked up, then looked closer, and then ran to get my father. While this was happening, I knew something was trying to scare me. I couldn't see anything, but I could feel something was there, up in the ceiling near the corner of the room.

My father came down and viewed the situation. He brushed it off as though they were the roofing nails. But I told him and my mother that the nails were too long for regular roofing nails. How would a three-year-old know that? He looked again, then went outside to quickly see if anything had fallen on the roof. Nothing. When he came back inside, he looked at the nails and made sure there were no leaks. Without any major problems, he left it alone and had it fixed a few days later.

That night, I slept in my bed and watched. I wasn't calm, but I wasn't afraid either. It was as if I had knowledge of the boogie man and was just waiting to see what else it was going to do.

That night, nothing else happened. I didn't know it at the time, but that spiritual experience would be the first of many in my life. One which I would never forget. There was also a part of me that somehow remembered choosing my parents before coming in as a baby because I knew they would help me adjust to this world. I don't know how I knew, but I knew.

My parents grew up on opposite sides of the spectrum. My father grew up in the south side of Chicago, being the oldest of nine children to two working-class parents. His mother was a nurse, and his father worked at a foundry and also was a church choir director. Even though I never met my grandfather on my father's side, I developed a spiritual relationship with him, which I'll explain later. Eventually, my grandfather moved his family to rural Ohio in order to give his wife and children a better chance of growing up outside of the city streets of Chicago. However, starting over wasn't easy. The family lived in a two-bedroom trailer for quite some time. And my father had to parent his eight younger brothers and sisters.

My mother grew up in east Ohio to Jewish parents, the youngest of two. Her father owned and operated a jewelry business and her mother was a school teacher. The family lived in a middle to upper class neighborhood. My parents met at Kent State University in the early 1970s. My father was present during the 1970 protests of the Vietnam War at Kent State University and the death of four university students who were shot and killed by the US National Guard. Everyone in that town remembers and commemorates the loss of those four students who were killed by their own government. And since I was a child, it was my first seeding into the reality that the government didn't always have the people's best interest at heart.

Another big lesson as a child was diversity and the complexities of racial dynamics in the world. The town I grew up in was amazing in a lot of ways but also had its growing pains as more racial and gender diversity was coming through from the seventies into the eighties. This was a time when mixed-race couples were almost forbidden. Racial dynamics also showed up in my mother's relationship to her parents. As a white Jewish woman, she was basically disowned for falling in love with and marrying a Black man. My parents were in their early twenties when they married. Her parents stopped helping her in any way and my father was not welcome in her family's home. It wasn't until my older sister was born that my grandparents began to accept our family into their lives. My parents endured their young adult life to give my sister and eventually give me a chance to grow up in a diverse world.

Growing up mixed race, I had to learn how to be a chameleon. I "fit in," but not completely. I had to navigate different cultural norms because it can feel as though you're never fully accepted. I always lived between two worlds, which forced me to see both sides of every story, a paradigm that has remained the centerpiece for my life into adulthood. The same went for playing sports and being a dancer; my football friends thought a boy dancing was kind of weird and my dance teachers never loved the idea of me getting hurt, let alone coming into class with black eyes, or smelling like a locker room right after a football practice. These experiences always left me feeling *in between* and subconsciously feeling on an island a lot of times.

Growing up, I was a *very* hyperactive kid. I was diagnosed with ADHD as doctors began seeing a rise in this new disorder in the early eighties. I remember a story of my parents taking me to our family doctor, who told them to put me in as many activities as possible to help me focus and exert energy. I'm so thankful he didn't suggest medications and that my family didn't push for them either. I was four years old. I know a part of me would have felt out of touch and I wouldn't be the same person. It's just something I always knew.

So, at four years old, my family put me into wrestling, which I loved and hated at the same time. But it gave me the discipline and focus I needed. I wrestled for eight years and also played football for twelve years, which was my favorite sport. Some of my closest friends to this day are the guys I played with from peewee league through high school. There was a bigger sense of brotherhood that I realized I always appreciated in team sports; people from different demographics coming together to accomplish one particular goal, everyone focused until they reached it. It was the potential to put all differences aside and just "win." It created a community which I realized later in life is what I needed.

Music was also a huge part of my family growing up. Everyone in my family was usually singing and dancing. My uncle and sister would put on talent shows for the family, sometimes making me their extra character or "stand in." My family inspired me. My sister was in the choir, and I remember her being a great singer. I sang in the choirs from elementary school all the way through high school. Luckily, my sister went to the same school before me, setting a record of the "talented and well-behaved student" until I showed up!

Dance was always a part of my life. The best thing about the late eighties and early nineties, is everyone was dancing; everyone! People were dancing on TV in music videos, in films, at parties, and family gatherings. It was a part of the culture. It was all about fun and who could get loose on the dance floor! After a few years of dancing for fun and in front of audiences, I realized dance was my thing. By age eight, I started going to dance class. I was one of maybe two male dancers at that time, which brought its own set of problems and benefits. I began going to different studios throughout the years, usually thirty to forty-five minutes away from where we lived just to get better training. And by age ten, I was training and competing.

The dance competition circuit was a world of big hair and sequined costumes! Dance competitions could become intense! When I mean intense, I mean students, teachers, and parents could end up arguing and screaming at each other or the judges. That's just how it was back then, and other teams and parents welcomed the competition! People came to win! And it made everyone work harder to become the best they could be for themselves and their team.

I believe that a competitive attitude, most importantly a healthy one, is truly beneficial in most areas in a person's life. It allows them to understand what discipline means and gives them a determination to strive for more in life. However, like anything in sports and the performing arts, perfectionism can take over and potentially become detrimental to a person's way of thinking and being. I was one of those people. Those early years formed me into a person that was always learning, having to work well with others, being disciplined and goal oriented, and having passion. Looking back, I don't know how my parents kept it all together with their work schedules and the busy schedules of my sister and me. I feel very lucky.

Fast forward to my early teenage years: My family traveled a lot driving all over the country for dance competitions. Every summer, we would drive to visit my uncle who lived in New York City. Going to New York at such a young age opened my eyes to everything. I loved that city from the moment I crossed the George Washington Bridge! I was fascinated from hearing the salsa and bachata music blasting from apartment windows, seeing drag queens in full dress and make-up walking through Times Square, the sounds of the taxis, the rumbling of the subways, the smoke from the stacks, the lights of the city, the Broadway shows…I wanted it all! I wanted all the weird, all the strange, all the exciting things that New York had to offer. I was in love! It felt like home, a place where a person goes to be free.

Each year, as I experienced more of New York and other places in the country, I was fascinated by how small-minded people were. In Ohio, most people never left or traveled. Sometimes when I returned, it felt like stepping back in time. I would share my stories and for them, nothing had changed. Unbeknownst to them, they weren't experiencing what was out in the world. But I also noticed that in New York, most people didn't leave their neighborhood or travel either. And their way of thinking and living was also limited. I knew people in both places that were completely fine with staying in one place. But they were missing out on a world of experience! And I finally began to understand, people didn't know what they didn't know. Living a simple life is one thing. And in fact, I think it's beautiful. But most people do not want to know or expand past their comfort zones. Our comfort zones can actually be the boxes that keep us prisoners to ourselves and others. People can't see that their thoughts and beliefs are mostly what their parents and towns gave them. The comfort zones and small-mindedness are what have kept individuals, communities, and society as a whole, in a loop. I started to notice these loops of belief and realized they are the traps. More on this later.

These earlier years of living between many worlds taught me many things. Most importantly, how to be very comfortable with myself regardless of what people say. I got picked on all the time…and I mean, all the time. I was made fun of for my race and was called gay because I liked to dance and perform.

You name it, I dealt with it repeatedly for years. But I was also a fighter. I didn't always win my fights, but I definitely punched a few people in the mouth for constantly making fun of me. I was more emotional about someone else being picked on than I was for myself. Because I knew how hate reached the heart and isolated a person. Don't get me wrong, I made fun of people too. I was a kid, and it's not something I'm proud of either. But it happens in childhood, and it doesn't feel good to anyone. The only reason it stopped bothering me was after something one of my favorite coaches told me.

"Seth, when someone makes fun of you or pushes you down, you have to be smarter than them. Always remember, short memory, thick skin."

Short memory, thick skin. This means when someone makes fun of you or something gets you down, don't allow it to stay in your memory bank. In order to not let it affect you, have a thicker skin to negative words and don't take it personally. I think this saying has saved me from a lot of trouble throughout the years. It's no coincidence that it came from a Black man who I viewed as another father figure. He and my father have the same build, same skin tone, and the same amount of resilience. It's the same message that many men of color have had to hear in one form or another for decades, if not centuries. I think it could be useful for everyone, though. Because sometimes in this crazy human experience, it's healthy to acknowledge your emotions to know what you're feeling. But sometimes it's also important to remember, "short memory, thick skin." It's a saying and a tool that could be the only thing to keep you going sometimes.

By sixteen, I was getting really good at dance. I was training at least twenty hours a week, traveling to take master classes and learning from some of the best. I was in it! And one night a performance I will never forget changed my life. My family surprised me with tickets to see the Alvin Ailey company while they were on tour in Cleveland. I had known of Alvin Ailey from my uncle. He got me a book on Alvin and what it took to have one of the first all-black dance companies in the world. He was built like a football player and danced powerfully and gracefully. He had passed away many years prior. But his legacy lived on in the company. That night, we sat in the house right orchestra about halfway from the stage. I will never forget the music and the movement of the dancers. I had never seen such elegance, power, and grace in dancers before! By the time the group performed *Revelations,* a company repertoire piece, I was crying. I finally knew exactly what I wanted. I wanted to be them, as good as them. I wanted *that*! I didn't know what it was going to take, but I was willing to do anything to get that good.

Lucky for me, Alvin Ailey had a BFA dance program with Fordham University in New York. I had two years of training to try and make it into the school. I had to finally listen to my dance teachers, bite the bullet, and take more ballet classes. I gave up some competition and some choir in order to train at a conservatory the last two years of high school. I also had to get my grades up, like way up. I was smoking so much weed freshman and sophomore years, I almost wasn't eligible to play sports, let alone save an overall GPA throughout high school. I'm not proud of it, but I smoked a lot of weed in those years, and it was obvious to parents and teachers. To me, it was better than getting drunk, which is what a lot of kids did. But I somehow stayed on top of things, usually. And now, it was all going to have to change.

I cut down on smoking and started to work harder. I would work during lunch periods to study and finish homework. With ADHD, some subjects were easier for me to read on my own. I would study every chance I had between choir, football practice, and dance class five nights a week. I moved a lot and still don't know how I did it all. But it was worth it.

Two years later, after visiting and applying to only three colleges, I eventually was accepted into the BFA at Ailey-Fordham. I was excited, but I knew everything was going to change. I was going to miss my family, my friends, my girlfriend, my teachers, and my coaches, who all supported me. They were my foundation, and they believed in my crazy dream. They were home. And I was going to miss them. But I had to represent. And I had to make my dreams come true for me and them.

Meditation and Reese's

Two weeks after graduation, I left my hometown and was working at the Hershey theme park in Pennsylvania dancing in a show six days a week. I lived in an apartment complex that was next to the Reese's candy factory. Every night and every morning, the entire neighborhood smelled of chocolate and peanut butter! Not bad for a first apartment. I had a great apartment and my first professional job where I was making a living for myself through performing. I was paying rent, taking care of myself, and slowly becoming an adult.

It was this summer that I also began reading more. I noticed I really liked reading when I got to choose the subject. That summer, I was stuck on two topics of erotic art and meditation. I was really into pin-up girls, the culture of bondage, and overall erotic art and history. I don't exactly remember what triggered it. But looking back, I wanted to understand what we as humans find beautiful. And why do we think of something as beautiful? The truth that I found is that the idea of beauty and erotic art comes from some twisted places. I realized eroticism, like most things, is a spectrum. Some of it is dark and twisted. And some of it is beautiful and liberating. That was the furthest conclusion that I wanted to find.

When it came to learning about meditation, I bounced between two books I couldn't get enough of. The first book was *Meditation* by Osho. And the other book was *Autobiography of a Yogi*, by Paramahansa Yogananda. I was reading about amazing Yogi's that could levitate or completely leave their physical body. They could heal themselves and others or go to astral planes of existence. Many nights, I would meditate for hours on my bedroom floor. And within a few weeks, I found myself slowly separating from my body when in meditation. At one point, I remember leaving my body, floating up, and looking down at my body on the bedroom floor, with a cord attached between the two bodies. It was wild and exciting to me! But that first experience I became scared and ended up crashing back down into my body. "What the fuck was that?" I thought. I didn't fully understand. But it was working, and I would continue to try; some nights being successful, other nights, not so much.

Throughout those months, I felt calmer. I was beginning to tap into a realm outside of the body, sometimes traveling to places I didn't understand. But mostly, it was about quieting the mind into a place of no thought. There is a lot of freedom in that space. A freedom from overthinking, worries, and unnecessary emotions that sometimes cloud the mind. That freedom created a peace for me, a peace I had never felt before in that way. So many nights after the show, I would eat, shower, and get to meditation as soon as I could. It was a practice I maintained for years to come.

By mid-summer, I was having experiences I couldn't explain to others. So, I kept it quiet and just focused on performing. One show in particular, I was dancing with my partner in a number we had performed countless times. In turning her, I caught an elbow in the face, right between the eyes. And trust me, I had been hit harder. I had three previous concussions to prove it. But this one was different. I remember seeing the lights go blurry, and thought, "Oh, shit." I don't even remember if I finished the show. And in fact, I lost track of time.

For a couple of weeks, I lost partial memory. I could remember some things, but not other things, like people's names. The rest of the summer I had to go to cognitive therapy, playing children's games and memory games to get better. It was not fun and even somewhat slightly embarrassing. I don't even think I finished the rest of the show that summer. I would sleep a lot during the day, go to therapy and physical therapy, and at night, I continued meditating. I think the combination of the cognitive therapy, plus the nightly meditation helped me heal and brought me back to my normal self-quicker. By the end of summer, as I finally felt better, it was already time to leave for New York and start school.

Who Am I?

I was eighteen years old, living in New York City and going to college. I was training every day at the Alvin Ailey School dancing with the best of the best modern dancers in the country; all from different cities, different racial and economic backgrounds, all in one place, sweating, bleeding, and training their asses off to become the best dancers they could. In those studios, with those African drums, the diversity, and everyone raising the bar, I was in my new home.

My freshman year I would explore all over the city any chance I had. Harlem was my favorite though. Harlem was like my heart. It held jewels of culture from the food, the music, and fashion if you knew how to find them. I would walk 125th Street, always seeing what the vendors had to offer. One vendor, by the name of RA, used to sell DVDs. He had a collection of dubbed DVDs ranging from subjects on spirituality, aliens, religion, black history, galactic history, you name it.

I started buying one or two DVDs at a time, coming back up to Harlem for more when I was done. The information contained in those DVDs was mind blowing, almost hard to believe. Some of it seemed a little conspiracy theory-ish. But most of the information in the documentaries, especially those pertaining to UFOs, aliens, or space programs, came directly from astronauts or people inside the space programs, and retired government agents. When it came to the spiritual or religious histories, there were always some physical remnants in ancient buildings and objects that were buried in the sand for hundreds of thousands of years. To me, there was proof of ancient history, the true history of the Earth and beyond.

For a year straight, I probably purchased twenty to thirty DVDs. Sometimes I would buy doubles or triples and send them back to my friends in Ohio. This was my first dive into the rabbit hole, and I was consumed. After a year of intense research, I had to take a break from it all. I realized later; I wasn't meant to understand it all at that time; it was only a seeding. The ideas needed water to be absorbed by the sponge of my mind. And that integration would take a few years.

By sophomore year, I knew things were changing. I'd had enough of school. I was rarely showing up for classes and became depressed. I remember being so frustrated with history and art history after researching all that I had discovered, I felt like I was going to explode! The information felt one sided as I was learning one version of history told from an approved academic perspective. And on the other hand, I was getting a totally different version of history from the DVDs and the books I was getting on my own. Something wasn't matching up. In dance, I still loved my training. But we weren't allowed to train at any other studios with different teachers. We weren't even allowed to audition for shows or anything outside of the school. I didn't like being told what I could and could not do, especially when I was on partial scholarship and paying for the rest of school myself. I eventually stopped showing up to almost all of my classes. I kept exploring the city, partying a lot more, and only returned to the dorm room to shower and sleep.

Eventually, I had a breakdown. I missed my ex-girlfriend, hated school, hated the dorms, and had a week where I just lost it. One day in my dorm room, I threw my desk chair at the window in frustration. The chair didn't go through the window, but I guess it scared my roommates. I only remember waking up the next morning to my father and the dean of the school standing over me. Wait, Ohio was an eight-hour drive. The school must have called my father, who must have driven through the night. "Uh-oh!"

The dean told me that I faced expulsion and would have to pay for the window. My father wanted me to come home to Ohio, which I didn't want to do. I told them both I would take two weeks off from school, go to the school counselor, and go back to classes. But I didn't. Instead, I started auditioning for music videos, tours, shows, anything. I was willing to do anything to not give up on my dream. I felt like if I went home, my path was going to completely end, and I was going to be miserable. And after a while, someone at the school caught wind I was auditioning, and I was again told I wasn't allowed to do it. I never did well with authority. So, I left.

For eight to nine months, I slept at different friends' houses and squatted in abandoned buildings in the lower east side of Manhattan. I even slept in different parks when I didn't have anywhere to go. Back then, before New York was gentrified, abandoned buildings that housed homeless had an understood tier system. Usually, the first floor was a common area, the second floor was for sleeping, and the third floor was for people who wanted to party. Some buildings were completely for drug addicts. Most buildings didn't have water, electricity, or heat. Some even had entire floors and ceilings missing between floors, or stairways with no sidewalls. I would shower at a gym or a friend's house. I didn't tell anyone, because I only needed a place to sleep. I always had somewhere to be—auditions, parties, friends' band rehearsals. Having enough food was the hard part. I was always hungry.

Luckily, during the last three months of jumping around, a college friend let me stay in an open apartment at his parents' brownstone. The apartment was about to go through renovation, and I had one month before the contractors started. The deal was, I had to be out by 7 a.m. and couldn't return until 5 p.m. when the contractors were done. There was a bathroom and kitchen which weren't always usable because of the construction, but I didn't care. I had a place to stay, and I was grateful. That time in my life I had some of the funniest experiences of my life. I felt free, I was doing what I wanted. But I was auditioning like my life depended on it. In a way it did. But mostly, I was ready to perform. I didn't have any specific artist I wanted to perform with or any specific show. I just needed to be on stage. Then, an opportunity came.

I was able to get a dance agent. They were sending me on auditions, a few here and there as I didn't have much for a resume. I was able to book a few small dance gigs, mostly live performances with unknown recording artists. Pretty soon after, I got a call for a major recording artist. At the time, it was going to be just like any other audition. Except 2,000 dancers from New York and all over the world showed up. There were so many people the audition ended up taking three days! The first and second day were long, sweaty, and competitive with a lot of characters in the room. When I say characters, sometimes people show up to auditions almost as though they were in costume playing a character. I guess sometimes it worked, but I just showed up as myself. I never had expectations I would make it to the end; I just wanted to do my best. But I was still very competitive. I didn't talk with friends. I didn't play games. I was focused. After day three, I was in the final group. We were told the production company still needed to hold auditions in LA and they would let our agents know when the final call back was.

A few weeks later, I booked a music video for an Italian recording artist for a three-week gig. The production company flew dancers from New York to Italy for a two-week rehearsal and one week of filming. I was happy. I was getting paid to work in Italy, in an industry I wanted to be in. Most importantly, I was going to eat well and come home with some money. Then, one week into rehearsal, myself and another dancer got a call from our agent. They wanted us to fly to LA for final call backs from the other audition. We didn't know what to do. We had a gig that was paying really well that we would have to leave and pay to fly ourselves halfway across the globe just for an audition we didn't know if we would book. A day later, our agent called and said the recording artist was going to pay for our flight if we could come to the audition. The opportunity was too good to pass up. But the Italian recording artist and his team were pissed. They called our agent and told us we would never work in Italy again. He was actually a huge artist in Italy, and he was probably right. We said, "fuck it," and left. Whatever, dude.

After an extremely long flight we landed in Los Angeles and immediately went to the audition jet lagged, tired, and hungry. There were only about forty to fifty dancers for the final call back. After two different dance routines the creative team cut the dancers down to twenty-two. They were only hiring eighteen. After the next call of dancers, I went to the waiting room and realized I was one of four dancers sitting there. Then, I heard a scream of excitement coming from the rehearsal room…shit. I didn't make it. I thought about the job in Italy I left that was a great paying gig in order to audition. Gone. I was exhausted, hungry, and barely had any money to get home to New York. But wait, I didn't have a home in New York. I had a sawdusty bedroom in an apartment I only had a couple weeks left to stay in. So, I broke down and decided to go home to Ohio.

By then, my parents knew I'd dropped out of school. There was nothing they could do about it. The first two days home were defeating. I had nothing left in my body or mind; I felt numb. "Did I mess up? Should I have stayed in school? Do I stay in Ohio? Will I go back to New York? How will I make money once I'm back? Where will I stay?" My mind had the questions, but life had no answers. On the third day, my father and I went to a high school basketball game my cousin was coaching. I was sitting in the stands, happy to see my cousin's team winning. Then, right before halftime, I got a missed call from my agent. I ran out of the gym to call him. He told me the creative team from the audition called him and said they'd made a mistake. They might have wanted me on the tour and asked if I was available. I said, "Fuck, yeah, I'm available!"

He said to give him some time to get back to me. I walked back into the gym nervous, excited, and trying to keep my cool. My dad saw my face and asked what happened. I told him my agent called me to see if I was available for the tour. My dad threw his fists in the air and started shouting. I literally grabbed his arms and told him to chill, that it wasn't official yet. More than anything, I was too afraid to get my hopes up. He grabbed me by the arm, and we walked outside.

We were both pacing trying to calm ourselves down. As halftime ended, I got some candy on the way back in and we sat. Luckily the game was good, but we were anxious. Then, with about three minutes left in the fourth quarter, my agent called. I looked at the phone, looked at my dad, and picked it up. I sank down to the floor between the bleacher seats. The agent began telling me I was officially booked for the Madonna Re-Invention Tour and I would have to leave for LA in a couple of days to train for two months of rehearsals and eight months of tour. I hung up and told my dad, both of us now shouting and jumping in celebration. When I pulled away from his hug, I looked around to see everyone in the gym looking at us like we lost our minds. We didn't realize it, but a timeout was called, and both teams were also staring at us. My cousin even looked up at us like, "Yo, chill!" We left the gym too excited to sit still and waited in the parking lot until the end of the game. The journey began.

Madonna

A week later, I moved to LA. We rehearsed ten to twelve hours a day for two months straight. That level of focus and dedication to the process of creating something great is what I loved. Performing is its own euphoria. But something about rehearsals, the creative process of finding the right choreography, changing the story, prop rehearsal, is a process I love as an artist. And working with other artists who are just as hungry and love the process as much as I do, is a blessing.

Working with her specifically was exactly like working with one of the Greats of the music industry. I was not a fan, but I did respect her because I knew she was a Great. No matter what anyone says, she was a trailblazer in music, fashion, and culture throughout the world. Not only that, but she was also one of the hardest working people I have ever met. She would go from music rehearsal for four to five hours, then come directly into dance rehearsal for another four to five hours, every day, for two months. And she sang live! Not that she needed it, but she had my respect since day one. And it made me want to work just as hard. To me, real leadership is setting an example.

Luckily for me, I seemed to catch her at an amazing time in her life. She was married with two young kids and was on top of her game even at forty-five! She also had an affinity for her spiritual life which I liked as she was practicing Kabbalah. She wanted us, the dancers and musicians, to join in her practice. We would have classes after rehearsal sometimes which we all went along with at first. But it wasn't too long after that most of us weren't interested. I think it was something that felt forced, even though people respected the practice and appreciated her wanting to share it with us.

I remember, she wanted to be called Ester, and I laughed in her face. I simply said, "Ok."

She would say, "Come on, Seth. You should learn about this stuff, you're a Jew."

I would tell her, "Thank you, but I'm good. Even my mom wasn't a practicing Jew."

But mostly, I already knew I didn't want to abide by one religion or practice. They all were beautiful to me in their own right. I just wanted to source the truth. There was also something about the Kabbalah tree of life symbol that bothered me. It felt like something was missing. But I couldn't explain it even if I tried. It just felt "off." And that symbol was actually the reason I rejected all teachings I started receiving. It took fifteen years before I understood why. More of which I will share in later chapters.

Fast forward. I'm traveling the world, dancing on stage with one of the biggest names in music, performing for 30,000 to 100,000 people. My closest friends and family would come watch me perform. Seeing them in the crowd, losing their minds with excitement was a life moment I'll never forget. It was as if we all made it! Because of their support, we all were winning! They not only got to watch me with one of the world's greatest performers, but they also were able to have a VIP experience during and after the show with me. Sometimes we did too much. But we were young. I had what felt like keys to every city, groupies ready at every party, and so much growth as a person and performer. I busted my ass to be there, but I knew the work was not finished. Just because you make it, doesn't mean you've made it. Success means maintaining a high level of professionalism and execution. And I learned that lesson from working with some of the best.

Throughout that tour, the audiences gave so much energy back to the performers. Within the first few shows I saw the power of energy through music and performance in a way I had never imagined. I had always felt that music was powerful, which is why I loved to dance. As dancers we were there to tell a story, support the artist, and give the audience energy. The audience is also attending for the artist and their energy through music. But it was an exchange. The only way to describe performing in front of tens of thousands of people, is like having the ability to control the ocean. The artist, performers, musicians, lighting, set movements—it all changes and creates different feelings that are blasted to the audience. The audience roars or swoons and has emotional ups and downs just like the waves of the ocean. But those on stage and behind the scenes are controlling the ocean.

I loved performing like my life depended on it. But the energy return and love from an audience is almost like being high. You can feed off of it. (And if you've felt that, you understand). It's not surprising when I see big name music artists and actors have huge egos. In their world, everyone loves them. It can become an addiction to the ego to always feel love and get attention as a performer. But at some point, most people have to come down from the mountain and touch reality. For some, they rarely have to touch the ground again. For better or worse, who is to say?

Lastly, I will say it was an honor to work with her. She took care of us at that time. And I grew professionally and personally in ways I may not have had the chance to. I saw the world, from the richest of the rich, to the poorest of the poor. I flew on private planes and had access to places I never would have had access to. But I watched. And I realized that energy and power through performance are some of the most influential tools that can sway masses in ways they would never understand. That power can be used in many ways, which has a fine line.

Broadway

After the tour, I moved back to New York and booked my first Broadway show, the revival of *Sweet Charity*. I was excited because it was one of my favorite Broadway shows that I had studied. The choreography for that show was originally from Bob Fosse, one of my favorite choreographers/directors of all time. He created a language of dance and movement in a way that blazed his own trail within theater and film. And to this day, his style is used in many famous dance pieces in musical videos and on stage.

In rehearsals, everyone knew each other and had done shows together before. No one knew who I was in the theater world, and I was ok with that. I had just come off a major tour, but theater from the inside out is a different community and a different way of performing. The talent in the show was exceptional! The actors, dancers, musicians, everyone was on top of their game. And I knew I had a lot to learn and prove. And I wanted to level up as a performer. As we finalized rehearsals, I knew I was about to *eat* onstage when we opened. For the non-performers, when a person *eats*, it's like they were fully in the moment, confident, and owning the stage. The performer and the audience both know when the performance is *eating*; it's like a guttural feeling. And when you have other cast members who match your energy, the experience onstage is unlike any other feeling, it's magic!

The show eventually toured for a few months for an out-of-town trial where we traveled to different major cities to gain exposure and build towards a potential Broadway opening. The shows were great and I tended to party a lot. I still had a young mentality coming off the Madonna tour that after shows meant a good party. I was 21 and too cool for my own good. As the tour continued and some friends joined me in certain cities, we turned up even more! I was still on top of my game when it came to doing the actual show. But everything was happening fast and usually in a blur. I didn't remember a lot because well, I was high as a kite most of the time. I had a rock star mentality and so did my friends. But by the end of the tour, the show was almost not going to make it. The star performer broke her ankle which almost ended chances of potentially transferring to Broadway. There was nothing anyone could do. The replacement went on for the remaining performances while the lead actress healed. And after a few months, we got word that the transfer to Broadway would still happen.

When we finally opened on Broadway, my family was so happy for me. All the work they did inspiring me and getting me to classes, paid off. My uncle was ecstatic. He had been a mentor of mine since I was a kid. And he was actually the reason I knew of Bob Fosse's movement and was the first to show me *Sweet Charity* the movie. He himself is a performer who also toured with recording artists and doing theater. He and my father's wealth of Broadway knowledge and history were the reasons I knew anything about it. And my first opening night on Broadway felt like my whole family made it. Dancing with them at the after party was the first time my family was together since my parents' divorce. It felt like, no matter what, the family could come together again to celebrate a mutual success. And that was my highlight.

The next six months, I quickly became familiar with doing eight shows a week on Broadway. At times it was exhausting, but every night was fun! If you love the show you're doing and have a great cast it doesn't feel like work. I remember times in certain production numbers when I would connect with a cast member before a dance break, with a look like, "Yeah, let's let them have it!" And the two of us would dance our asses off. It was for us just as much as the audience. I would have some moments with different cast members just to be silly and have fun on stage and keep things interesting. I also would see what I could do as a performer to keep the show fresh each night and try different things to gain a different reaction from the audience. Looking back, I was again realizing how an audience could be moved and influenced by what was happening on stage. They fell in love with the characters or performers. They wanted to root for them. And in any show or any movie, everyone as an audience member picks a character that is similar to them, or who they wish they could be in real life. The energy from the crowd was my fuel some nights. And again, subconsciously I realized the power of energy and energy exchange.

Even when I wasn't doing the show, I was living my best life. By twenty-two, I owned a three-bedroom condo in New York, gave my sister a deposit on her home in Atlanta, and owned two cars, a BMW and a 1966 Cadillac. I had money, an amazing experience in my show, pretty girls around me, and things were beginning to pick up in my career. I was feeling myself. And you couldn't tell me anything. I had come from dropping out of school, homelessness, and touring, to a Broadway show. I wouldn't brag because that's not how I was raised. But I was definitely in full swagger mode.

Then, I injured my knee during the show one night. I couldn't walk on it. And I had to leave the show due to injury. It would take me six months of physical therapy just to be able to dance again. But I was determined to get back onstage. And eventually, I was performing in commercials, music videos, award shows, and concerts with recording artists. One of those artists was Jennifer Lopez.

Wake Up

I was performing in a few cities on a promo tour for her new album with three other dancers. We were flying back home from London, and I was sitting next to one of the dancers, a woman whom I'd eventually date. We were having one of those silent moments after hours of good conversation, that moment where both people let go. I remember I was trying to fall asleep when something happened.

For a moment, maybe a few minutes, reality split. To some it would feel or look like an anxiety attack. But I could feel something in another time that was existing in the present moment. I saw another reality and *looked* in. I *felt* into what I now realize was a potential future timeline on Earth. It felt like something wasn't right in the world, something I couldn't explain. But it was a feeling you get right before something bad is about to happen. Unfortunately, this "when," was "now," and "eventually." It was hard for me to breathe and come back into my body. She noticed I was struggling and tried to calm me down. But all I could say was, "Something isn't right! Something is wrong!"

"With you?" she said.

"No, in the world! Something isn't right!" I replied with a short breath. And I started crying. It was as though I felt the lie, the deception, and a worry of the future, all at once.

It took me hours to calm down. But even longer to try and understand what that moment was. Was that my first look into the future? It took me weeks to feel centered again. But this triggered a major fear of the future in thinking humanity would be destroyed. For years, I was unconsciously trying to control what I could. I woke up every morning with anxiety about what I was going to accomplish in a day, a week, a year, a lifetime. I smoked a lot of weed just to calm down. And it wasn't until a few years later that I realized that moment was the beginning of an awakening. And so, I returned to my regularly scheduled programming.

In the Heights

After the tour and a few other gigs, I booked my second Broadway show, *In The Heights*. When I arrived, everyone was young and hungry to make something great. Even the veterans of Broadway that were in our cast, came in ready to make something special. My weird ass came in the first day of our table read wearing gold grills in my mouth, tops and bottoms. I was on something different. And I was going to bring that to the stage. And everyone, every single person in that cast was talented in a way that got me excited before we even opened the show. It was one of my favorite shows as a person and as an artist. The story was real; the cast was close in friendship and amazing on stage. It felt like home.

I was in such awe of the process. We were a part of building an original show, which also allowed me to have my first small principal role. I didn't understand what it meant at the time, which I laugh at now. But I got to be a small lead in the show. And I wasn't going to take that for granted. During our off-Broadway run and moving onto Broadway, we were a tight-knit cast and people loved our show. We had momentum.

During that process we were also being filmed for a documentary about the process of the show. And one day, while sitting in the theater waiting to start our tech rehearsal, the director pulled me outside and started to walk me right into Times Square. I didn't know if I was getting fired or getting a raise; it was just weird that we were walking further into Times Square five minutes before rehearsal.

Then I saw it. The creative team of the show put up a seven-story billboard of *me* in Times Square! I was a freaking poster boy for the show! It was wild! But even with that, I felt the pressure to be great. I felt like I had more responsibility to bring the energy of the poster to the stage every night. And the cast and creatives did not disappoint! The show felt alive every night! And I loved every part of the experience. The show became a major success winning four Tony Awards! And once we as a cast knew the show would continue to run, I wanted to do more in my free time.

Entrepreneurship

During that time of the show, I was traveling to Hoboken, New Jersey, starting my first business and building out a 3,000 square foot film studio and separate dance studio with my business partner. It took eight months to get up and running. We literally built it from the ground up—the walls, reframed the plumbing and electric, everything. The studio became a rental space for music video and production shoots. Meanwhile, I was using the dance studio for my own personal projects. We were making money slowly but surely with bookings. I was creating projects in my studio with friends and having parties whenever we felt like it. But after a couple of years of eight shows a week and running a business I started to burn out. The art that I loved had become work; a chance to buy the next car or the next house. Something felt a little "off." I was at one of the highest highs in my career and in life, and it still felt like something was missing. What was it?

In a random decision, which I tend to make from time to time, I decided to start camping, something I never had time to do growing up as a kid. I was a suburban kid turned city kid; I loved the streets. But I needed a new experience.

During my second camping trip ever, I set up my campsite and decided to go on a hike. A few hours in, I realized I was lost. I came across a pack of coyotes and spotted them before they spotted me. Fear boiled up. I started to walk/run in a different direction, getting me further from my original campsite. I was lost for most of the day. Eventually, I came to a road and found someone to drive me back to my car which was a few miles away.

On my car ride home, I was upset. I realized I didn't know how to survive in the woods. Survive? I mean, humanity has lived in nature for hundreds of thousands of years, perhaps millions. And within a hundred years we somehow forgot. I forgot. I was not ok with that feeling. I was not ok with myself as a human and as a man that I did not at least know some of the basics. That feeling was the seed that eventually sprouted and grew.

THE CALLING

The First Call

Eventually, the cast found out our show was going to end. A few months before closing I realized I was going to have a little more time on my hands. I had a choice to find another show or tour and continue building my career. Or I could pay attention to my internal feelings. I prayed on it. And very quickly, it was clear it was time to do something different in my life. Getting lost in the woods still bothered me. And the fear bothered me more than actually being lost, hungry, and thirsty. Within a month, I found a survival school in southern New Jersey called the Tracker School and began taking classes that summer. The "school" was a five-mile drive into a national forest reserve down a barely maintained dirt road. It was completely off grid, there were bucket showers for bathing or a pond for rinsing, outdoor compost toilets, an outdoor kitchen, and small gardens with edible and medicinal planets. All the water came from a well, and the structures were pole barn style with tarped roofs. This was the *woods* woods. And from the moment I arrived and took it all in I knew I was going to love it!

We had classes in the day and camped in the woods at night. The whole experience was brand new to me. There were a mix of expert outdoorsmen, ex-military, and regular people just wanting to learn new skills. We made debris huts, Mandan lodges, and other natural shelters from the surrounding environment. Shelter was the foundation and most important survival skill. It is the first of the Sacred Four. The Sacred Four is like a natural order for animals and humans. It is also an easy mental format to know what to do when in a survival situation. Again, Shelter is always the first priority. Second, is water; how to locate it, filter and purify, and most importantly, how to honor the water. Fire is third in the sacred four depending on the survival situation. Sometimes, fire may be needed first if it's cold. We learned how to make primitive bow drill and hand drill fires, make natural tinder bundles, and tried different types of wood for heating and cooking. The fourth in the sacred order is Food. Humans can survive a lot longer without food than they can without water or warmth. We learned about edible and medicinal plants, animal tracking, and overall awareness of the environment we were a part of. We had to learn how to energetically drop into the baseline of nature, moving slower, quieter, and with more awareness. These were skills humans have had for centuries. It felt right. And within a week I started to feel "in." In my body, in my natural environment, and most importantly, in the right place.

Earth Mother, Talk to Me

At the end of my first week the teachers held a sweat lodge ceremony. I had never done a sweat lodge before, but I was all for it. The ceremony of a sweat lodge is very sacred, like all ceremonies. One by one, people crawled through the entrance of a small dome-shaped lodge made of bent tree saplings. It was covered by raw hides of deer, elk, or moose. Modern coverings use blankets and tarps to keep the heat inside of the lodge. The overall shape looks like the shape of a turtle shell meant to represent Earth Mother. Inside, people sat on the bare ground in a circle or multiple circles around the central pit. Everyone wore bathing suits or light coverings as the process was meant to make us sweat. Once everyone was settled, a fire keeper brought in huge red-hot rocks that had been buried beneath a fire for hours and placed them in the center pit of the lodge. The elder running the ceremony brushed off any ash to keep the stones clean from debris. Once all the rocks were in the pit, they closed the door and everything went pitch black. The ceremony began.

As they threw water on the hot rocks, the heat quickly rose, the steam spreading within the lodge from the low-lying roof. I quickly felt the warmth of the steam on my body and put my hands on the ground, feeling the coolness of the dirt floor. The elder began singing a native American song. I closed my eyes. It felt like only a few minutes before I thought I was hearing things. At some point, I heard the moaning of a woman's voice in pain. It was a low, drawn-out moan. I thought it was a woman within the ceremony. But I realized it wasn't coming from inside the lodge. I even thought it was coming from outside the lodge until I began having visions. I saw a woman running, then falling to the ground in a dress. She was trying to save her child from something. She had been running for a long time and seemed she had run out of energy to go further. She was reaching out to me. What did she want? What did she need? It took me a few moments, but she kept saying that she *was* the Earth.

When I made the connection, I could feel the Earth underneath me, and I could feel myself inside of her. Her moaning, her pain, was in my body now. She had been running from other humans trying to harm her and her children. She was only trying to protect her children, that's it. The feeling of despair felt like the weight of the world was on top of me and it was hard to breathe. I laid on the dirt floor that was now turning to mud from my sweat and the sweat of those around me. I was gripping my hands in the mud trying to grasp something. I started crying. Her pain was coming out of me. I wanted to protect her just as much as she wanted to protect me. What was I to do?

What felt like only twenty minutes ended up being an hour as the door of the lodge swung open, and it was over. A wave of fresh air came into the lodge. People slowly crawled out, a few wanting to leave quicker than others. I sat for a minute, then went out slowly. Coming out of the lodge I looked up to see the stars; there were so many! I felt like I just came out of a womb, feeling reborn as a child of the Earth. The elder and teachers whispered to us to go find a spot on the land to sit. I did and began walking slowly down a sandy path. My eyes were adjusted to night vision and there was no need for a flashlight. I wanted to be far from everyone. I found a pine tree tucked deep in the blueberry bushes and sat against it. I briefly looked up at the stars in amazement then closed my eyes. I could still hear her voice. I still felt her pain. I felt like she called me; she brought me home. I was a child, a baby on this Earth. I knew nothing about my true home. I let it all sink in. I sat in the dark in meditation for maybe thirty minutes to an hour.

Time was irrelevant to me. I eventually went to the small pond, took a dip to wash off, and went to bed. I slept deeper than I'd ever slept before.

The next morning was the last day of class, and I knew everything had changed. I was calm, quiet, and grateful all at the same time.

A few days later when I arrived back in New York it was back to business as usual. But I wasn't the same. It took me a few months to be around people. The outside world was now moving too fast and too chaotic. How could I explain the experience I'd just went through? I felt like I was on a different plane of existence.

Months passed. I was still running the film and dance studio but not doing any shows or even auditioning. I began hiking a lot more and had a few solo camping trips. But I wanted more experiences, and I decided to volunteer for the school for their Fall program. Only this time, the classes for the season were being held in a camp in the Redwoods of Northern California.

Within weeks I flew out to Sacramento, rented a car, and drove up to the mountains. As I entered the Redwood Forest, I felt like I'd entered another world! The trees and the landscape felt so large and majestic! I knew it was going to be an amazing experience.

Energetic Baseline

I spent about three weeks at the camp helping in the kitchen and with classes. I was able to take a philosophy class. Not philosophy of western academia, but of Native American philosophy of the earth, spirit, self, and the creator. Two to three times a day, we as students would go to a *sit spot*, a dedicated place in the forest away from others, to work on one of the exercises or simply to surrender to "nothingness." It took everyone time to slow down their mind enough to expand their awareness. But once you surrendered and dropped into yourself, you became the observer. You began thinking less and less and feeling more, attached to none of it. Your awareness expanded within yourself, what you were feeling, what was hidden, what was needed. You became more aware of your outside environment without the need for sight.

My sit spot happened to be really far away from others and the main camp during this time, to the point where I couldn't hear the call to return to camp. I would just do the work and show up late sometimes. My spot was by a river, with the top of the mountain ridge line maybe fifty feet above me. At sunset, I could always feel the shift. It was like the animals were getting ready for the night and doing their last-minute things. But one thing that stood out was the energy of mountain lions. Even though I never saw them, I could feel when they were close or on the ridge line behind and above me. I had been in the woods for a while but knew I still had a human smell. I wasn't afraid of them. They didn't give me a reason to be afraid. And after a few days of being in this sit spot, I could feel them getting closer to my area trying to understand who or what was there. I put out the energy so they could come close, but not too close.

A couple nights later, they eventually did. I felt three or four of them within fifty yards of me. Again, my eyes were closed, but it was like I dropped into a different plane and could see things without the need of my eyesight. I could see them in my vision, sniffing and moving closer. At one point they stopped. It was the first time I felt my outer energy wall be touched. That sphere, or energy wall turned to the color red in my mind's eye. I could feel they wanted to come closer, but I didn't let them. Instead, I slowly stood up and realized I'd learned what I needed from the exercise and from nature. I wanted to give them their space, so I decided to walk back to my tent in the dark. In my mind I thanked the lions for coming so close and teaching me. We both were curious, and I'd learned I didn't need to fear them and they didn't need to fear me.

In the final week something shifted. After a deep, late-night meditation I opened my eyes and was confused; the night almost looked like the day! But how? I stood up and looked around. I could see in the dark! For real! As I began to walk back towards my campsite, I looked down at my feet and saw an iridescent glow around the leaves on the ground. I didn't know it at the time, but everything was bioluminescent. I looked up at the trees and started to see them glow slightly in different colors. I stopped again and looked around. It felt like I was in a different world. After a few minutes, I kept walking. This time the glow was getting brighter around the leaves on the ground. By the time I reached the field and stepped on the grass, the glow started to fade. But when I looked into the forest behind me, I could still see it all glowing. To this day, it is one of the most beautiful experiences I've ever had!

I learned once you find the natural baseline of yourself and your environment, you begin to *feel* the changes. You begin to have a *knowing*. And once you get the hang of it working through the gatekeepers in your mind, you begin to have a practice. A person can then move from their practice into having this awareness as a part of their daily way of living. But that balance is a fine line. Balance is something you learn throughout your lifetime.

That winter I went back to New York humbled and grateful. This school and the Earth were teaching me lessons that changed my life. And it was only the beginning.

The Second Call

Eventually, I felt my second *calling*. The following spring, the primitive school put out an email that they were looking for interns for their upcoming spring season in 2012. I was interested right away. I called the office directly and spoke with the director of the program whom I worked with before in previous classes. He said he was looking for someone to start within two weeks. It was a fast turnaround. And it only took twenty-four hours to decide. I was nervous to leave everything behind, but I could feel the pull in my heart to take a chance. I didn't know when I would have an opportunity like that again in my life. So another twenty-four hours later I told my agents I was taking a leave of absence for six months and told my business partner who would have to take care of our operations for that same time period. We had things under control by then and he was ok with it. I quickly packed up what I needed for six months in the woods, put my affairs in order, and I left. Peace out, homies!

"Let go of everything you know. Empty your cup." - Tom Brown

Tracker

Living and working in the woods was like leaving society behind almost completely. Myself and three other interns were tasked to take care of the kitchen, order food for classes, cook for classes, care for the land when needed, and set up and help during classes when needed. Luckily, I had a good crew to work with. Two of them were much younger than me, and the other was my age. I was twenty-eight. We did work-trade where each month we would acquire one free class for our time. It was worth it. Helping run the school was a great feeling. I lived outside, and this was my opportunity to give my intention, my time, and my energy back to the school, the students, and the Earth. Other interns and caretakers had come before me. I just needed to fill the open slot and do the best I could. That's what I feel life is in some ways; we're here to take over where others left off, each generation making it better for the next.

For the whole summer I lived in a tent, again, the furthest away from others. It's not that I don't like people, I love people. But I find being the furthest one out brings not only peace and quiet, but it lets the outside come closer in. It's like getting to live on the boundary between two worlds without interference. That way of living has become a major theme in my life; being far out in nature, working on spiritual and physical skills every day, and surrendering. The process brings out many things in a person if they allow it. To start, it's humbling to return to Earth Mother realizing you're no more important than a grasshopper or a tree. We matter and we don't. The biggest blessing and realization is that Earth Mother provides everything we need—shelter, water, fire, food, music, inspiration to dance, materials for most of our modern day products, steel, iron, rubber, minerals for electronics, everything! Another benefit of living close to nature for extended periods of time, is that the experience can bring a person to a different level of awareness. Eventually, the spiritual world will touch you and communicate with you. Whether you feel the dark, the light, the neutral, it's all on the same spectrum of spirit. And this time period is where I tapped back into the spiritual.

Every once in a while, when walking to my tent at night, I felt things shifting on the landscape. It was almost like things were walking and flying around. Sometimes, I would feel a cold breeze quickly go past as if someone just walked right by me. One night while in my tent, I could hear something walking through the woods. My tent area was surrounded by thick, high-bush blueberries. The area was so dense there was absolutely no way a person or animal could walk directly through it. At first I was confused. Then I realized, I wasn't alone.

For a few weeks, on random nights, I would hear and feel this *thing*. I realized it had to be a spirit. If I got up to go pee at night, I could sometimes feel it watching me. I told it to, "Back up!" I was tired, and it needed to go somewhere else. A few weeks later it was mostly quiet, no weird feelings, nothing. Then, a girl I was dating came to visit me. At first, she didn't believe me when I told her I was going to live in the woods for six months. Who does that? There were no classes for a week, and she decided to visit for two days. We got to walk the land, swim in the freshwater pond, lay in the sun, and had a fire the first night under the stars. But around midnight, the spirit came back.

We were both falling asleep, but I could feel it nearby. Within seconds it came right towards my tent! It sounded like a

250-pound man was running straight through the thick bushes; the bushes were actually moving and cracking. The girl woke up and almost shouted. I quickly put my hand on her mouth to stop the scream. Then I yelled at the spirit commanding it to go away. It just stopped what felt like ten to fifteen feet away. She looked at me with wide eyes. I signaled to be quiet. I yelled out again and commanded it to leave. I felt the spirit retract a little bit, but not fully leave. I got my head lamp and knife and raced out of the tent in boxers, shining the light in a 180-degree view, then 360…nothing. I could see where it would have been standing. Another intern must have heard me yell. They yelled out and asked if I was ok. I shouted back, "Yes!" and told them something was messing with me.

They shouted, "Uh-huh!" and that was it. I went back into my tent. The girl was shaking, but I told her it was ok. Although she was spiritually inclined herself, she couldn't believe what just happened. I was just relieved someone else heard and felt what I did. It was confirmation I wasn't making any of it up.

A few weeks after the incident, I started to feel a presence just outside my tent area towards the walking path to central camp. It felt like a man who was leaning up against a tree. It didn't feel bad or good, just neutral. It took me a long time, maybe a month or so, to finally identify it. Over time it would get closer and lean up against a tree next to my tent. I asked who it was.

An inner voice said, "James." My grandfather? I felt the spirit shake its head, "yes."

The funny thing is, I never met my grandfather before. He passed away before I was born. Again, I thought I was making it up. He shared some things with me I can't quite recall. But it's almost like he showed himself to me and what he looked like.

It was hard for me to accept. This was the first time I had open communication with a spirit. First, I could hear the Earth and even began to feel her. Now, I was interacting with and talking to spirits. My friends were going to think I'd lost it. But I wasn't losing it. I was losing the distractions from my mind, pulling the curtains (plural) from my eyes, and finally beginning to return to life beyond the material plane.

The remaining few months, I continued to communicate with different spirits on the other side, but mostly my grandfather and ancestors. I continued to help out with classes, which led to less time working on skills I wanted to master. But it was a constant reminder I wasn't interning for myself; it was to help the students and school. I did, however, manage to build a larger primitive shelter which I was able to enjoy and sleep in for a few weeks before my internship was over. One of the last days in the shelter, two of the other interns came in and sat with me. We all knew our lives were going to change. We spoke about getting land together and leaving society to live closer to the Earth. As we were leaving the area after our conversation, I remember looking back at them and the shelter and feeling a deep knowing that I was going to make that potential a reality. I had to make it happen.

Living my vision, the vision within my heart and living close to nature were the only things that really mattered to me. These experiences of learning and integrating with Earth Mother are part of every human's birthright. Knowledge and relationship with Earth and sky have been in our ancestry for centuries; it's a part of what makes us human. I had found my way back to the Earth and surrendered. I found that unknown part that was missing in my life; the realization that I am a part of a bigger vision of remembering who we are, caretaking the Earth and keeping this ancestral knowledge alive.

IV

REINTEGRATION

Returning to Society

If you've ever seen the film *Into the Wild*, you will understand this next part. If you haven't, I highly suggest watching it. The feeling is exactly what happened next. After my internship, I was heading back to my film studio. This was October 2012. Driving out of the forest after six months, off the dirt roads and onto the highways full of traffic, passing shopping malls and a swarm of movement is extremely difficult. I was overwhelmed by the amount of traffic and how to navigate it. But mostly, I couldn't believe the type of feeling I got returning to society. It felt like I was returning to a chaotic world. It was so fast and felt so manufactured. The temperature was much warmer, and the air smelled bad. I could feel people's energy like it was on blast and became so overwhelmed I almost felt sick.

When I finally made it back to my studio, it was too overwhelming to be out in the world during the day. I would only go outside in the evening when the baseline was a little more settled. One evening, I remember sitting on the entrance stairs to the studio and looking out at a patch of trees across from the studio. I always saw it, but I never *saw* it. That little patch was alive! Not only with the trees, and plants, but full of life with birds, raccoons, squirrels, rabbits, and crickets. I sat and smiled and was thankful for that little area. I gave it some energetic love from afar and I immediately felt it return the energy. I heard the whippoorwill birds call from that forest, the same ones I'd heard over the last six months. I didn't even know they were out there, but they were! It was a reminder that the experiences I had were real and to hold them close to my heart.

Within a month of returning, Hurricane Sandy was making its way North towards New York and New Jersey. I could feel the energy of this storm. I had been working on paying attention to the weather patterns over the last few months by trying to predict if rain was coming in for the day, in order to make any necessary adjustments for the class. But this storm was going to be bad. I could feel the buildup and stirring it held. We had four days before it would reach our area, and I immediately started packing some bags and essentials. I found a tall parking garage and took my 1966 Cadillac, my prize possession at the time, to the highest floor in the parking garage just before the roof of the building. I put the cover on the car and secured it. I told my business partner and friends they should consider leaving the area for a few days. No one felt it was going to be that bad. They even laughed. I shrugged my shoulders and left for a friend's house an hour north.

Two days later, Hurricane Sandy hit. The destruction and flooding up the East Coast were one of the worst in years. Three days after the initial hit, I called my business partner to check on him. He told me he and some of our friends were stuck, running out of food, and the flooding in the area was up to the windshield on his truck. He also went downstairs to the studio, which had flooded about one to two feet. But the floor of our studio was already five feet above street level which meant there was seven feet of water in the streets! Five days after the storm I drove back to check out the damage. The flooding was still so bad, I had to park my car five blocks away. I walked up to a railroad track that overlooked the studio and other warehouses and apartment complexes in the area. You could see the water covering the streets that were still closed off. I saw two Coast Guard inflatable boats rescuing people from second-story windows to take them to safety. I looked to see if I could drive through or wade through to check on the studio, but there was no way.

A few weeks later, my business partner and I had a decision to make. The first option was to wait eight to nine months to see if we were eligible for insurance money to rebuild. Remember, thousands of homes, schools, and essential business were also flooded. Non-residential buildings or businesses would be the last on the list for claim money. We couldn't even get an insurance adjuster to look at our building. They were so busy. If we waited to rebuild, we would have mold all throughout our studio with no guarantee of insurance money. If we did rebuild, we would spend money out-of-pocket rebuilding the green screen and other studios, spending thousands we didn't have. I was already tired of the business and my partner after four years. I immediately knew it was time to move on. I wasn't even upset. It was the holidays, and all I wanted to do was see my family. So, I packed the rest of my stuff and put it in storage to lighten my load for the next part of my journey.

Grandpa Speaks Through Me

I went to Ohio for a week to visit family. The first day back I drove to see my dad at work on his lunch break. I briefly told him about my experience in the woods and then used the topic to tell him I was looking for land to build an off-grid cabin somewhere in upstate New York.

He leaned his elbow on the desk, gave me a scanning look as he does and asked… "Why?"

"I don't know, something's calling me," I replied.

"What is it now?" he said, wondering what happened to me while I was in the woods.

I replied, "I don't know. I just need to be in nature." Then, something started shifting. In my mind I went, "Uh oh!"

I knew a message was coming through. It was my grandfather.

Cautiously I said, "Dad, this might be weird, but I'm getting a message coming through."

He raised his eyebrows. I was trying to control the little pulsating I first had when getting messages from ancestors or other beings. I asked if I could close the door to his office.

He said, "Yes." I closed the door and faced him.

I continued, "Ok, this could seem weird, and you may not believe me, but I don't care. But there is someone in the room with us and I think I know who's coming through."

"Who is it?" he asked.

I cried a little, and said, "I think it's Grandpa."

He squinted his face like, "What?"

I continued, "*Your* dad."

He said, "Oh, ok. Well, what does he want to say?"

It took me a minute. Then, the messages came through. I won't share all of them. But I remember within the first three sentences, something I said struck my father, something only *his* dad would know. I remember my grandfather saying something along the lines of he knew how hard my father had it growing up, having to be the oldest of all his siblings.

At some point my grandfather said to my dad, "…and stop being so hard-headed."

My dad looked at me stunned! He said, "Dad, is that you? Seth, is he in you?"

I said, "No, but I can hear him and see him somewhat." (By the way, when this was happening, I was speaking in my regular voice. It didn't change. I usually look at a spot on the wall to focus or close my eyes.)

My dad started crying. I couldn't remember the last time I saw or heard my father cry. But he knew it was real. (Remember, I'd never met my grandfather before.)

My father fought the tears and said, "What does he want?"

"Dad, he just wants you to know he loves you. He's around. You can talk to him yourself. You can talk to him, and he can guide you if you need. But he hasn't gone anywhere, he's just on the other side. It's like they can call us here, like if we're on the other side of the planet. But most people can't hear the phone ringing. They don't believe it, so they drown it out," I replied.

My dad couldn't believe it. He did, but it was so new to him. He looked at me and said, "So this is what you've been working on out there?"

I replied, "Yeah, kind of. This and many other things. I just had to go home to nature to hear more clearly. Grandpa was out there with me when I was working at the primitive school. But it took me the first few months before I could see him and know it was him. It's like he was my introduction."

Shocked, all the doubt my father had, all the worry (maybe not all), disappeared.

New Beginnings

By the beginning of 2013, I knew I was going to be in a bit of a transition. When I returned from Ohio to New York, I stayed at a friend's house for a few months. By April, I reached out to my godfather, who had a two-story apartment in Queens. The downstairs apartment had three bedrooms but needed a lot of renovation. Because I didn't have a lot of money, I worked out a deal that I would renovate the apartment over a year while I got back on my feet and found my next job. He agreed, and I moved in. But by summer, I'd moved again to Los Angeles for more work.

During that summer, I created an e-commerce fitness start-up company with a girl I dated. We decided to move in together to save money and work on the business together. I found myself working twelve-to-fourteen-hour days six days a week and within six months found myself overworked. I had become a workaholic because I saw the opportunity to make millions and lost sight of everything else. The business had a lot of potential, but I was miserable.

I felt lost. And working hard felt like the only way out. I was trying to figure out what the next step was.

First Ayahuasca Ceremony

By the end of 2013, I was getting a call to do plant medicine. My girlfriend at the time told me about ayahuasca about a year before but I was never intrigued enough to look deeper into plant medicine. But I felt like I was hearing the plant call me, sometimes even in dreams. I began to feel the plant medicine as a female spirit, and I knew it was a confirmation. I found out that the shaman my girlfriend went to years before was actually going to be holding another ceremony in Los Angeles. I scheduled a one-day journey which was to be my first ayahuasca ceremony. I had a few weeks to begin my dieta, cleansing my body of toxins and removing meat, dairy, sugar, and salt, among other things from my diet.

A week later the ceremony was set to take place. When I found out the location, it was in an undisclosed warehouse. I didn't like the feeling from the outside but when I went inside, it was clearly set up as a ceremonial event space. There was soft lighting, candles, and thick padded floor pillows to use. I grabbed three of them and set myself up in the corner in order to have only one person next to me and the ability to see everything in front of me. There were about twenty to twenty-five participants, but most seemed to talk and lounge like it was just another night. I only saw two other people that I remember really settling in and creating their own space and spiritual boundary. This was LA, which explained that lack of prep. But it was still interesting to view. I was there for maybe thirty minutes before the shaman came in, a tall, late fifty-something French man with fair skin and long hair. He entered in a white t-shirt and plain jeans. A younger white male apprentice and a native elder to the area was also there to assist. As soon as the elder took his place I could feel his presence. I was chillin' in my own space, but I looked up because I felt his eyes and energy slowly scanning the room. He looked at me observing him and we both just nodded our heads.

Before the ceremony began they lowered the lights and lit a few candles; one near the shaman, and a few others by the exit doors in order to find the bathroom during the ceremony. When the ceremony was ready to begin, each person went up to get their cup of ayahuasca from the shaman. When it was time for me, I was already in prayer. I set the intention to open myself up and learn what I needed to find out. The shaman poured the ayahuasca in a shot glass everyone was using. I wasn't a fan of that. He blew a mixture of tobacco smoke and other herbs over my head and then blew over the cup. He offered me the glass, and I took a drink part way. The mixture had the warmth, texture, and a little bit of the taste of hot chocolate. But that quickly dissipated to the *real* taste, which tasted like something I can't explain. I drank what was left, thanked the shaman, and walked over to my area. Normally, I like to lie down when going into meditation, but I decided to sit in an upright position as the ceremony began.

Once everyone had taken their cup the shaman said a few prayers. Then he began shaking a rattle and sang a song between a whisper and a whistle with his mouth. About five to ten minutes into the ceremony I saw a lot of people lay down. I don't know why, but I knew I needed to sit upright in order to journey. At some point, I lost track of time and started seeing beautiful shapes and colors. I could see them with my eyes open. And when I closed my eyes, the images were a little more intense. I began to hear people around the room start to purge. Some purged quietly and others sounded aggressive like they were releasing demons. I just let it happen in understanding. I think I even said out loud, "Yes! Let it go!"

It was beautiful. The experience was similar to mushrooms, but not the same. This journey of watching the room, listening to the shaman sing, and enjoying a bit of a light show happened for maybe an hour which quickly went by for me. Then, the shaman asked if anyone would like a second cup. Only four or five of us raised our hands. I think everyone else was asleep or still on their journey.

Immediately after I took my second cup, my legs were wobbly and I found it hard to make it back to my seat. I wanted to lie down, but I stayed sitting up. Within a minute or so, I began to purge. It wasn't as intense, but I could see a little bit of black stuff at the bottom of the bucket with almost no substance. Weird. I felt like I lost my whole stomach. As I settled back in, the visions came in even stronger. I began to see the energetic field in the room. It looked like a grid that was moving mostly horizontally, almost like a 2D grid from the 1980s. This field grid reached about three feet above the ground. Then, I looked around the room. Most people looked like they were squirming, uncomfortable. I remember getting a feeling some people didn't want to do the work; they were only there to journey or trip. I felt pain and trauma stored up within the people. They looked like little children wanting to be rocked to sleep. I sent out love to everyone. I felt like my brothers and sisters were sick and couldn't get the pain or sickness out.

As I looked back to the shaman, I saw a light inside of him. I squinted my eyes and looked again. He was glowing from the inside with bright white light! I could see him working on a different plane, though I didn't know it at the time. It was as if a layer had peeled off from the real world. His younger apprentice also had a small white light inside of him. His light wasn't as strong or as visible, but I could see it just enough to know he had it too. I couldn't believe what my eyes were seeing. It looked like a scene from The Matrix. The rest of the journey I was trying to watch everything he was doing. I couldn't see with my eyes or my vision yet, but I knew he was moving energy. I tried to look further and watch spiritually to what was happening. I received the same message that people were sick with darkness in their body. I eventually received the message to go back into my own journey. So, I closed my eyes and allowed the rest of my journey to be beautiful colors and shapes swirling in my vision. Hearing the rattle, the light drumming melodies of the songs, was amazing! I felt like I was being cradled by the sound. I was tired but felt awake. I felt different from everyone I was around, but I didn't know why. I made sure I was being humble. But I felt different, like I understood this work.

Reintegration

By the time it was over, I felt tired and went home and slept for twelve hours that night. When a person returns from a plant ceremony or from any type of spiritual retreat, reintegration into daily life can sometimes be difficult. I know for me every time I returned from a long retreat in the jungle or stayed in the mountains for extended periods, cities, traffic, or airports were extremely overwhelming energetically. When you're on retreat, your central nervous system is returning to its natural baseline. Or when in ceremony, some people are blasting off to other dimensions or speaking with their ancestors. These are experiences that change a person's life forever. And integrating all the knowledge and experience can be met with a brick wall once the person steps back into society. Most people go into isolation for a few more days or weeks to give their systems more time to integrate. The energies of the outside world, the phone and computers, regular conversations, sounds, and movement, can all be overstimulating.

Another tricky part is returning to a spouse or friends and family who have not shared the same experience. It's hard to explain. This person just went through deep healing either facing trauma, finding their peace, seeing the world or worlds with new eyes, or all of the above. Everything is at the surface. And sometimes, the people and the world we have to return to, just isn't matching the vibration.

So, I suggest taking it slow. I journaled to catalogue the experiences and feelings in order to put them in context and review at later times when needed. Over the next few weeks, I felt calm again. Something triggered in me, like a memory or feeling that I had looked into a realm I remembered and was somehow working toward. But I soon had to get back to building the start-up company.

What Comes Next

I spent the rest of the year working long hours having meetings with potential investors, advisors, and sponsors. By 2014 my partner and I moved to Florida as we figured it would be a good place to run our company. My cousin had a three-bedroom condo he wanted to rent out in Ft Lauderdale, and it worked out perfectly. But after the first few months I realized, I had moved to an area where I had no friends and no community, and it started to catch up to me. I shipped out my 1966 Cadillac to have something fun to do. But after a few drives to and from the beach, it wasn't as satisfying.

For nine months I did everything I could to make the business and the partnership work. But I was still miserable, and I wasn't following my heart. I was so tired by the end of it I didn't even care about the money anymore. My partner and I couldn't communicate anymore, and we both decided to call it quits. I sold all the furniture we'd purchased for the condo, shipped my car, and moved back to New York with no idea of what was coming next.

I moved back into my godfather's three-bedroom apartment and had two friends move in who helped me finish renovating the rest of the apartment from the year before. Within a month a friend called me to let me know the creative team from our last Broadway show had been working on a new idea titled, *Hamilton* for an off-Broadway run. I heard the music and got a brief description of the story, neither of which made sense to me. But since I knew the production team, I was ready to create again. I auditioned and booked the job.

Hamilton

That winter, rehearsals for the off-Broadway version began. Working in New York City again felt weird and overstimulating. I also hadn't really danced or performed since my last Broadway show which was almost three years prior. And I knew I had to make some effort to feel like myself again in the rehearsal studio. Luckily, I had friends in the show that I was excited to create with again. My dance partner and cast became my saving grace that helped me get out of my funk.

Initially, the process of this show still didn't make sense to me. I didn't fully understand the story in the way we were portraying it through movement or the music. We were rapping about presidents and financial systems, congressional hearings and back-room meetings and…what were we doing? A makeshift set was built in the rehearsal studio, but the overall picture was still hard for me to imagine. I was questioning if I should even do the show. But we had to trust the creative team and the process. I got to create moments in the show that were personal to me, forcing me back into creating something that fit the show and brought something new to the stage.

It wasn't until we reached the stage for the off-Broadway tech rehearsals and even a few weeks of performances that I finally understood how the show came together and how the audience was reacting to it. The cast started to mesh as we found our power onstage; the moments of intensity we could amplify and the moments where we could let the story breathe. It was almost a three-hour show, so letting the story and your feet rest was important.

Pretty quickly, the audiences were packed and celebrities started filling the small 300-seat theater after the first month. It was amazing to work from the ground up again and to be a part of creating something that was special. It was even more special to be in a show where you can find something different each night in the music and lyrics, the story, the choreography, and with other actors. Finding new moments within the show after doing it over and over and over again, is something every artist dreams of. It is a lesson in trusting the creative process. And simply proves the creative genius that created the show.

The problem was we weren't making much money. In fact, the entire cast was losing money. An off-Broadway contract doesn't pay the rate a person needs to live in New York City. Performers are willing to take a financial loss to be a part of a show they believe in, in hopes that the show and themselves as performers, transfer to Broadway. By the end of the three-month run, we were told we would be transferring to Broadway, but the show would be extending our off-Broadway run for another three months. I was happy the transfer would be happening. But by the end of the three months, plus the two months of rehearsal, I had gone deep into my savings just to pay the bills. I already lived way below my means with two roommates and the idea of having to use more of my savings for the next three months of extension to make it through, did not excite me. But I continued because the show was fun, the responses were amazing, and I believed in what we were building.

Broadway – One Last Time

A show like Hamilton only comes around once in a generation. The show was a creative masterpiece, and this was before it was a worldwide sensation. But by the time we made it to rehearsals for Broadway, something felt different. The energy had shifted. The show was already a phenomenon. Tickets were sold out a year in advance. The work had paid off, and for a moment, it felt like security.

As a dancer, I was offered base pay. Minimum. After all the hard work from the previous six months—after two previous Broadway shows and major tours—there was no room to negotiate. My agent was told flat out: take it or leave it. I wasn't alone. Even veteran performers in the ensemble got the same deal. We were told we should feel "lucky" to be there. The refusal to negotiate sent a message: we were replaceable. I realized—even in the midst of greatness, you can be undervalued—but showing up with integrity is still a choice. People I had known for years acted brand new—entitled, walking around with inflated egos. This set a terrible tone. From the moment we started performing our cast was disintegrating from the inside out. And yet, we delivered onstage and chose to perform with heart. Our performances on stage were amazing, but inside we were fractured.

After a while the ensemble fought for more. And eventually, we got a slight increase—what felt like a blanket offer to quiet the noise. I started to detach. I think others did too. I would go out usually once a week and have a drink which led to three or four bourbons by the end of the night. As a performer in theater, you only get one day off—which usually consists of sleeping to let your body and voice recover, doing laundry, and attending appointments. Going out to have a drink felt good to let go from the show and I felt like I needed it to take away some of the pain in my body and mind. But six months in, I realized I was drinking heavier than I ever had before. It wasn't often, but it was a lot in one night for me. I was performing in one of the most groundbreaking shows, meeting every celebrity and attending every fancy party, and I realized deep down I was angry and unhappy and I couldn't suppress it.

Still, there were moments that kept me going. The show still meant something. It was reshaping Broadway. Young people of color saw themselves in powerful, intelligent roles—not as sidekicks or stereotypes, but as leaders. That kind of representation mattered deeply. And when we performed at the White House for President Obama, I felt proud. Proud to be part of something that symbolized change. It seemed as though a game changing president and a game changing Broadway show were setting the stage for a new America. But even there, the illusion cracked.

We toured the Treasury Department and learned about the 2008 financial crisis—how the government bailed out all the banks, even the ones that caused the crisis. The story was delivered casually, like it was just another tour stop. But for me, it was personal. My family, amongst millions of other families in America, lost our home because of that crisis. Hearing it brushed off like it was justified? I couldn't stay quiet. I walked out. As much as I love this country, I think we can still hold it accountable. It reminded me there were important ways the country was still failing us. But it also made me wonder deeper about the people that were portrayed in our show. One one hand, they took the country into the next part of its evolution. But some of them also had blood on their hands from slavery. It made me realize that life and everything I was noticing was ironic. And that revolution or evolution is both beautiful and ugly at the same time. We just can't talk about the ugly.

As the show went on, societal tensions increased as racial injustice, police violence, and political division dominated the news. Unarmed black men were being killed at an alarming rate with no justice. We wanted our show to take a stand as the cast of the show. We asked the producers to allow us to speak out against the violence but were met with resistance or silence. In fact, most Broadway casts asked their shows for support, none of which allowed their cast to cross reference the shows they were in. So many performers of all ethnicities met in Times Square anyway in solidarity for the victims and their families. We stood together, without support from our shows. We were representing change onstage, but not when it came to black and brown bodies in real life. And for me, that broke my heart.

Is real progress, truth? Or what it looks like to the general public? Are we as people and a country working so hard to keep the presentation of ourselves that we will smile against the falsehoods and allow our integrity to falter? It made me look at myself and what I was a part of. "Am I really who I say I am? Are *they* really who they say they are? Am I becoming the person I say I want to become? Am I *really* progressive or true to what I represent? Or am I also propping up the show?"

On one hand, we were all putting up this show that shouted, "We're changing the game! There's a revolution!" But behind the scenes, everyone and everything was a mess. It was like a micro to the macro of what was happening in the country; silently fracturing, crumbling. This was America.

By the time we made it to the Tony Awards, I was exhausted. And the night before the Tony's there was a terrible shooting at a gay club, killing innocent people who were simply living their lives. We performed without our usual prop guns as a gesture of respect. We won 11 of the 16 Tony awards we were nominated for. And when I arrived at the after party to celebrate, I remember my friends and family being so proud. I got hugs, smiles, and congratulations but it was ironic to be celebrating huge wins, when so much had happened in the past twenty-four hours, let alone the previous six months. That night, I felt equally proud and sad.

After the Tony Awards a lot of the cast started to leave the show. Eventually, I stepped into one of the lead roles which was one of my favorite characters. But a few months in, things were changing even further. I had been seeing and feeling butterfly energy for a few days. And one night during a show while I was sitting backstage between numbers, I had a vision. I was emerging from a cocoon. The message was clear, it was time to evolve.

Weeks later, another message arrived: "Remember, grandfather (my mentors' mentor) had to leave his people to learn different medicines." Grandfather taught my mentor to follow his big Vision. My mentor following his own personal Vision was the reason the Tracker School started. It was where I reconnected with the Earth and the sacred. And the message was clear - I was being called to leave and explore a new path, to live in alignment with a deeper truth. When my contract was done, my journey with Hamilton and with Broadway would end.

There's power in knowing when to close a chapter. Growth asks us to leave comfort behind. But taking my final bow was bittersweet. I was proud, I was exhausted, and I was ready. I had seen the duality of greatness: its beauty and its burden. And I've learned to embrace duality; to hold the beauty and the brokenness at the same time. To speak the truth even when it's uncomfortable. And to keep evolving, even when the next step is uncertain.

Let's Go to the Woods

That summer turned out to be one of the best summers of my life! A friend of mine called me about a summer camp where he taught primitive skills. They were in need of a trip leader for their backpacking trips. And yeah—after Broadway, I went to summer camp. I had to get wilderness EMT certified and I decided it would be great knowledge to have. My very first impression of the EMT course was that the information was so important. And I felt as though everyone needed this basic knowledge. CPR, bone breaks, stopping bleeding, and safety measures were some of the critical protocols we learned. I took the course seriously as I would be leading kids ages seven to eighteen on one- to five-day backpacking trips through the Appalachian Mountains.

I already knew some of the trails we would be hiking on. And the ones I'd never hiked I scouted on my own, planned breaks by age group, and mentally prepared for worst-case scenarios. Once summer camp began, it was fun taking kids from New York City backpacking in the woods. Most had never done it before. And to be completely honest, there were many times it was strange for me to come from leading the biggest Broadway show to becoming a camp trip leader. But it was easy and fun for me because kids from NYC are hilarious and have a worldly understanding growing up in a large city. I let them have fun but quickly set the tone from the beginning of each hike. They had to quickly push past limits while on the trail. And once they fell in line and got to relax at the campsite, they really loved it. I learned that a lot of the kids liked the discipline of having to push through. They felt accomplished even if it was a one day, five-mile hike to the campsite. Structure and discipline coming from someone other than their parents or teachers was different to them. I shared with them; I didn't talk down to them like children. I didn't want to boss anyone around. But when I needed their attention, it was because I cared and had to think about their safety, and they understood.

We would talk about plants and trees and birds along the way. My friend was teaching all the kids primitive skills back at camp every day and this was their test to make sure they learned what he was teaching in real time. Every time we arrived at a campsite they had to set up tents by themselves. If they had trouble, they needed to ask for help from what I called "their little tribe." Then, if they wanted a fire, they had to collect wood themselves and start the fire. I was only there to help and give them tips. When it came time for dinner, I didn't tend to the fire or cook for them. If they were hungry, they had to cook. This was nature and no one was going to baby them, especially not me.

Every time a kid would complain I would tell them, "You have a little tribe, complain to them and see what they have to say." Or, "Imagine if you were out here alone, what would you do? Would the trees care? Would the deer care that you're hungry and don't want to cook for yourself?" I had to do it that way. I had to make it real for them at first, and play time would come after. And it always did when everyone was fed and just got to run around barefoot. These kids were free, away from their phones, with the forest as their playground.

The older groups were my favorite. Even though I was double their age, I was young enough to relate to what they had going on in their lives. The younger kids definitely had a lot more questions, but the teenagers seemed to have specific questions that led to what they really wanted to know. I know it was nice for them to have someone older to talk to that wasn't going to bullshit them. A trip leader or counselor seemed easier for them to talk to because they didn't have to be told what to do or be disciplined by them on a day-to-day basis. Trust was built over the summer and especially on the longer trips. Kids would share more as trust was earned, and I felt honored to have their trust. Usually, after the first day on longer trips everyone settled into the experience and had a lot of fun. The longer hikes became more of a fun challenge and exploration for them rather than a trip from A to B. Every so often I would stop briefly and ask them, "Where is the water? Where is the food? Where are the animals? Where is a good shelter area?" Eventually, I would go for a while without saying it and I could hear them start to consult with each other on different parts of the trail. My little mini tribe. We were awesome!

One trip became unforgettable. On a five-day hike, a strange man at a shelter made one of my campers uncomfortable. Twice. I pulled him aside, made my position clear, and when his energy didn't shift, I made a call. We quietly packed up at sunset and moved to another site, hiking two hours in the dark. The next morning, we debriefed the situation. I taught them the value of intuition, boundaries, and knowing when to deescalate instead of escalate. Even though you want to teach someone a lesson, nothing is worth an unexpected knife fight. I knew I was crazy enough if something went down I would handle it. But I also knew he was crazy too. Sometimes your safety is more important than proving a point.

We continued on with the remaining two days of the five-day hike and had an amazing time! We were all learning, eating wild berries, making fires, and enjoying the nights. At the end of completing the five-day hike, I gave the kids their trail names. Most hikers have trail names given to them. And by the last day, the kids called me ChipMonk. They said, "Because you're always hustling like a chipmunk in the mornings, but once we set up camp, you chill like a monk." It was actually the perfect name. It was so good, I got a chipmunk, as a monk, tattooed on my leg. Those kids and the experiences we had meant a lot to me. I felt like I was giving back knowledge to the next generation and my heart felt full. That summer reminded me that no matter how far you go, your purpose will always pull you toward service. And mine was just beginning. The summer only got better when I got called by a friend to go across the country for a gathering.

V

DOWNLOADS

Finding My Tribe

I was invited by friends to visit Mount Shasta in Northern California. I felt an immediate response to go and that August I flew into Los Angeles and took a ten-hour road trip with a friend to the mountain. I arrived at one of the most beautiful forests I had ever seen! The beauty and energy of the area is hard to describe. It felt like all tension was released the moment I drove up from the small town to the top of the mountain. The areas around the top of the mountain feel angelic, crystalline, and pure. The baseline creates a calmness that is rare even for a national state park. This forest doesn't attract the typical oversized American RV family trips or alcoholics that want to get drunk. It's almost as though the spiritual protectors keep that energy out of the mountain. This first visit to Mount Shasta was for a very special reason. The very first day I remember there were around one hundred people on the mountain, all gathered for the solar eclipse the following day. Everyone was walking around meeting and talking with friends and strangers. I met a friend who I would end up having a soul connection with. We'll call her Wally; she was like my soul sister. Wally and I found ourselves at a tree and we immediately connected. When all of a sudden, a cute little chipmunk crawled right up a boulder and over to us. I had some trail mix in my bag and put an almond in my hand. The chipmunk, cautious, yet curious, eventually scrambled over and ate the almond right out of my hand! The connection was there.

Then, we heard tuning forks behind us. It was a sound and energetic vibration that caught our attention immediately. We both looked at each other and realized we had to go sit in the circle that was gathering. The two people playing the tuning forks struck them again and my entire spine contracted and then straightened. I could feel my body's central nervous system light up and come online. It felt like we were in a vortex of sound. Others started to join the circle and without anyone leading we all began meditating. For around thirty minutes the group connected spiritually while listening to the tuning forks and a singing bowl. By the end, everyone opened their eyes with smiles on their faces. We knew the ceremony for the week had begun.

That night, a few of us went to a waterfall cave. It was beautiful. It was a different type of energy from the rest of the mountain range. You could walk deep into the cave. And as we sat down, we all felt like we weren't supposed to be in the cave just yet and that we should wait until sunset. Strangers, yet all mutually acquainted through one friend, quickly became in sync as everyone was aware and listening. So, we all exited the cave and walked further down the trail, finding a place to sit overlooking a river. We played music, sang songs, and just enjoyed the area. After an hour, I had to walk away to do a private sit with myself. I realized we were all settling down in preparation for the ceremony we didn't know we were about to have.

Looking back, the spiritual forest protectors of that area were watching us to feel our energy to see if they were going to interact with us and allow us in the cave. Fortunately, it felt like they gave us permission. The lesson in this is that **you must ask the forest if you may enter**. Without permission, you may be walking into an animal nursing its young and not be aware of it. The forest may not want human activity. And some lands need time to heal energetically from being forested or over use. You could even walk into an area that is chemically contaminated, and because you didn't ask permission, you end up getting sick. The forest is home to others and we should all enter with consent the same way we would ask for an invitation to enter someone's home. The other beautiful lesson is that complete strangers can become like soul family in the matter of hours the way it happened for us that week. We were all fascinated with each other and met with a limited facade. It created synchronization almost instantly. So, in short, **vibrate your truth and you'll find your soul tribe.**

Right after sunset we all decided it was time to return into the cave. When we settled, the energy from the cave was intense. Everyone felt there were beings there waiting for visitors. The seven of us went into meditation. Someone started to hum and everyone eventually joined in, creating a harmonic. We all immediately felt these beings. Some people saw them as tall white light energy forms, some with faces. I didn't see them as clearly, but I felt energies flying past me and around me almost as though they were dancing. It didn't last long, maybe twenty to thirty minutes. But it was beautiful, and it was one of my first shared spiritual experiences with new people. A shared experience is different. They are moments where you can look at someone and know something real and special happened. The experience is true when people can confirm something happening in real time, instead of you thinking to yourself that it didn't *really* happen.

We all walked out of there changed. As we left and began to walk up the mountain, the temperature got really warm, and then hot. We knew some energy was moving through. Then, everyone stopped. We could hear the beings or something in the cave humming and singing back to us, like their way of confirming what we experienced was real. It went on for a few minutes before it finally stopped. We went up to our cars laughing and hugging. This was my introduction into Shasta. Late that night I had to jump into my friend's tent, as my old tent had collapsed and it was too cold to sleep outside in just my sleeping bag. He asked what I was doing and I told him to just move over and get comfortable, I didn't leave him much of an option.

Day Two: The Eclipse. I woke up early in the morning and felt relaxed. After coffee, I walked around the mountain a bit with my friends. Later that morning, we met a young man on the mountain in a green wool poncho. He was hermit-like, gypsy-like. He did some martial arts with a feather in his mouth, just outside of the group that had formed. He then sat with a didgeridoo. One person passing by touched him; another hugged him. He eventually came and sat near me, and I said, "Hello," but he didn't respond. I couldn't feel out or understand his energy. But he started beatboxing to the drum circle. It felt like he was living super close to the earth.

After the drum circle when everyone was leaving, I wanted to connect with him but didn't make the effort. I went down to the parking lot and felt someone walk past. It was him. I told him I wanted to connect with him and told him my name, but he didn't respond. Instead, he gave me a hug heart to heart, and we had three long breaths together in the hug. He felt like me; a probable me in some other timeline. He was my brother and he was free. I received all of that without words in a thirty-second hug. I asked him how long he had been out there, and he counted four fingers on his left hand. I asked him if he could speak or was choosing not to and he again put up four fingers and laughed a little even though he was choosing to be mute. I told him thank you. I told him I felt his medicine. He had a purity and oneness emanating from him. And looking eye to eye with him, he had an almost animal-like gaze. I knew that feeling. I had gotten close to that feeling of not being in the world but fully being immersed in the natural one. And as he walked back to the forest, I thought to myself, "I never met a rich man this free."

By late afternoon, everyone was assembling and settling in on different parts of the mountain. My friend and I found a spot halfway up the mountain tucked into a thicket of trees. But I realized I forgot my water and I had to run down the mountain to get it. As soon as I tried to hike back up, I immediately felt like I was going to purge. Uh-oh! I tried to walk up more and it was no use, I wasn't going to make it. I immediately looked for the nearest bush that was at least taller than knee height. The problem was, there aren't many trees or bushes at the top of the mountain. I saw the closest shrubbery, ran over, and immediately started to take a poop. Nature was taking its course and I knew I was purging. Unfortunately, a small family of four was walking up a trail and couldn't see I was there. I tried to wave them off, but they were completely oblivious. They didn't see me until they were about fifty feet away and when the father looked up, all I could do was smile and wave. He quickly pushed his family forward, but the kids were curious and shocked. I yelled out, "Sorry! Nature calls!"

Luckily, I had the essentials I needed in my backpack to clean up and start heading back up the mountain. Source said it had to get me ready and clear for the download. Ok, cool.

As soon as I sat back down, the solar eclipse started, and it was intense. I immediately dropped into a still place and closed my eyes. The energy was getting even more intense. I found my solar glasses, looked at the sun, and saw the eclipse happening. I stared through the glasses and my body started to move. The sun felt like it was giving off plasma which came in cyclical waves toward my body, starting through the crown chakra in powerful white frequency light. The plasma energy continued down through my chakras, into the earth, and back towards the sun. It was a continuous flow of plasma energy. I felt like I was eating the sun. I said a prayer of gratitude. I put my friends and family in protection and love in white-light orbs. Just then, the natives of the land were on different mountain peaks and began howling. It brought chills to my body. This eclipse was clearly important. After their first few calls, we all began howling. I let out three howls and began sobbing heavily. I had not cried in a long time. The howl activated something inside me. I knew I was where I needed to be. I felt the call and followed my heart. I then realized that I was thirty-three years old, and I finally felt the inner "Click" I was looking for. It felt like my inner operating system came online, or as though I had a system reboot within my mind, body, and spirit. I was thankful. Something shifted and I would have to learn to walk in spiritual embodiment, taking each step with awareness and love. I was seeing with my third eye now.

I heard someone in the distance say, "**Just believe. Make a wish. Believe with your heart. Ask for your heart's desire. Ask the spirits and your guides to guide you through any pain or fear. If you want to be happy, just look up to the stars.**"

After the eclipse, my friend and I slowly walked down the mountain. Some people were crying from the energy from the eclipse. Others had big smiles on their faces. When I arrived at the valley section of the mountain, I saw my soul brother who was also getting over tears. He and I hugged, knowing we all just experienced a collective transformation. We couldn't do much the rest of the day except lay on the land and look at the trees and sky - no thoughts no emotions, just being. At the fire that night, a lot of people gathered in shock and awe about what happened. The energy was high in everyone. We had all shifted.

I woke up the next morning to the beautiful mountain. My body still wanted to purge a little. A small drum circle was starting on the mountain. My little crew made breakfast to the soft drumming and it seemed like everyone on the mountain was sharing their food and fruit. There was so much love, so much release, and so much diversity. Everyone was smiling, and it felt like how the world should be—full of care, hugs, listening, sharing, non-judgement, freedom, music, dancing, truth, minimalism—all led by the heart. It felt like how the New Earth would be, and maybe it already was.

That week I met an older gentleman named Meerkat. He was such a pure soul and the second person where I felt I had never met a rich man that free. It seems some of the people who roam with the wind or live that close to nature have the winds, the waters, the trees, the Earth, and Spirit that fills them. And I learned a valuable lesson that **there is purity, a real Christ-like purity in the world. Those people usually tend to live and stay in nature.**

Over the four days of being on the mountain the communication between our small group became telepathic. We always knew where other people were in spirit. We would communicate to another friend in our minds and they would appear. On the last day, I was in the meadow lying by the water for an hour before we had to leave. In my mind I could hear/feel one of my friends telling me to come out. I packed up and walked out to see the rest of my friends waiting in the car for me. I asked if they'd called me and everyone laughed…they did. I jumped in the car, gave my thanks to the mountain, and we started our journey back. Something about that mountain and the people it attracts is different from anywhere else I've traveled in the world. During the first couple of hours on our drive to the airport hawks were flying in the same direction as our car.

When I got back to LA, I flew out that night back to New York to figure out the next part of my journey, which was quickly changing.

The Return

Flying back into New York after a long trip in nature is always strange. The city looked like a circuit board, buildings in almost perfect order, at different sizes, resembling the inside of a computer. The city began to feel like a matrix to me and it didn't feel good. Within a few days I began looking for land as soon as I could. The dream that started in 2012 of building an off-grid cabin was getting louder.

Within two weeks of being back, I began driving all around New York state searching for homes and undeveloped land. I noticed that the areas and land I was looking at just didn't feel good. I had hiked many areas within an hour's distance of the city. But even the land and towns two to three hours further away felt depleted. In short, there had been a lot of mining over the last one hundred years, and I could spiritually feel the areas were still trying to recover. The mining made me concerned about the water and health of the land. I also started to notice the trees were all less than a hundred years old. I spoke to a close friend of mine who told me more about the history of logging in the US and how many times the land had been raped of its trees for usable lumber. The history of it all is sad. Kings in Europe were claiming old-growth forests in the Americas after hearing of them from expeditions they sent out. They had never stepped foot on the land themselves, yet felt they were able to claim land that belonged to natives, in order to have lumber for their ships. The entitlement is almost unimaginable, but it really happened. And the lands across this country are the evidence.

This led me to look even further for land that felt right. There were many times when I saw a property that *looked* great! But I would walk the land and talk to the trees and elements. Most of the time I would get clear images or a guttural feeling that it wasn't the right place. A lot of damage had been done and most areas just wanted to heal. This broke my heart. After six months of searching, I had to take a break. Another lesson that it wasn't the right time yet.

Downloads

The rest of the year included more insights. I had many breakthroughs and downloads and was still holding all the love from finding my new tribe. Randomly, two books appeared in my life. I don't even remember ordering them, but I knew the information was important to me. From both books I learned more about galactic history and dimensional timelines. Through all my reading and personal meditations, I kept feeling a major timeline shift between 2017-2022. Why was I receiving this timeline? I realized it was a second ascension window. I had a strong heart and gut feeling of leaving people behind. I felt like I was going to leave the planet. I felt it and I knew it. I began to have more questions. What planet am I from? Who were the helpers in the cave at Shasta? They were clearly there waiting for us. I needed to be open to receive answers from my angels. I began speaking to them a lot and began to get more insight as I continued to study and meditate. Months later I was seeing visions of a snake and hearing a woman's voice. I realized it was Mama Ayahuasca, and I was getting called again. I wasn't exactly excited and I sat with the idea of journeying again. But I know a call when I feel it. And that December, I decided to go to Peru for a week-long ceremony in the jungle with a well-known shaman.

Return to Mama Aya

The thing about energetic and spiritual work is I'm very particular about who I work with or who I allow to work on me. The place I decided to go to was recommended by two different friends. I wasn't in any rush or looking for a place to go. It just came up in conversation when I was talking about going into the jungle this time to work with the medicine. Those friends who had no relation to each other both led me to a man in Iquitos, Peru, who had been working with plant medicine for over thirty years. A very important factor for me is working with masters of their craft, not someone that has just started. I had been in ceremony a few times before with and without plant medicine. And I knew that opening yourself up spiritually, especially with plant medicine, can leave you vulnerable in the spiritual realms.

Ceremony begins the moment a person decides they will be doing the ceremony, even though the physical part may not happen for weeks, months, or even years. It's the person's responsibility to prepare and know how to hold space for themselves. But if a shaman is not a master of the ceremony, it can have negative effects during and after the ceremony. They could open spiritual doors they may not know how to close. Or they could be working with other entities that are not in the best interest of a person. In preparation of working with Aya I did my two-week diet again. I didn't have sugar, salt, oils, meat, dairy, or a lot of other foods in order to detox and become clear. I stayed disciplined with my diet.

When I arrived in Peru, I had to take a long taxi ride to a hotel for the night. The thing about Iquitos, Peru, is it can be very hot and humid. It gets so hot that most people don't go outside between noon and 4 p.m. And most hotels and restaurants don't have AC; it is the jungle, after all. That night, I slept as best I could underneath a small ceiling fan.

By morning, the retreat guests loaded onto a van that took us to a small entrance on the Amazon River. We all went in a "dug out" boat with a tarped roof and a small motor. After about thirty minutes on the Amazon River, we arrived on the shores of a very small village of no more than thirty people. We walked through the village on muddy roads with stray dogs passing us or following us partway. After about another hour-long hike we finally made it to the retreat center deep in the jungle.

Once at the retreat space, we were assigned small huts with raised wood floors, screened in walls, and a grass thatched roof. The size of the hut was large enough for a small bed, desk, hammock, and toilet. I loved it! I could see the jungle almost 360 degrees. It was simple, and all I needed. The rest of the first day involved relaxing into the environment of the jungle, allowing the body and mind to find a natural baseline. That night we had our first purge with no plant medicine. I did a purge that consisted of drinking a lot of water in a short amount of time in order to cleanse the body. I'll be honest, it sucks. You chug water until it feels like your belly is about to explode and you have to drink until the point of throwing up. Not fun. After the water purge, each person meets with the shaman who decides what plant drinks you will have to further clear and heal your system. Each person takes different plants depending on their needs, addictions, trauma, anxiety, you name it. The plant medicine comes in a shot glass that you take every morning and it's usually disgusting every time but is there to help you cleanse the body.

The second day is continued relaxation to rest the body and mind until the ceremony begins in the evening. The ceremony usually begins at sunset in what is called a maloca; a large circular structure that has mesh netting as the walls to keep out the bugs, rough wood floors, and a grass thatched roof. This allows for the outside connection to Mother Nature. Mapacho tobacco cigarettes are offered to people taking the journey during or after the ceremony. Each person has their own floor mat and pillow to make the journey comfortable. Once everyone is settled in, they approach the shaman one by one to receive their first shot glass of ayahuasca. The concoction looks like brown hot chocolate. It's made up of ayahuasca vine and leaves that act as a catalyst for the DMT.

On the first night of the ceremony when I approached the shaman, I was already in meditation, in thanksgiving for the ceremony. I spoke my intention, drank the shot, and almost couldn't keep it down from the taste. I went back to my floor mat and waited. Once everyone had their first cup, the shaman slowly began using his rattle and softly sang his icaro chant. To me, an icaro is a catalyst for the medicine. It's like a song that summons the plant medicine to come forth and work her magic. Each icaro has a specific sound that is personal to the shamen themselves that creates a different field throughout different parts of the ceremony. The first part feels like the shaman is opening up the portal or removing the veil between the physical world and the spiritual realms. The song is soft, nurturing, and in gratitude. As I dropped deeper into meditation, it was as if I could see the shaman in his spiritual form at the edge of two worlds, pulling back the curtain to allow the spiritual world to open. As the singing and shakers intensify, the energy of the song calls Aya in the form of a snake or black jaguar to come forth from the jungles of the spirit realm. She arrives slowly the way any animal would. She lets her presence be known softly, coming in vision, so as to not scare you. Her presence feels wise, sometimes motherly, and intense. It's a person's own fears that pushes her away, or their open heart that brings her in closer. And in this ceremony, I wanted to go all the way in. She came to me as a large snake, bigger than me in size and looked at me face to face. I sat up and put my back against a post as if in honor of the elder arriving. She had my attention, and I wanted to give her my respect. She scanned me, almost to see who I was and if I was ready. I stayed in a state of gratitude. And I subconsciously told her, "I'm ready."

Then, she got bigger, and I saw the rest of her body. She opened her mouth and swallowed my entire body. I got quiet; internally quiet in a way I'd never felt before. My mind, my thoughts, just blank. I felt like I was floating in a sea of blackness, but I wasn't scared. I just waited. I could hear the shaman sing the icaro and it started to change in tempo and cadence. It made my body get chills. My only thought was, "Here we go."

My body began dancing like a snake. From a seated position, I physically swayed my body right to left. It felt good. It was me, but it was Mama Aya working through me. I opened my eyes to the room of the maloca which was lit only by one candle. Though it was dark, I saw most people lying down, almost like they were sleeping. I closed my eyes and quickly drop into my journey. The swaying continued, and I let go of everything around me. I sat up to my knees to allow the dance to happen, but I was conscious enough to not make a sight of myself and to not distract others. At some point, I let myself go further. I was enjoying the song; it felt like it was my favorite song. After a while when I opened my eyes again, I looked up at the roof of the maloka. With my third eye I could see past it to the cosmos and I could see all the stars. I was happy.

I Became A Tiger

I looked down at where the floor was and saw a huge hole, like a portal opening. It mirrored the sky, but I could tell it was going underground. As above, so below. I put both hands on the floor and it felt as though I had claws. I stretched my back, then stretched each leg behind me one at a time. I looked down at my arms and hands. I saw my fur and paws, and long claws. I could tell I was shifting and then realized I became a tiger! I felt so good, like I was in my body again. I remembered being a Bengal tiger; free, strong, and powerful! I continued to dance like a tiger on all fours. I was a protector. I wanted to protect my brothers and sisters. I realized the portal I saw below me was a portal from the underworld. I could see beings from below wanting to come up into the physical realm. But I growled and hissed at them to stay down. I wouldn't let them come up and interfere. I was protecting the dimension and Aya made me strong. I flexed my claws a little more and stretched out my body. I saw more entities wanting to come up again, and I hissed them away.

A message came through, "Be still like Tiger; observe. Wait and see what presents itself. The perfect hunt. Bravery. Courage."

I remembered a mentor once telling me, **"The man with courage is not one who doesn't feel fear; he's the one who conquers fear."** And that message came up strong that night.

After maybe an hour or so, I slowly came down from the vision and had to use the restroom. When I came out of the restroom, Aya spoke to me again, saying she would never bite me. And I had a strange feeling that I had been to this time and space before. I found that interesting. I looked up and stared at all the stars. It felt like I was looking for something. After a minute or so, I saw lights moving in the shadows, little orbs of white light and they were dancing and getting closer. I don't know why, but I knew they were family. I looked up and saw a star. My heart beamed. It felt like my home star. I saw a shooting star that travelled a little too long and seemed to land in the tree line. Was the star actually a ship? Did they come to get me? The lights came in closer, maybe two or three of them, and I started to see them form.

"Don't be scared, they're coming to get you." The light orbs said telepathically.

I wanted to put on my headlamp, but they quickly said, "No light. They don't like the light, it's too much."

Just then, one of the shaman's helpers came out and asked if I was ok.

"Yes." I replied.

And he asked me to come back into the maloca. I went back with him.

When I sat down, I kept my eyes open and looked at the others. I saw my brothers and sisters asleep or in pain. They were shifting on their floor mats, and I could tell they were working through issues. I saw the shaman working his magic and realized I was seeing him on the spiritual plane. In the physical, he was to my right with his head down, shaking his rattle in his right hand and singing the icaros. When I looked ahead with a wider vision or closed my eyes, he was in the space spiritually walking around to each person. He was trying to wake them up, softly. Wake them up from their slumber. But no one was waking up.

I heard a bird call from outside start to sound. But in the spiritual plane, it wasn't just a call; it was like an alarm clock to wake up. I heard Mama Aya say, "**We are here to wake up as many people as we can. But then, we will have to leave those who still want to sleep.**"

I closed my eyes. I felt like I was in a Matrix pod. Even though my eyes were closed, I could look around the room and see more people in pods. The pods were always full of new people, like sleeping babies. The purge is like them trying to get out of the artificial womb. The coughs like air bubbles.

I heard the beings from outside speak to me. "**We are here to raise people up, because the Law of One is to help everyone. We want everyone to know love, to feel love, to be loved.**"

I kept feeling like I was in school. The light orbs outside were waiting for me to come play, but I needed to stay inside and learn. "You have a gift. It doesn't come easy, but you must work on it. Work from the heart, not the mind. Being taught right now. In class. Be here now. Know your baseline."

The messages I was receiving were all pointing to a collective healing and reawakening within humanity. I realized there are different roles to be filled to help people wake up; speakers, teachers, shamans, prophets, and the like. In the present moment, I could see the shaman was doing his part by moving energy through people with the medicine, waking them up and helping them heal deep traumas. I felt like I was going to have a role in helping others too. I just didn't know what that would look like or where to begin. But I knew I was in my own container of healing and receiving messages for my own remembrance. I could leave the "when and how," for another time and just focus on the present moment.

After a few hours, I slowly came down from the medicine back into my body. When the ceremony was over, I immediately went to bed. My mind and body were still. I was calm and quickly fell asleep.

Sirius B

The second night of the ceremony I quickly went into myself in deep surrender. I surrendered to Earth and saw geometric codes and colors. Then, I saw light at the top of the maloca. It looked to be a light the size of a star, and I felt myself go through it - fast. I shot through a light portal and realized I was on another planet; a military base of some sort. I saw a plane or a ship fly over, but I wasn't allowed to follow it. I was only allowed to observe. It was docking on a floating planet to my left. The planet where I stood didn't have a lot of oxygen and the ground was dusty and more brown/reddish in color. It was like I was on a separate base to view ships coming in and out. I knew Earth was always home. But Earth was a little separate from where I was on this journey. I knew I had been to this place before, in this same time and space. I knew I could travel and had a personal spaceship. I felt/heard, "Sirius B."

Sirius B? I thought it was just a star. But in the vision, it felt like a planet that was an international base station. I was in a group like the military, but for the Light. I felt different. I shook my head "yes." I remembered holding this post. I held that post as a Light protector, the same way our airports now have security. Except we were traveling to different planets and star systems. The remembrance felt lucid, as though I was really there. I could look back to the light I came through down towards my right foot. The star or light was a Light highway. One could travel through light highways if they held the light within them. I knew I was connecting to the stars and to the multiverse. I eventually came down from remembering this lifetime and found myself back in the present moment with full knowing I had lived or worked there before.

The Tree of Life

As the ceremony continued, I surrendered even deeper. I purged that night, and it was like the rest of the darkness was pulled from me. The congestion in my heart was gone. Aya showed me my medicine, and it was dance (Duh)! When I dance, I open the hearts of people and dance with spirit. Aya and the spirits love dancing. After the purge I closed my eyes, and this time, I laid down. Immediately I heard, "Protect the tree."

I was transported to what felt like inner Earth. I saw a huge tree and went to sit by it. I had been to inner Earth before in other meditations and sitting at other sacred sites. But this tree felt different. There were others sitting around the tree also protecting and learning from it. It was beautiful. I felt lucid and the moment felt as though all of this was happening in real time and I just happened to drop in. This was the Tree of Life, which helps us remember our origins and to get back to love. The Tree was a spiritual imprint on the Earth and within human DNA.

Part of the spiritual war is that the dark side wants to cut off the tree. If they cut off the Tree of Life, people will be cut off and forget where they came from, which is love, light, and God Source. If they cut people off from the tree, their souls will be stuck. They won't remember anymore and the darkness will be able to scare or manipulate them and feed off their fear and bioelectricity. This war over the Tree of Life imprint is one reason we fight, which is to protect the tree connected to Earth so people can wake up and be free again.

I protect the tree by getting close to the Earth and learning her ways with my brothers and sisters. Helping people return to her as well. If we don't learn the medicine, it will be lost. I felt sad because I knew there would be a time, we would have to leave society and leave people behind. None of us want to leave them because we believe love and connection to Source is everyone's birthright. But the time was coming soon. The sight of this beautiful tree was magic. It glistened with different colors, and was right-side-up no matter if you were at the roots or branches. It confirmed the phrase, "as above, so below."

When I came down from the vision, I purged again. Then, Mama Aya asked me if I was ready to see the world of darkness? I was only halfway ready and I was unsure. But I decided there was no better time and the shift quickly happened. In my third eye vision, the darkness came in from my right, like a scene change. I then understood why the shaman had to spit and blow his nose and cough, because every time he goes to that place, he has to get it out of his system. He's like a firefighter who goes back in for more. He goes back to wake more people up and get them to safety. He sits there like a parent singing his song with his shaker gently trying to wake up the children. I was thankful to him, to Mama Aya, Earth Mother, and Creator.

I was eager to learn more. But most importantly, I was eager to do God's work. All this information—my past lives, the spiritual war, the sacred Tree of life—showed me I was here to remember and recollect myself so I could move into the next part of my life mission with a better understanding of what has happened universally.

Light At The End of The Tunnel

The third night, I took my first cup, a larger dose than the other two nights. I felt like I was blasting off quickly! I closed my eyes and had an image of walking through a golden light temple with sick brothers and sisters on either side. I noticed I was taller than everyone else. Growth codes; 333, 333. Aya asked me if I wanted to see the darkness again, if I was ready to see where the shamans go. I said, "Yes." I went into a cave full of darkness, entities, and insects. I was riding on the back of the anaconda. I was a white orb. The darkness would try to reach out, but they couldn't touch me. I wasn't scared, but she said, "It gets deeper."

I turned into a man, back in Egypt. I saw a geometric shape on the ground; it was a crown. "King," she said.

I am a king. I have been fighting off the darkness for a long time. My staff had a spinning crown on top of it. I could throw energy and electricity from it. Then I heard, "Star Children, come home," two or three times. I was being pulled into a portal in the sky, but I had to let go of my staff. I didn't need to fight and protect anymore. My whole body was being pulled through, but I was trying to bring my staff. I had to let it go, and I did.

I came back to the present day, but I was back in darkness. I was still and calm physically. Then, I felt like I started dying. I knew it wasn't a physical death, so I tried to calm my mind and relax. I couldn't move but I could breathe. I had the visual of ants and insects beginning to take me, eating me. I started smiling and said, "You can take my body, but you can't take me, motherfuckers! The "king me" was stabbing me with the staff saying, "Die, die, die!"

That was aggressive. It was like the older part of my soul was trying to quicken the process, because it was time to move on. Then, more insects. They were trying to tell me they were my god. I was them. I said, "No, I am of the Light." I prayed to God for truth and clarity. I started to come out of the darkness. The music began to slow down and eventually the shaman stopped singing. His apprentice asked if anyone wanted a second cup.

And slowly, I peeled myself off of the floor and made my way to him. I took my second cup.

I made it back to my floor mat and pillow and everything began to intensify. I was confused about what was real. If the messages I was getting were real, if the New Earth was real, or if it was just in my mind. I prayed to God and Aya again. I laid down on my side, but the sound of the icaro triggered me to lay on my back. I felt how beautiful Earth was, how special she was. I started traveling to outer space, but a spiral was coming into the top of my head. They said it was the codes, and that I would understand them soon. I started to travel in my own personal spaceship. I was in the far future. People were traveling in the cosmos to a floating city. They were docking. Like a futuristic *Jetsons*. It felt like the place I would study, work, or visit. It wasn't home, but I would go a lot. I was happy. I enjoyed coming out of the doubt and back into knowing. I enjoyed the experience and the rest of the icaros for the next few hours.

That night when I went to bed, I knew something was changing. I had the feeling again that I chose to leave. I was tired of fighting on this planet; it goes on and on. I was ready for something new.

The next morning. I woke up with a lot of anxiety. The feeling like I always need to or should be doing something. But I don't. I'm taking the carrot on the stick off my head. Fuck that carrot! I could feel like my heart was opening further, like a lotus flower. I kept seeing the flower over my heart chakra. I needed a good cry, a good release. I was thankful for my path and my tribe and that I no longer accepted societal programming. I only accepted the natural truth. I was ready for the next ceremony.

My Exit

The fourth night, the shaman's assistant knew I had been deep in my journey the whole week. He told the shaman to offer me three cups in the first sitting that night. Something about it felt off to me about the assistant. I could tell the shaman even asked him if that was going to be ok. The shaman looked at me. I told him whatever they suggested, and I took all three shots. That shit was too intense right away. I started by seeing white lights from the upper left side of my head. Then, I felt the darkness collect on the left side of the maloca. It was a collective darkness that wasn't mine. I couldn't hold my space, and I wasn't grounded. My personal darkness started coming through. I saw the underbelly of insects and their legs, like maybe I had insects inside of me. I tried to stand, but I could barely walk. I was so weak. I asked the assistant to take me to the bathroom and as I stood up the experience got more intense. It was the feeling of being trapped, like I couldn't breathe.

I asked for the "cutting serum" of lemon, salt, and onion, which helps stop the medicine in order to come down from the ride. It is something they give people who don't want to journey anymore. But it wasn't helping. I felt like I needed air and sat outside of the bathroom. I didn't know what to feel. I was so uncomfortable, like I didn't know if I needed to cry, sleep, laugh, poop, pee, anything. I just felt like I needed more help and asked the assistant to bring me more serum to cut the medicine. I could see past him and see the stars. The serum made me throw up immediately, and I felt like I had to go to the bathroom again. But as I tried to walk into the bathroom, I couldn't breathe and I felt like there was darkness in the bathrooms from all the purging. I somehow knew it was a place of releasing darkness and I couldn't close the door. I didn't want to be left alone. I just wanted to cry and for it to be over.

When I sat back down outside, I remember the assistant putting his hand over my back telling me it was going to be ok. But I couldn't breathe. I felt like I was taking fewer breaths and getting less oxygen. I felt like I was about to die in real life because I knew I was still mentally present. From the sky I saw a bright white light almost as a portal opening, in front and above me. Aya or a female voice said, "Are you ready to go?" as though I had the choice to die and move forward.

But I was scared, and I didn't want to die. I thought about my mother and her hearing I died in the jungle. I wasn't ready for her to bear that. I thought for a moment and realized; this was it. This is why I felt like I was leaving the past few years. But I replied, "No! I'm not ready to go!" And the light quickly went away. I immediately came back into my body and slowly, terribly slowly, started coming down. It felt like forever. I didn't like the feeling that I didn't have control of my mind or what was happening. Maybe that's the process of letting go of control. But I didn't feel safe. Maybe I should have died in surrender to the Light. I just couldn't tell if it was a death with the medicine or an actual death. But now, looking back, I'm thankful that I had a choice. Thank God! I tried to slowly stand up, but I still didn't have any strength. I knew the assistant needed to be close to the maloca. But every time we got close, I could feel the darkness inside and I couldn't go in there. I couldn't be in and around other people's darkness. There was a part of me that said, "You don't need to be here. This isn't yours; this is their process." I tried to get closer again, but immediately something inside me said, "Absolutely not, it's too thick of darkness in there." It's a voice I trusted, maybe one of my personal tools of knowing. So, the assistant took me into the smaller maloca and I laid down.

I was so tired. Was this Mama Aya showing me the deeper parts of darkness? Was this where the real shamans go? Was there relief knowing there is Light beyond all of it? I just wanted it to be over, to be fully back on Earth and grounded. I think I was afraid to die because I wasn't fully ready to let go. I wasn't ready to let go of family or friends. But I know these are still just physical attachments. I know that one day I will have to leave it all behind. I will have to shed my physical self to fly like a butterfly. I guess I have some more learning and loving to do, even though I thought I was ready to leave. But I know when the moment comes to surrender, when we all have to surrender to the Light, we will leave it all behind. There's nothing to take with us and there is no going back. We will be so much lighter, and the release of all things will be powerful and beautiful. I know that now.

A lot of time passed, at least it felt that way. I remember being so tired and still hearing the sounds of the shaman singing his icaros. I could tell the shaman was doing a lot of work in the darkness. But there were a few times I couldn't tell if I trusted him. I was trying to see if he was working for the insect people. But then I remembered he and his people did work for the Earth, and I decided not to let my mind spin out further. But I couldn't fall asleep. I didn't trust falling asleep. I was praying to God and the Light to come in and help me. I remember telling Mama Ayahuasca her medicine was too strong, and I wanted it to stop. I saw her as a snake retreating back into a tree. I said, "Thank you," and kept praying for the Light. At some point I remember taking a deep breath. Mama Aya said, "**This is freedom. Breath, choosing to live, choosing to discover.**"

I felt a colorful bird with big wings spread across my chest. Freedom. I felt and saw the lotus flower on my chest slowly opening its petals. It was all about love and opening the heart. Love was the center, the zero-point energy.

Once I had the strength, I went outside from the secondary maloca. I still didn't want to go into the main maloca. I knew the energy was intense and I felt that the ceremony was going to end early. And it did. As I sat outside, I slowly came back into my body. I kept feeling like I needed to leave the next morning. I remembered another person left the day before and I wondered if he had the same feeling too. I called a friend I trusted early the next morning, and she said, "Yeah, you need to go." Even now I feel like I trusted my gut and my heart and made the right decision to leave early.

When I was trying to leave Peru, the flights kept getting mixed up. Mama Ayahuasca kept showing me to trust myself with everything—leaving, flights, going to the woods, all of it. Eventually I made it home and needed a lot of time to integrate the lessons. One of them being that no matter where I go, no matter where I travel: "**The answer is always inside of me. The answer is always simple. Life is about truth in simplicity.**"

When I finally returned home, I felt humbled from the experience. I had made it back from what felt like the "spiritual deep end." In retrospect, Mama Aya showed me the place in spirit where the shaman goes to do their work. I learned in a new way how we can walk in spirit, travel in spirit, and work in spiritual realms. When we know we hold the light, we can heal ourselves and others. We can face darkness without fear and understand that facing darkness is not always a fight, sometimes it's a letting go. And even if darkness takes a long time to release and heal, and all we can do is hold our Light, eventually, we make it through.

I then took stock of everything I was learning and downloading the past few years. **The entire time period was about DNA and upgrading to our original angelic blueprint. The DNA was connected to our memory—remembering our galactic and**

spiritual history and remembering ourselves in the process. It was time to heal all the trauma that we had been through as a human species and a planet on all planes of existence. I started to "see" and remember more, and it all made sense to me. This was remembrance I was seeking without even knowing it. And it was only the foundation for what was to come.

I meditated a minimum of two to four hours a day. I kept traveling in spirit and received so much information. Things were getting clearer. The Tree of Life, time, and timelines became very important. And after reading fanatically, my research began to confirm the information I was getting spiritually. It was like I was relearning knowledge I already knew in my soul. I could understand the unity and the linear layout of God, Spirit, and Time. I will break it down into the easiest way I can for those who are not used to understanding energy in dimensional time.

VI
GOD IN DIMENSIONALITY

Dimensions

There are many timelines existing at once. The past, present, and future are all happening simultaneously. And somehow, all possibilities still have a structure. Different potential timelines exist separately yet they can also overlap or be experienced consciously. A dimension represents time and space. Each dimension holds a certain vibration or density. Some dimensions like Earth are denser. As we move into higher dimensions, we physically become less dense. Our physical makeup actually becomes less carbon based and more crystalline in its structure. Our ability to learn, heal, and to evolve comes much easier. However, in order to reach higher dimensions, we must learn the lessons here on Earth, first. One of the simplest lessons yet hardest for humanity to achieve individually and as a whole is unconditional love.

Dimension = Time + Space (from a human perspective)

There are fifteen dimensions within what is called a time matrix.

Dimensions are grouped together in threes which create a harmonic universe.

Harmonic Universe = 3 Dimensions

Think of the dimensions like grades in grade school. We start in first grade then move on to second grade, third grade, and so forth. Now, think of the Harmonic Universes like physical schools containing a certain number of grade levels. For instance…

Dimensions 1-3 within Harmonic Universe 1 (HU-1) is similar to elementary school.

Dimensions 4-6 within Harmonic Universe 2 (HU-2) is similar to middle school.

Dimensions 7-9 within Harmonic Universe 3 (HU-3) is similar to high school.

Dimensions 10-12 within Harmonic Universe 4 (HU-4) is similar to college.

Dimensions 13-15 within Harmonic Universe 5 (HU-5) is similar to getting a master's degree.

Beyond this Time Matrix there are more matrices with other timeline potentials. But for the human consciousness there are fifteen within spiritual reach. I once felt we could not know what lies beyond in the higher dimensions or higher harmonic universes. But I believe now there are a few who actually can see and travel beyond fifteen dimensions. It's great to know the other dimensions exist but understanding the first twelve to fifteen is our main focus.

Within each of these dimensions, in this "life school," are different lessons for a soul. A soul must learn the lessons in Harmonic Universe 1 (elementary school), before they graduate to Harmonic Universe 2 (middle school). Education and progression are the reasons why humans who want to evolve can only "touch" the upper realms at first. A person can only "step in the classroom" of higher dimensions or realms and observe, initially. There are spiritual and etheric gatekeepers in the higher realms protecting the dimensions. Spirits, angels, and higher vibrational beings can "drop down" to help us learn and guide us towards evolution the same way a middle schooler helps his siblings in elementary school with their lessons. But just like our older brothers and sisters, it's difficult for "older" energies to lower themselves into a slower dimension to teach their little siblings.

Currently, we live between dimensions three through five on a fourth density. We've barely graduated to middle school in our time matrix. However, we and the Earth Mother are ascending towards a less dense reality in the fifth dimension in the second Harmonic Universe (HU-2). Most of humanity is in the third and fourth dimensions with a potential to understand higher dimensions at this time. The same is for us in our fundamental understanding of the universe. For humans existing in a third-dimensional consciousness the idea of teleportation, self-healing, unconditional love, or a healthy and self-sustaining society, isn't even in their perception. But it doesn't mean that it doesn't exist.

The densities of physicality also lessen as you move up in dimensions. Some beings have a less emotional extremes as they don't live in the mind and live more from the heart. But beings of darkness can also exist in the upper-dimensional realms. And they too deal in less emotionality, but they are not connected to a heart frequency. Light and dark are spectrums on the same scale.

In higher realms, there also seems to be time compression. This is not exact, but to give an example, imagine one month in higher dimensions is equivalent to a decade in this lower dimension. And the higher up in consciousness levels is shorter in time "up there" but longer here on Earth. I have yet to confirm this, but it is something that I've personally experienced.

Viewing Dimensions Like a Radio

Dimensions are planes of existence that can be reached through consciousness expansion. Another way to view the totality of dimensions is to visualize them as frequency bands, similar to an old radio. On radios, there are different stations to "tune into." By changing the dial on the radio, or in other words changing the energetic frequency, a person can tap into or join another station/ or place of frequency. If you want to be in a lower frequency, you can tune into anger or destruction. If you want peace, love, and abundance you can tune into higher realms. So the question is: *"What are you tuning into?"*

Viewing Dimensions Like Spheres

These different planes or dimensions can also be viewed in their truest form as spheres within spheres, similar to an onion. Dimension 1-3 would be the core, the most dense layers. Further out would be dimensions 4-6, 7-9, and 10-12. Dimensions 12-15 would be the least dense and furthest layers out near the onion skin.

The planet itself is multidimensional. In lower dimensions where it is denser, the planetary version is Earth. A few layers out is her higher or less dense self as Tara. Even further out still, in even less density and her highest version, is herself as Gaia. It's similar to this version of you being most like the inner core. Your "higher selves" or the higher versions of you are the outer, less dense spheres.

Gatekeepers

As I stated before, there are gatekeepers between dimensions. Some of the gatekeepers may be of the darkness, using fear, anger, or confusion to keep a person blocked from moving forward or upward in their evolution. Those malevolent beings want to keep humans continuing the process of siphoning their energy and they don't want to lose their energetic food source. There are also beings of Light at some of the gates. The gatekeepers of Light ensure that as a person is moving upward in their evolution, they understand the rules on these higher levels. It's as though they "look" into or "tap" into a person's heart space. At some point, a person can no longer hold certain fears, anger, regret, jealousy, envy, and lower energies. The energy at higher levels won't allow that energy to seep into its ranks. There is no place for that. It's like a third grader stepping into the sixth grade; everyone knows how to take care of themselves and has a much deeper understanding of learning.

Viewing Timelines

Timelines exist within dimensions and there are multiple timelines happening at once in each dimension. Let me give an example; imagine electric power lines that go down a road. The power lines represent multiple timelines. Now, the energy is the same in all the lines which all come from the same power source. The same thing happens with multiple timelines existing at the same time. All of their energy comes from the same source. But the electrons (animals or humans) are not always aware of the other electrons (animals, humans, or beings) in other powerlines. But it doesn't mean they don't exist.

What if we could step outside these dimensions and view them happening at once? Would we then see what God sees? There are many different ways to view the same concept of dimensions within our time matrix. I hope one of the examples helps readers visually understand the higher levels of consciousness, and the fact that there is much more going on beyond this realm.

God as a Mandala

When I zoomed out to see the bigger picture, I began to see God as a mandala, expressing and experiencing itself as an inhale and exhale through time. Each exhale was a push of creation and expression happening over millions of years! Imagine all the life that came and went throughout millions of years. Then, imagine all those lives and creation happening in one exhale, starting to contract and collapse on the inhale. The inhale is the return of creation to itself happening over millions of years. Then, it exhales again, creating an entirely new expression, an entirely new era or epoch of life that happens over another million years.

Another visual concept is something I call, "the mandala of time matrices." Visualize God's point of view as a tree. Then, imagine each "branch" is a time matrix and each "leaf" is a dimensional experience. Each season that passes is a new expression of the God Tree learning and experiencing itself through each branch and leaf until it reaches winter or death. It returns to its original self, only to sprout again. It's never ending. Even stillness is momentary. A creator is meant to create.

If you were a God, would you be bored in nothingness having every potential inside of you? Wouldn't you want to experience all that you create? Wouldn't you want to express through the infinite parts that are connected?

God Source itself must be neutral in its expression. It's the only thing that makes sense in my heart, because I never understood suffering. The reality of suffering bothered me to the core of my being. But this was my human viewpoint. From the viewpoint of

Source, all the suffering, the slavery, the hate on the planet, all the love, creativity, joy, and innovation are happening at the same time. Maybe we wouldn't appreciate the good without the bad? If we can view God Source as a mandala experiencing everything in neutral expression then everything just is.

Fractals

Zooming in from the macro, we as humans are tiny fractals that contain the entire multiverse. We are holographic. The moment a person begins to realize the implications that they are a small holographic fractal containing all things, their life begins to change. It doesn't mean that you are all knowing; only God Source knows and experiences everything. But it is possible to answer your own questions from within and be a co-creator in your life. This realization only makes life a lot more interesting and maybe more digestible and peaceful when you realize you are a part of the One and everyone you meet is you. **Everyone you see or meet is also God, expressing itself through that unique individual.** Which is why we shouldn't judge people. It is God living another trillionth experience of itself through that individual.

From one perspective, it might seem like a selfish endeavor for God to have all of these experiences through us. But imagine if you could experience everything happening at once. For some, it might seem overwhelming. But the individuation from a singular source gives us a freedom we don't realize we have. It gives us a chance to experience more than one lifestyle, or job, or whatever it is we want to experience! We even get to learn through other people's experiences without actually having to live through some of the experiences ourselves. When we talk to our family or friends about joy, heartache, and loss, we feel it too. It's because we are one and the same. It means we get to share experiences through feeling. And we won't have to experience some of the lessons as long as we learn from what is being shared through others. It's the original social learning where experiences can be felt.

Being holographic also means that everything you want to understand, know, and become is already inside of you. Every potential reality or lifestyle is being lived at the same time. All of the fractals are connected forever throughout time. Which brings us to what are called the Akashic Records. The Akashic Records are holographic records that contain everything that ever was, is, and will be. We have our own personal Akashic Records inside our DNA. That is why some people can remember their past lives. Those experiences get recorded forever. It's like the end of the movie *Interstellar*, where Matthew McConaughey is traveling in the rainbow stream and sees the different parts of his life; from the moment he saw the dust from the open window, to the time he left his daughter. From inside the Akash, he could only view – but everything we do affects the Akash. We can go back and change and heal events which create a ripple effect through the rest of the library past, present, and future. We're all strung together by everything that has or will ever happen. Wild.

The Trinity Head

As God is what is considered One Source, there was an individuation that happened throughout creation. The first individuation came in a trinity of Holy Mother, Holy Father, and Holy Christ-Sophia or Child. This trinity is represented in sound, color, and frequency. It was the first split of female/male principle and energetics; electric and magnetic frequencies. But together they created the third "Golden Light" frequency. The Golden Light or Golden Child represents both Holy Father and Holy Mother energies combined and tha t's what makes it special. The Golden Child brings with it mastery of both elements and creates a harmonic. But most religions only point to the Holy Father principles. The He/Him of it all is limited in perspective of principles and ways of being. Once the Holy Mother was removed, on purpose, is when imbalance took place across all dimensions.

In current times, this understanding is very important. These times are about returning to the balance of divine masculine and divine feminine principles as a whole. The Holy Mother of 15D and Holy Father God of 13D are rebirthing a new Golden Child of 14D dimensional energy, an energy higher in frequency than this planet has ever felt! This energy is going to birth a new reality of Golden Light or the Golden Age of universal balance. All who are healed or trying to heal will see in time.

FINDING HOME

Finding Home

In continuing the story - after coming back from Peru at the end of December I knew it was time to move to nature. I spent eighty percent of my time in the city and twenty percent of my time in the forest and I wanted to flip those percentages. And with so many downloads and life-altering experiences I was ready to take a break from all the physical and spiritual journeying.

In Spring of 2018 I started looking for land again. I had searched so many places the year prior throughout three different states. None of it resonated with me. It was either too far, too expensive, or the lands simply felt disturbed or unhealthy. But by late summer, my friend CC called me to check out Vermont. A week later as I drove north and entered the state, I looked at the mountains, felt the health of the trees and the land, and immediately knew it was where I wanted to be! The waters felt pure, the communities felt welcoming. And it was worth the four-hour drive from New York. Unfortunately, after a few more weeks of searching there wasn't a home or land I could afford and I was losing hope.

I drove back to check out potential places three different times between summer and fall. On my third trip there, again after finding nothing, I gave up and started driving back to New York. Two hours into my drive CC called me and said she'd found a property on a random website that looked incredible and was available to see the next day. Even though I was exhausted from the previous week of searching, I could tell from the tone of her voice that the property she found could be something special. As much as I wanted to go home to my bed, I turned the car around and went back to her place to spend the night to check out the place the next morning.

We woke up early to visit the land. It was a subdivision off of a larger plot of land on a dead-end road. It was secluded, but only twelve minutes from town. It was also for sale by the owners who would be our neighbors. As soon as we walked the land, we *knew* it was something special! The land definitely needed caretaking as the area had been logged multiple times throughout the years. But the air, the water, and the whole energy of the land felt good to us. As we walked down an old logging road, my friend reached her hand out as if to touch the air and a huge leaf floated down and landed directly in her hand. It was a sign! This is where we were supposed to be. We found a small circle of trees and said our prayers - if we were meant to be on that land, the process would happen on its own. We were in complete surrender to the outcome. We walked back to the owners and I put in an offer. They were very particular about who they wanted to sell to. We spoke to them and hit it off immediately. Luckily for us, they felt like we were the right fit! They were interested and we decided to talk over the following few days. I gave my friend a hug, took a look back at the land, and got in my car and drove back to New York. I was in surrender to whatever the future was going to bring.

The night I returned home to New York, I had a very clear dream: I was in a field near the woods, I was kind of just standing there. My friend, Justin, was in my dream; waving at me from the tree line to come into the forest, to come home. I knew his spirit was talking to me in my dream, but physically, we had not spoken in many years. The next day, I called him and found out that he had moved with his girlfriend to the same area of Vermont where I was looking for land! The last time I spoke to him, he was in a completely different state! I told him about the dream and he just laughed, not surprised. To me, it was a very clear sign. The beginning of many that year.

The next few weeks, I began selling items I didn't need. I already had eight huge bins full of stuff ready for me to take to where I was moving. I was organizing tools, dehydrated food, work clothes, you name it. I feel like I had them packed for a few years and they sat in storage. After a few weeks of being back in my apartment and while negotiations for the land were happening it was really hard at times not to get too excited. But the signs were very clear. And one night, I had another dream.

Power Animals

I was on a moving train with an open top. It was heading north through open country. I looked down from the train and saw sheep, then I saw people facing towards the passing train. The people and the sheep were one and the same, both unaware that the train was moving right in front of their faces. I saw a man wearing the same red wool shirt I wore in the winter time. He had glasses and was bald and was just staring as though he didn't even see the train. He was a version of me I was leaving behind, still unaware with the sheep. Then, a black moose started chasing the train. My friend CC, the one who called me to Vermont, was also on the train with me. The train took off faster and faster as we left it all behind.

We ended up in an old barn next to a little town that was lit up at night. The moose met us there in the barn. CC and I were on a high-rise platform, almost like a hay loft. The moose came up to us directly, bringing its face close in. We were nervous at first, but I reached out my hand and he nibbled on it. He was friendly. Then he kept making purging sounds. He kept doing it until I purged. I realized he was a messenger. A black moose, different from the rest, was there to tell me to, "Let it all go. Release all of it. It's ok." He was showing us the arrival to the place we were meant to be. We just had to get on the train.

Moose medicine means using intuition and intelligence to see what fits and what does not. It means taking authority to make your own choices in life and to not feel ashamed or pressured if what you choose is different from those around you. Individuality is a strength. And the mythology of ancient ways teaches that the moose has the ability to shape shift and is linked to magic. The skills of magic and moose medicine are enhanced through studying. And people with the Moose as a power animal are born with their inner eyes already open.

I have other power animals as well. The Eagle always reminds me to soar above and look at the bigger picture, to not get caught up with the worries of the lower world. It reminds me to fly high and to focus on the smallest details when needed. My tiger teaches me to be stealthy and to use energy efficiently. Tigers sleep fourteen hours a day which is pretty sweet because I excel in napping. But tigers also love to play and only use their strength and fierceness when needed. My elephant teaches me to have grace —to slow down and enjoy the walk, the journey in life. The black bear, who visits me periodically, teaches me to play, have fun, and chill. But also, be fierce when needed.

The Land

By mid-December, the owners and I had come to a deal to

close on the land. I was more than excited! A six-year dream was finally becoming a reality and it was only the beginning. As I drove north, I heard myself say internally, "**Where I'm going there is no applause.**" I felt a release in my entire body and I knew it was the next phase of letting go of my old life.

When I arrived in Vermont, I stayed at my best friend CC's small studio apartment above an old barn. There was just enough room for a small bed, a love seat, a round kitchen table and two windows overlooking the snow-dusted prairie. The bathtub was behind the headboard of the bed and the toilet and sink were in the bathroom the size of a closet. It was small but homey. And for both of us, after living in tents or primitive shelters for extended periods of time, this was all that was needed. But that night, something happened that changed both of our lives forever.

CC was playing a 528 hertz music playlist on her phone. As we started to fall asleep, I began to have vivid visions. Energies were coming into the room, and I asked CC if she was asleep. I felt bad for bothering her, but she said she was also feeling things in the room. I looked at the clock, and it was midnight going from December eleventh into December twelfth, 12/12. I told her that I was about to get a download and told her not to be weirded out as it was still new to channel in front of someone. I let her know that I might make funny sounds and faces.

She said, "Go for it." Then, I went in.

I started seeing a Native American man with long black hair and a spear sharpened slightly on one side. It was less weapon and was more for everyday use. I described that I started seeing another man that looked similar, but not quite the same as the other one I was seeing. CC sat up in her bed. I couldn't look at her because I was in my vision, but I could feel and hear her sit directly up in a flash. She said, "Do you know who that is?"

"No." I replied.

She explained who it was. They were the lineage of ancient Apache Scouts that once walked the Earth and were now here to help us. They were our ancestors in a way, not by blood, but by spirit. They began to tell me that not many people try to connect with them or ask for their guidance. We both started crying. They were there. I was seeing them and we both felt them. I told CC I was seeing a grandmother figure too. She started freaking out, also knowing who it was. I was still clueless. But I felt her kindness and her warmth. They taught us many things that night that I'm not allowed to share who they are nor all the messages. But their message was simply this:

"We are all things. We are all things. We are all things."

The depth of that statement, "We are all things," still fascinates me to this day. What they mean is we literally *are all things;* we are the air, the earth, the stars, the cosmos, all humans, all beings, everything that ever has, and ever will exist. And with that, we are not bound. We are limitless! We truly are free! We are also responsible for our actions, as they are conscious. But even then, we are every possibility that has or potentially could ever happen.

The entire channel lasted for about an hour. We were up at least until 2 a.m. feeling grateful, dumbfounded, and at a loss for words. We knew we were blessed going into the next chapter of our journey. We kept our promise to ourselves, to the lineage, and to Earth Mother.

The next day, the day before my birthday, we were allowed to be on the property. CC, her partner, and I decided to hold a pipe ceremony in honor of the land and it welcomed us. We knew we were caretakers of the land now and a part of something bigger than us! That night we decided to camp on the property and found a spot down an old log road as it was the easiest to navigate with over four feet of snow on the ground. We each stamped out our tent areas and set up camp. We made a fire, had a quick dinner, and looked at the stars. It was beautiful! But it was also really cold. We called it an early night and headed for our tents. Within minutes of settling in, an owl landed on a tree branch just outside my tent and gave a strange and loud screech. It spoke two more times over a few minutes and flew away. There was a lot of movement and spiritual activity outside my tent. I said to myself, "I'm alive. I may be cold, but I am alive." I was in heaven.

The following morning was like magic. The way the sun struck the pure white snow was like a dream. The birds were singing and we could hear the river close by. We had morning coffee and had to pack up our gear to move on with the day. I had to get ready for Los Angeles. In order to find more work and to wait out the winter, I decided it would be best to go to LA and stay with a close friend for a few months. I told CC and her partner I would see them in the Spring, and I headed for the airport. A new chapter was beginning, but not that quickly.

Between Two Worlds

Being back in the city and within society I felt 50 percent in the world and 50 percent out of it. My being was between two worlds. I felt like I was traveling to new heights consciously but also still wanting things in the physical. I was listening to the call, and I was awake. But I was scared to miss out, and I felt stuck and indecisive between two worlds. Back in LA, I was standing outside on my friend's porch one night and felt a subtle, yet major shift. The wind changed that night and it felt different. It's like the wind was saying something so I tuned in and listened. The feeling of the wind made me drop my shoulders…it was about surrender, letting go. Letting go of the ego, surrendering to the Earth and the unknown.

But deep down, I felt a little lonely. My friend group had diminished drastically, and I was trying to figure out where I fit in. Even though I never felt like I fit in and usually stood alone or with a chosen few, I was longing for a tribe, which really meant family and like-minded people. My family at this time felt like it was spread thin—mom, sister, uncles, aunts and cousins all living throughout the country, only seeing each other maybe once or twice a year. But I missed them more. I had to ask myself, what kind of family/tribe do I want? What I felt was a family or community that was self-aware, led by love, proactive, fun, and also wanted to live consciously. Where they were, I still didn't know.

By April, I was getting signs again. I saw a floating solo angel with a trumpet flying east to west in a dream. "Leave Babylon."

I had another dream where I saw my friend Justin again, waving me to the tree line. My inner voice was telling me, "Go home, Seth. Go back to the vision. All signs and arrows point in that direction. Nature." And I remember my mentor saying, "The children of the Earth must run to the wild places."

Before leaving New York City for good, I had another dream where I heard, "The train is leaving the station. All aboard!" I only knew getting on the train meant I had to get on to leave society again. Which is why I knew it was time to leave the city. I remembered a friend said something I'll never forget: **"The path** doesn't move, the people on it do."

So, I listened. I left Babylon, I followed my heart and went to the tree line, and I returned to the wild places.

Working Hard

By Spring, I had everything I needed in my car and left New York for good. After a few days in Vermont, it was time to set up what I needed and to go even deeper to further my skills, my medicine, and to truly live in the sanctuary of the Earth. I didn't want to walk in fear anymore. And I could hear my inner voice say, "What are your intentions?" I knew I wanted to walk in power, in knowing, in activation. I felt ready for a personal phoenix. I had been caring too much about what other people thought. I didn't know where my tribe was, but I knew they would come.

With a new beginning it was time to assess that land and my new home. The land itself is beautiful but had been heavily forested multiple times and still had deep trenches where large logging trucks had driven through. Most of the trees, minus a few pines, were younger than fifty years. The thing about most of this country, is the land has been forested for its lumber and natural resources so many times, it's hard to fathom. There are few areas outside of national parks where the trees are a hundred years or older. With this knowledge, my job was to take care of this land over time to bring it back to optimal health. And I think if people did this all over the world, taking care of their little section of lands and waters, this planet could thrive again.

I found a place on the land that was fairly flat to set up my tent. I bought a larger six-person tent in order to stand and move around, since I was going to be living in it for the summer and fall seasons. During the day I would roam the land, cut trees that had fallen or tend to an area that needed clearing. I had never used a chainsaw before. Luckily, CC and her partner helped me and taught me necessary skills. Each day was about listening to the land—what trees needed cut and which ones didn't. I would ask the land, "What do you need? What can I give?" And over time it began to answer me. I would walk and it would say, "Clear these small trees," or "We can't breathe here." So, I would. And immediately within a few days I could feel the difference in the area. The wind could move through, and it almost felt like some of the older trees were stretching their branches. A big indicator of trees fighting for sunlight is if the branches start higher up on the tree. That means they will forgo their lower branches because there's too much competition below. I started to see this very quickly. There were other areas on the land where I could hear, "This section needs clearing, but don't worry about it right now."

Over time I began asking, "Where is the home? Where will I be able to set up permanently?"

It became very clear that it was close to my tent area. So, I decided to put in my driveway with the help of my friends. We taught ourselves how to use a Bobcat excavator to clear tree stumps and level the land. Surprisingly, I picked up how to use the machine very quickly. I had a truck driver bring in stone for the driveway and over two days we would move the piles and level them out until I had a driveway. Once the driveway was in, it was clear exactly where the homesite would be. So, I began taking down more trees until I cleared another acre of land.

All day every day, I was smelly, dirty, and sore. It was a lot of work and some of the hardest physical labor I had ever done. I was used to doing eight shows a week as a performer. But labor as a part-time lumberjack, part-time construction worker is different. I was strong in a different way, and I loved it. At night, I felt like I could rest easily. And some days if I was just too tired, I would lay on the land and just feel what was happening. I would pay attention to which direction the wind was coming from or try to predict when a storm was coming in and how heavy the rainfall was going to be. Some days, when it did rain heavily, I would walk around the homesite area and watch to see where the water would shed, I could tell where water would gather, and in some areas, flood. I was trying to pay attention to all the signs, all of which concluded that I was going to be building in the right area.

Other times, I would pass an area and feel, "This is where the deer lay." If I walked around the area, I could see the depressions in the tall grass which would confirm what I felt. In other areas, I would hear/feel, "This is where the bears are. Don't go here." And I would respond, "Word. I'm not going there."

Mother Bear

One day at sunset after a long day's work and a cold outdoor shower, I decided to lay down in my tent early. I had just moved my queen-sized mattress into the tent which thankfully fit just right to still give me enough room to move around. After so much manual labor I needed to sleep on a real mattress, and it felt like the biggest treat. After a few minutes of lying down, I felt something come into my area. I was still lying down, but the feeling got stronger. I was getting good at sensing between spiritual and physical things. And whatever this was felt physical and big. It felt like a bear! I sat up, unzipped one of the windows further to look out through the mesh screen; nothing. So, I laid back down. A minute or two later I felt it again. There was definitely something out there, but I didn't hear anything or see anything. Less than a minute later, to my north window I could hear something scampering from underneath the brush. Just then, two small bear cubs appeared, strolling towards my tent area.

"Cute, but where's mamma bear?" I thought. Then, rest assured, mamma bear came right after them. My heart started pounding, but I told myself there was no reason to continue to be afraid of the animals. I wanted to have some communion with them, so I slowly sat up further, grabbed my machete, faced the window, and just watched.

The cubs slowly walked past my tent sniffing for food along the way. One was so close if I would have reached through my tent, I would have touched it. Then, the mamma bear began to sniff the air. She must have been about 200 pounds, maybe larger. She was big and beautiful. Her hair was black and against the sunset she looked majestic! As she got within twenty feet, I spoke softly through the mesh window.

"Hello, grandmother bear. I just want you to know I'm here and I don't want to scare you."

Her head lifted slightly as she looked towards my tent.

I spoke again, "Hello grandmother bear. It's me, Seth. I just want you to know I'm here to take care of the land and I'm happy to see you. Please come slowly."

She kept slowly strolling towards my tent. My heart was pounding, and I took some deep breaths. I told myself to chill out and started pushing out love towards her. I did pull my machete out of its sheath, but I could tell I didn't need to. Mamma bear walked right up to the screen, sniffed the tent, her wet nose two feet from mine. She sniffed again, looked around, and kept strolling with her cubs past my tent, unbothered. Once my heart dropped from my throat, I shouted, "That was fucking awesome!" And throughout the summer I would hear her and the cubs in different parts of the woods. And I would let them be. Bears are cool, but from afar.

My Team

Even though I was having amazing experiences, being by myself started to shift things. Being in the woods with others is one thing. But for my first summer out on the land I was mostly by myself. Being by yourself for months on end only seeing people a few times was different. I would only see people if I had to stop into town, which was rare. I had to ask myself some serious questions. "Why am I out here in the woods?" My response to myself was that I wanted to live my vision. I loved the Earth and was seeking Oneness with the animals, plants, trees, rocks, soils, winds, rain, sun, stars, and all things. I wanted to grow my own food and drink my own water. I didn't want to contribute to the pollution of this Earth. This way of life forced me to buy only what I needed and to use more of what was around me. It made me think about the products I bought, used, and disregarded, all of which eventually go into the Earth. I didn't want to be a slave to the created consumer economy. I wanted to be wild and free. I wanted relationships and contact with spirits and ETs. I was going to caretake and help the land as it did the same for me. It was hard work but there was no drama in the mountains. I had peace. These were my reasons. Reasons I would check in with when money was tight, or my body hurt, or even when intense loneliness set in. And loneliness did set in. In ways I didn't see coming.

I went to my ceremony spot one night. And another elder in spirit was there to speak to me.

He said: "Need warrior spirit. You need less than you think." He was referring to the truck I was buying, the feeling I needed more tools, and all the extra trips to town I was taking just to get coffee and see other humans after months of loneliness. My energy started to go all over the place, and I realized I didn't have anyone to consult. He continued, "Master the basics. Keep it simple. Let go. You need less. Move like the ancient scouts."

Then Black Bear came in spirit as well. "Stay up here." Meaning in the woods. "Are you listening? Why don't you trust yourself or your guidance?" I wasn't sure. Because it was all so new to me and there weren't many people to talk to about it. Black Bear reminded me of the sheep dream on the train and that the train was leaving and leaving the sheep behind. Loneliness was taking its toll, but I could feel this was another phase of complete surrender. I remembered my teacher Tom wandered the lands for ten-plus years and his mentor, Grandfather, roamed most of his life to gather medicine.

But in some ways, I was feeling guilt for always going away to work on myself. I felt selfish, like I was not helping enough. But I could hear my higher self say, "All of this is adding up. All will be revealed. All of this is leading somewhere. Scattered, wave coming." Scattered? Maybe I was overwhelmed and felt scattered. But I could feel that this meant something else, like something was coming or happening in the world I couldn't quite see. My Higher Self continued: "Ark—create your Ark." Over time the message was becoming clear and a lot of what didn't make sense would. And like Noah, I needed to stay focused and keep working on the land. I had to move in faith. It felt like I was leaving—leaving the Earth or leaving society. It was like I chose to leave. I scanned through everyone I loved in my mind. No matter what, I loved everyone. I loved everyone.

A few weeks later, I could feel the elder spirit sitting on the boulder in front of my tent. I wasn't sure if I felt worthy or honorable to be in his presence. He told me to relax. He said, "You're one of us, the lineage." And I cried. He looked around and said, "These are your friends—the animals, the spirits. Don't be afraid." I felt more than grateful. Then as he was leaving, he said, "They're coming." I thought, "Who's coming?"

Then, four people appeared in spirit. I could see them in the spiritual plane very clearly. They were my age. They wanted to show me something but I was nervous to work with them. A few became frustrated with my lack of trust. Eventually, I went with them to an in-between space between worlds, almost like a lobby. I was confused and not sure why I was there. Then, one of the girls shuffled her hands and was making geometric light shapes. She would throw one and it would open up a gateway. She would create another shape and throw it in another direction creating another portal. The lights and geometric shapes were like keys that were there to help people get to where they needed to go. I'm not sure where these people who needed help were coming from. It felt like they would be walking into these other realms physically and not necessarily through death. I began to wonder why they were showing me this.

"You've been freed." One girl said. "You're not working your whole life waiting to retire at sixty-five like some carrot dangling in front of your face. Now, what do you want to do with this freedom?" I asked, "What is my responsibility with this freedom? I want to do what I came to Earth to do. To learn, understand, incorporate, help people, shine my light, and leave." The girl then wiped dead skin off of my third eye. "You can see now." She said, "What we're trying to show and tell you is that what you've experienced in all these places is real. Must show the people." I was confused. "Like to write or make a movie? Is this my duty on Earth?" I asked. She replied, "Where is your time spent? On distractions? You can attract things like a magnet if you are a vibrational match. Integration. First, is the awakening to true self, power, love, remembering who you are. It's not about escaping this world. It's about loving here. About embracing change." I sat back in my tent and simply responded, "Word."

They turned as they were about to leave and they all looked back at me. I stayed in tune with them briefly, then as quickly as they came, they left. I opened my eyes and looked outside of my tent. The elder was gone, but the message was clear. I had a team. They felt true, like they were a part of me. And the message of awakening to who I am and not escaping this world, shifted my paradigm. It's about integrating everything I was learning on different realms, and making it real in my current life on Earth.

The rest of that month I toiled over this reality. For a few years, I really thought I was leaving this realm. I thought there was a percentage of people that were leaving. But I slowly began to realize this was a consciousness ascension, not a full physical one. My lessons, journeys and experiences were far from over.

VIII

GALACTIC MEMORY

ET Ant Visit

Later that summer as I arrived home one night, I could hear three coyotes howling. It was beautiful. After five minutes of howling, I walked to my tent site and heard an owl singing its song in a tree. The coyotes howled again. Once I settled in my tent, I felt something stalk towards me, but it wasn't physical. I was too tired from the day to look deeper. And if it turned out to be a large animal, I had my machete in case of an emergency. When I laid down and closed my eyes, I kept seeing a triangle. When I opened my eyes, I could see the triangle. I opened and closed my eyes multiple times and it was still there. In my mind I thought, "Oh, geez, here we go." I heard, "The triangle is in everything."

In an instant, I felt and saw in my vision what looked to be like large ant people. Again? Ants again? I asked, "Where are you from?" They replied, "A Nebula far, far away." I asked if they were of the light. "Yes. The same ones that helped the Hopi during the time of transition," they replied. I could feel they were somewhat in the physical form, and I could feel them right by my tent. But I was too afraid to open my tent and potentially see them. One said it was pulling an implant from my neck. When I saw it, I said, "That's it?"

They said, "That's it." It was so small.

Their demeanor was surprisingly funny and playful. They were nervous I would be afraid of their appearance. I said it wasn't their appearance; it was the coyotes howling that put me on high alert. When my third eye vision started to see them more clearly, I realized there were only two of them. And they were much taller than expected, maybe standing seven to eight feet.

"That's a tall ant," I thought. They must have heard my thoughts, and we all laughed. We both had jokes. I don't remember why they started to leave. But they said, "Take care of yourself before you can help others."

Then, I heard a rumbling like a plane, but this wasn't a plane. They said, "Do you hear us?"

Oh, dang! Was it a ship? They replied, "Do you believe us now?" "Yes," I replied. And then I heard the ship quietly take off to the east. The experience was interesting. It was my second interaction with these types of beings. I took it with a grain of salt, as they were trying to help me again. I didn't try to call them in again, just another notch on meeting a new, or old race of beings.

Sedona

By the end of summer, I felt a call to Sedona and decided to go with some friends. When I arrived in Sedona, the red rocks were stunning! It looked and felt like mountains from another world. And the vibration of the red rocks made my whole body vibrate. I knew I was in the right place and initially felt a graceful and loving divine feminine energy in Sedona. It felt like the presence of Earth Mother. I would see murals of different indigenous women outside of stores and I began to hear Earth Mother's voice guiding me everywhere I went. It was beautiful, and I felt so honored to see her and hear her voice so clearly again.

The next day, I went to have a healing session with a woman who has become special to me on my journey. She did past life regressions for clients, but her specialty was DNA upgrades. As soon as I walked into the door, it felt as though we knew each other. When I went into her home, it was full of Egyptian paintings, relics, and other spiritual books and decor. Her dog came right over to me, which she said was rare. Then, we both immediately felt a presence in the room. It was as if a door from another realm had opened. She said, "Oh, now I remember who you are!" as she looked over my shoulder.

My vision was not as sharp then. But I could feel a specific being and other beings coming in. She could see them clearly and we decided not to waste time and started the ceremony. She asked me to stand facing the fireplace. She told me she was going to use a small crystal rod and move it up and down my spine and maybe my arms. I told her I was ready. Within minutes my whole body began vibrating. My mouth started making sounds like the engine of a rocket that was getting ready to launch. And I felt a spiral come into me and into my vision. I felt like I was about to lift off the ground and levitate as she told me to breathe. I surrendered more, and my spirit "took off." I traveled quickly and landed in another realm.

Remembering Egypt

I remember I was standing on top of a hillside and looking over a beautiful valley. The land was gorgeous, but the civilization was gone, buildings in rubble. But it seemed enough time had passed that the greenery of the trees and grass had returned. I remembered this place; this was home. But where was everyone? It felt like I was gone, out there, in space or something. It felt like I had returned too late. And just then, the memories started flooding in. My heart grew heavy, and I started crying.

I remembered what happened. They were gone; my people were gone. I *was* too late. I was off fighting the war, and the war had hit home. The enemy completely destroyed the planet. I cried like a baby in that realm and fell to my knees.

In reality, in this woman's home I was also bawling like I hadn't cried in years. All I could say was, "They hurt my Earth, they hurt my momma!" This place was actually Tara, because it felt like a higher realm than Earth. But I didn't have a name for it at the time. Tara is our 5th dimensional home. It looks just like Earth, but it is higher vibrationally. We fell into 3D through many spiritual wars. And in 3D, we call the planet Earth. But in this vision, the planet Tara was gone. It was an extinct planet. I was angry, I was hurt, and I was confused about why anyone would do this. But it had already happened. The experience was so intense I had to slowly come down from the memory. I knew I needed to feel it. I knew I needed to remember. My heart needed to begin to heal. But I was overwhelmed.

I took a few deep breaths. The facilitator asked if I wanted to go on. I said, "Yes, I'm ready."

She said, "I knew you were strong. You're a galactic warrior." In my mind, I understood. But understanding is different from inner knowing. I knew it would all make sense, eventually. But I had to continue the journey in the session. She placed the crystal in a different part of my back, and I immediately began to travel again. This time, my heels were off the ground and my body arched backward as my entire body felt like it wanted to lift off the ground.

I remembered I was a general for an intergalactic army in ancient Egypt. Egypt has had a few renaissances. The one I remembered was during and just after the pyramids were built. For us, intergalactic travel and communication was a common thing, it's just what we did. During that time, we were never worried about war. We were trained to protect but never concerned about incoming conflict. We were a peaceful society with a lot of technology. We grew crops, but everyone knew about and used the technologies we had available. We could activate most of the technology with the energy coming from our hands or even our mind. Some tools, like the ankh or a staff, were used because it would accelerate and/or control the energies for different uses.

Intergalactic travel was telepathically and geometrically coded. The geometries we saw in our mind telepathically went into the computer of our spacecraft. We held physical master keys as well. But the geometrically coded keys were telekinetically and energetically programmed which was a specific science that aligned with the nature of the stars. The pyramids were not the only ones we had; there were many more. We used them like major intergalactic airports. Even as I write this, I get activated into the memory. The pyramids were an energetic portal. We used blue beams to accelerate travel and slow down incoming spaceships. I could still see them clearly. The alignment with the stars and other planets is when the pyramids were most useful. It was like "catching a window" into another time-space dimension for the users/passengers. Ships were used, but we could also travel galactically with our physical selves or consciousness. We could come and go as we pleased. It really was physics. Our bodies, cells, and cellular structure were built to do this. We could sort of "fizzle" out into and through the blue beam portal and go where we wanted to go based on memory, intention, and alignment. It was actually pretty easy.

The best way to describe it was like a scene from the original movie *Charlie and The Chocolate Factory*, when the character Mike "TV" goes into a life-size television set and is sent to another location. It's the same. It's the same as information traveling through wireless technology. What does that information and data travel "on"? It travels as organized frequencies on other bandwidths on the ether. Whether or not science makes sense to you, back then, we could just do it.

After the session, I cried some more. No wonder Earth Mother was talking to me so frequently while I was in Sedona. And I realized that since 2010 she had been calling me home back into nature and periodically letting me know she was with me. But now, she was guiding me to see and acknowledge what had happened to her, and me, throughout different lifetimes and in different realms. I had to see the different ways humanity and the planet fell. But most importantly, I had to let go of anger and fear. I realized as I wrote this book, she has always shown me that her essence is ok. But she still needs her warriors. And these visions continued all throughout the summer.

Egypt Infiltrated

Not long after I returned from Sedona, I decided to attend a sound bath my friend was having. I quickly dropped into meditation and heard an inner voice saying, "Follow the Light." Within minutes, I felt my consciousness travel, and I was at the river. I went to view what seemed like New Earth, then went into space and viewed Earth and the cosmos. I then went underground somewhere, in a hall. I saw an opening. I was shown the bridge, and I heard kids playing. I was at an in-between place. This place had peace; it was safe and everything was in harmony.

Then, I returned to Egypt. My vision quickly confirmed I was a warrior there. The armor on my chest was gold, and I had a gold spear. I knew I was a protector. I was trying to figure out why I was there and where everybody was. I felt the presence of a being, and I immediately killed it with my spear. I couldn't tell if it was good or bad. Then, as the vision went on, I felt another presence and slowly started to see a human form appear walking up a sand hill. It was another warrior and I heard him trying to talk to me and slowly walk towards me with his hands out like, "Don't hurt me." But I didn't trust him. I kept looking at light coming through the top of the pyramid with entities coming in from above. Something wasn't right. That's why no one was around. Infiltration. I yelled to the other warrior, "They lied to us! They lied to us! They lied to us!" I was angry and almost ready to kill the warrior talking to me. He knew, and I knew I was more powerful than them. I was angry, and I felt betrayed.

I took a deep breath and quickly dropped back into the original vision of New Earth. I was enjoying my time, and I played in the grassy valley teaching children. It was peaceful there. But I always kept an eye out in the cosmos. In my head I said, if they did it before, they'll do it again. My journey had my soul visiting two realms at once, the old and the new. In the new, I was still keeping an eye out for the children and all my people. Then something clicked and the message became clear. In order to be in a peaceful plane or planet, I had to let go of all the fear, the pain of war, and the need to always be in survival mode. It was another sign to drop the spear and move on. War in some realms would continue. But peace in other realms also existed. And I would have to let go of the past in order to live in peace.

As the sound bath ended and we sat getting back into our bodies, a woman to my left began staring at me. She then asked me if I was Egyptian. I started laughing and told her that I just experienced a lifetime of mine again in Egypt. The synchronicity did not surprise me. But the experience and the change that it created did. Something that needed to be healed for thousands of years finally showed up in this lifetime. And it was time to assess it, accept it, alchemize it, and let it go. These experiences and journeys are why I think true remembering is so important. It allows us to heal the baggage from lifetimes we didn't know we had. It gives us freedom. And the pain, suffering, fear, and karma no longer comes with us on our soul's evolution. That is the work we chose, because we chose to be sovereign and free.

Galactic Memory

One night, in my meditation I began to work in my sacred space. I felt myself shedding dead skin, my old warrior self, and all unnecessary things. My galactic family, power animals, spirit brother, grandfather, and newly acquainted ancestors were there. The ancestors showed up as three coyotes. It was a gathering of my team. I needed to make a choice about which team to work with- my more Earthly guides or my galactic guides. I didn't understand why I had to make a choice. But I could tell it wasn't a choice of one or the other; they would all be with me. It was more about choosing which medicine to work with to keep my focus. I thought and felt it through my heart. Then, I saw a white coffee cup with galactic symbols inside. It was empty of liquid; the symbols were floating inside the cup, and I drank from it. It was a conscious/unconscious decision to work with my galactic family.

Immediately, my spirit went home to the dimension I was from. I saw my family there - my wife and kids. I was finally let into a place I had been secretly traveling in spirit the previous year. I was welcomed and even celebrated in the middle of the circle. It was like I woke up from amnesia. I guess I had been fighting for them for a long time and didn't remember. Maybe it's good not to remember everything. I had put down the spear, and I was done fighting. It felt like I came home from a war and I didn't need to fight anymore; the war for me was over. I had found my family. They were in a different realm. It didn't take away my love for my family in this life. But I could look back and see Earth in the distance. Other ships and helpers were standing by as the New Earth separated from the old. A part of me was only there (here on Earth now) to finish the mission, help my tribe, and live my vision. I felt so much love for all. I felt One Love.

A few days later, I was standing outside on my friend's deck again. I felt called to sun gaze, where I would stare directly into the sunset. I could look at the sun with both eyes open and feel the sun codes and remember them. I looked out to the city below and started to have a flashback of multiple lifetimes—where I had stood on a mountain or hill, looking over the valleys and towns. Each time was the last time I saw them as they all had been destroyed from war, energy attacks, or alien invasion. I prayed that somehow in this moment, in this lifetime, that would never have to happen again.

Remembering Lemuria

A month later I was traveling to Hawaii to teach some dance classes. I made it a work vacation and arrived a week early, being that I had never been to the islands. I decided to camp the first week and rented a little spot for $20 a night next to a mountain. I spent the whole first week camping. It was awesome! One day I drove to Kiholo Bay and found a fish pond with beautiful red and blue dragonflies. I went into meditation and felt like I was slowly being surrounded by an ET race. They said they were the Lemurians. They told me they were fine and in a safe place. I asked why, when I returned to my Lemurian lifetime, everything was gone. They said I was still off fighting the galactic war. My anger over the negative alien invasion took over my entire being and I wanted to destroy all of them. *Them* was a group of different negative forces whose sole purpose was to take over other lands and planets.

When I briefly opened my eyes from the vision, I saw the blue dragonfly chasing two red dragonflies. It showed me that protection was my job. I became the aggressor out of anger over the destruction of my people and lands. The war turned me into a warrior, and I knew I lost myself in vengeance. It took me lifetimes to recover from the pain and grief of my people being wiped out. I almost feel like I had joined a bandit group like the Guardians of the Galaxy whose people and lands were also destroyed. But this was part of the reason why I was tired of fighting. I must put down the spear and fight differently. I thought, "What does all of this have to do with the *now*?" And I remembered Lemuria was an example of how we once lived and how we can live. A utopia can exist if the people and lands are in the right frequency.

I later went to the temple of Pu'uhonua. I immediately met a man my age working primitive skills in an A-frame grass hut. He was native to the area and we talked about his culture - how they lived, ate, traveled, and their beliefs. Everything was a ceremony for them. It was similar to what I was learning but never lived beyond a few months at a time. He was diligent in working on his project, so I stepped outside the shelter and walked towards the water to a group of palm trees.

I sat down but immediately was told by a spirit to stand up. I complied. I felt male and female warriors resting and watching around the area as if on a rest or lunch break. All of a sudden, this group of native Hawaiian warriors in spirit surrounded me almost to intimidate me. I could see through my third eye them making faces to scare me. They kept getting closer, quickly crossing into my threshold. I relaxed and said, "Thank you." The one in front of me backed up a little, realizing I wasn't afraid. He said, "You have heart." The energy calmed down. And they were thankful I saw and honored them. Then, they began chanting and dancing around me. I felt my warrior spirit come out, and I joined them. In the physical, I was just standing by a tree. But in spirit, I was dancing my ass off with them, making faces, and chanting. I was getting physically hot from the energy. But I needed to feel that warrior spirit again. Even though not much time had passed, maybe 20 minutes, the spirit protectors allowed me to have a full ceremony with them. I stayed for maybe five more minutes before giving thanks and exiting the space.

I walked back to the guy doing primitive skills and asked about the spirits on the land. I told him I felt a warrior woman watching me and couldn't understand why. I told him I felt a dragon or dragon energy by the trees. He was surprised and laughed. He said the statue he was carving was the deity I probably saw; that she was a human-reptilian whom he was honoring. He said they carved statues in order for the deities to have a vessel to enter for communion. After a year, they bury the sculptures to let them rest. I asked if the native people believed these deities, were cosmic beings. He said his great grandfather and those before him said their ancestors came from the Pleiades. He himself wasn't so sure, but he said they did build their temples in alignment with the stars. Each year, the Pleiades, Orion, and another system lined up perfectly; it was their time of celebration. Even the way the sun and the moonlight would hit certain parts of the temple was considered very sacred. I thanked him for taking the time to share with me. I left and went to the beach and swam in the water for the rest of the day.

The next day, I went to Akaka Falls. It was much more touristy than I expected but still very sacred. I walked around and saw the massive waterfalls. I wanted to play the flute, but there were too many people, and I didn't want to be seen. I walked further down a path, and to my right I saw a group of trees with vine-like branches reaching to the ground. It just so happened the hand railing that kept people on the walkway opened up and began again another twenty feet further. The trees canopied, and it was dark. I knew no one was going down there. Perfect. I crouched down and slid on my feet and hands because the roots were slippery, and the hillside was steep. I stopped and looked around. To my left was a tight grouping of trees with an opening in the middle of them creating a circle big enough for two people. I took my shoes off, brought my flute in, and lit some sage. I was in the belly of the trees. Something told me to close my eyes. I started seeing images of a woman. In my vision she changed races but always looked indigenous.

I said, "Earth Mother?" She replied, "Yes. It doesn't matter how you see me." She told me to slow down my mind. I put my hand on the trees and realized I was in a portal. Was this a Mother Arc? I sent her love from my heart through my hands. "But will you receive love?" she said. Was I not receiving the love? She replied, "Open your heart. You're home now." I opened my heart. She showed me to receive her love like a flowing waterfall, always giving. And I cried. I cried because I could see and hear and feel her. She was always giving and providing. She felt so much like a mother, and I felt held like a child.

I played two songs on the flute for her. Enough sunlight started to come through the canopy of the trees that it lit up the area inside but kept me hidden from the pathway. I could hear people stop and wonder where the music was coming from. But I just stayed hidden. The music was for Earth Mother and there was magic and love being shared. **It showed me that magic can be fifteen feet from you, but you won't know how to find it if you're not being led from your heart.** I had a lot to learn and many places to learn from. I had to remind myself to slow down. After an hour or so, when I came out of the tree portal and stepped back onto the pathway, I felt like I'd transferred back from another realm. There were a few people walking, and I felt like I shouldn't be around people the rest of the day. I drove back to my campsite to integrate and sit in silence.

The rest of the trip I had work to do, teaching dance classes at different studios. The students were great and hungry for knowledge. I was always greeted with fresh flower leis. It felt like a ceremony every time I was greeted by a group of people. There was so much love and welcome everywhere I went. I wish the rest of the world could have this baseline of ease and unconditional love. Everywhere I went I was met with smiles and open arms.

By the end of the trip, I realized the Earth and feminine presence were honored on these islands. The people honored the lands, and in turn she kept showing them her beauty. I kept hearing or feeling *Aurora* energy in my mind and in my body. I didn't know what the energy was but found out that Aurora is the feminine divine energy that assists in highly transformational periods. I felt a lot of divine feminine energy coming through me and into the world. The bigger message was **it was time for Earth Mother and the women on the planet to be truly free and sovereign**. I wanted to heal as a man to be able to not only provide for my partner but also become the man that women—my partner, my female friends, and women as a whole—could know that a shift was happening in men. I wanted to be better, and I left the island a changed man. I chose nature. I chose the truth. I chose happiness.

Galactic History

After having so much remembrance over the last couple years, I woke up again to a larger realization that humanity has an extensive galactic history. It took me back to the time when I was 18 years old and bought DVDs in Harlem about extraterrestrials. I realized a lot of it was true. What I had stored away as "too far out there" was not so impossible anymore. Almost a decade later, all the information I found confirmed most of what I remembered in ceremony or mediation and was experiencing. I wasn't looking for the confirmations, but I continued to find them in books or online research. I am not a galactic historian. I only know what I recall. But there are many researchers, authors, and speakers who have dedicated their lives to researching human, extraterrestrial, and galactic history. I would suggest researching some of them. There are also physical records all over this planet from the pyramids and tombs in Egypt, Central and South American pyramids, native drawings, and dwellings in North America, all of which are a tip of the iceberg to prove that most humans were cosmic citizens with an extensive galactic history. The writing is actually on the wall! The amount of proof is undeniable. More and more are being revealed, and the research will take you as far as you want to go.

The most important fact to note is that humans were meant to be caretakers of this planet—to maintain the forests, cultivate food and life by helping each other and the animals, and give gratitude to all things. We were meant to live in harmony; sing, dance, make art, play games, and be free. We were given the Garden of Eden, a place of purity. Gaia, the highest version of Earth, is Eden. It's not just a made-up story. Eden also exists here on Earth, but in the deeper parts of nature. We were given a very, very rare planet that is the perfect distance and alignment from a solar source, the Sun. Even though drastic temperatures, pole shifts, and cataclysms have happened multiple times over billions of years on this planet, it is still a relatively safe planet. Earth is so special in the fact that it provides countless food sources, shelter sources, water, oxygen, gravity, pleasant sounds and smells, animal and ecological diversity, and a mostly predictable weather pattern. Unfortunately, most people have lost touch with how grateful we are to coexist on such a beautiful planet with other species. We're quickly losing our ancient wisdom and losing touch with our sacred mission as caretakers of the planet.

We as humans did not just evolve from apes; that was one of many seedings. Many ancient cultures revealed that humans have been seeded four to five different times on this planet by other extra-terrestrial species for evolution. Meaning, some humans are actually hybrids of other extra-terrestrial species, with or without their knowledge or consent. For some extraterrestrial races, this planet was an experiment. And unfortunately, there is also a small population of humans and ETs that have been producing a false matrix system that has created slave races of humans for their own benefit. If it's hard to believe, there is public proof that companies create lab-grown babies of different species. This has happened on our planet for a long time and in multiple dimensions. If you can choose the eye color and intelligence of a child, what makes you think this technology of hybridization hasn't happened before?

There are negative, positive, and neutral races of extraterrestrials. They are a part of us – woven into our DNA, though the truth has long been hidden from most of humanity. There is evidence of many seedings in which extraterrestrials have bred with humans to create hybrids. It's not natural or human to destroy the planet when it's encoded for us to be her caretakers. So how did we go from our birthright of taking care of heaven on Earth and most of our indigenous ancestors having cosmic contact and cosmic relationships, to becoming alien to it all?

Unfortunately, there are also other negative ET races involved who very successfully mind wiped humans and turned them into slaves or destroyed our galactic history. Different negative races also created contracts with certain humans that were part of their genetic ET races and gave power to those few in order to control the masses. They used humans to mine for essential elements in the Earth for their technologies and have used humans as a major energy source to generate bio-electromagnetic energy. This unseen energy is a vital force that can be used, released, and stored. Believe me or not. But I remember all of this and have seen it in the spiritual realms beyond this Earthly veil.

Bio-electromagnetic energy or *force* energy was known by all when humanity flourished in different time periods. But after many spiritual wars there were eras of amnesia. And personal, planetary, and cosmic energy was manipulated, extracted, and used for very dark reasons. Humans being manipulated and used as an energy source is also why negative ETs have not wiped-out humanity completely. They would rather have a forever "food" source that they can keep alive to work for them, all the while living off of billions of free bio-electromagnetic energies in the form of fear, anger, despair, abuse, hate, jealousy, and the like. The negative ETs are so destructive and vampiric – they will kill their enemy, their alliances, and even their own kind. They exist in a physical and spiritual cannibal state of being.

True beings of Light don't need energy from other beings, as they hold Eternal Source energy to live from. Many ETs such as the Pleiadians, Arcturians, Sirians, and Lyrans are here to help the planet and humanity evolve and reach a higher level of consciousness and higher dimensional existence. The lessons are always about returning to love and oneness. The planet has been waiting to be loved. There are soul agreements between humans and guardian races to help humans repair their genetic mutations in order to ascend. These groups are only here to assist humans to be responsible for their own evolution. They've wanted me to speak for a long time.

Spiritual War

"The Fall," that has been recorded in many religious and spiritual teachings, was when a few beings closest to God Source decided to fracture away. Personal will and desire created this fracture from Divine will as these fallen beings or as some call them, fallen angels, wanted power and rule over different dominions. Hence, the known war between good and evil, or light and dark, broke out. Over time, the fallen intimidated others, used them, or recruited them. And as the darkness spread, needing other energy to sustain itself, life became denser in energy, dropping the vibration into lower dimensions further and further from original creation. This descent created more duality and diversity within the different dimensions. This war has been happening for millions of years. I only know this truth from the lifetimes I remember. But there are many galactic historians who have the spiritual ability to track further into history in more detail using the Akashic records. And these historians have dedicated their lives to returning our history.

The fallen angels, or negative aliens as they are now called, created many factions over time. Most people have heard of the reptilians, the Annunaki, the Orions, and many others. Some of these factions banded together in different periods to combine their powers for control. They made plans to take over many planets and races. And they did. This became known as the Negative Alien Agenda, or NAA.

From a God Source perspective this fracturing is a part of the bigger experience. God Source is mostly neutral, and the first separation was Mother God and Father God energies. They had divine children, but some children didn't want to follow their parents. It's similar to watching some of your children go off on their own, do bad things, and eventually those free will choices of the child negatively affect themselves and their family. But just because Mother God and Father God's children turned away doesn't mean they didn't keep their original divine powers. They still kept most of their powers and used them for negative reasons, like war, slavery, and suffering. The war has trickled down from the spiritual into the physical worlds where it still affects us today as different countries fight because of opposing views or conquest of lands. But if we look at the macro, wars that have been fought over land don't always result in the land being claimed. It's as though there is so much death and destruction only to gain inches. But for the original fallen ones who are actually behind most of the wars, there is a much deeper reason to keep them going.

Inverted Matrix

Earth has an organic energetic ley line system that is like the circulatory system of the planet. The ley lines criss-cross all over the planet, which creates an energetic grid. This grid of interconnected ley lines is like a natural energetic communication system, similar to the way a forest can communicate through its root system. Some ley lines that crisscross within the grids create energetic vortices and portals that transmit higher frequencies of information from different dimensions, allowing for interdimensional communication and even travel. Our ancient ancestors knew this. It's the same reason pyramids were built all over the world throughout different time periods. They were built on these vortices and portals known as stargates. In different time periods these pyramids helped energize people during specific astrological cycles and helped certain races travel to and from different parts of the planet and other planets in an instant.

These natural grids and vortices tie into the spiritual war as negative aliens from different dimensions used their technologies to run reversal currents and inverted frequencies through the natural ley lines and stargates. Over time, these inverted frequencies created an energetic overlay throughout the grid of the planet, which placed a frequency net over the planet known as the inverted matrix. The inverted matrix frequency net that runs inverted frequencies negatively affects different species and the planet. It can make people, animals, and the planet feel sick. Specifically, it can make humans confused, angry, or ready to fight. It also allows the negative races that control it the ability to take over planets through energetic distortions or misalignments during cosmic ascension periods. These periods of takeover stop the species and the planet from experiencing its organic evolution by keeping the vibrations low. How is this known? Many ancients, empaths and shamans have seen and felt it in the spiritual fields and realms. And we can all feel the distortions in our bodies, especially in war torn areas. This is what the spiritual war essentially comes down to, a war over the grids.

Our organic frequencies have harmonic states that are shown in nature, science, and quantum physics. Dis-harmonic frequencies have also shown up in these areas. This inverted matrix runs on a ten-base code, while the organic matrix runs on a twelve-base code. To make this even more personal, knowing the difference between ten and twelve-base code was the reason I felt uncomfortable with Kabbalah. It was missing two essential codes. And the true organic twelve-base code is why I and many others relate to the Tree of Life. The code is linked to our DNA, the Tree of Life, and base harmonics in this time matrix. The inverted grids' false matrices run a ten base code, removing two additional codes, which allows the NAA to run programs that allow for mind control, disillusionment, and sleeper software. Our organic light body can sustain itself. But a dark energy system keeps humans and the planet in disharmony in order to harvest energy and natural resources.

Energy As A Food Source

Whether you realize it or not, energy is the biggest unseen commodity. You emit, give off, and receive energy. Your body gives off more energy and heat than most electric heaters.

Unfortunately, if you're unaware of your energy or energetically shielding yourself, your energy can be fed off of. You can be used as an energetic source just like a battery, the same way it is explained in the movie, *The Matrix*. This siphoning can happen from the news media, sporting, music, or religious events. It's becoming more well known that people at large concerts feel like they're sucked into a part of a larger energy when attending. As I stated at the beginning of this book, one thing I knew as a performer was that I always fed off the energy of a crowd, whether I was tired or not. It was exhilarating, but I had no conscious intention to feed off the energy in a negative way. However, I believe some famous performers do understand what they're doing energetically. And some can't live without that energy, which is why they still try to perform in later stages in their careers. But once I left the industry, I didn't need that attention or energy the same way I did before.

Another example of energy consumption is like the movie *Monsters INC*. In short, monsters go to work every day, and their job is to scare children. The screams from frightened children are captured as energy, which is then used to power the city where the monsters live. The monster who gives the biggest scare/creates the most fear, captures more energy, and in turn they receive bigger praise and pay. Well, the same thing happens in our reality. There are negative entities that feed off of humans. They range from small leeches, the relationship handlers, to demons, and even artificial intelligence. Each of these negative entities has a different flavor they like to feed off of. Most feed off of fear, but some like anger, sex, doubt, ego, distraction, anything that keeps us out of positive alignment. Towards the end of *Monsters Inc*, the monster Sully accidentally makes a child laugh and realizes that laughter is more powerful than fear. *Monsters Inc* continues to promote fear and feed off the energy of children, but. Sully creates his own company to make children laugh because he realizes that the energy of laughter, love, and lightheartedness is so much more powerful than the energy of fear.

The point is, since the moment of our birth we are used as human batteries. We are used to fulfilling the worker-bee model, the consumer model, and over the last century, the role of fear-based citizens emitting fear-based energy. There is a reason you almost never see a happy news cycle. The media and corporations behind them pump fear into the human psyche 24/7/365. And it won't end because the negative entities that feed off of the false matrix are used to a certain amount of energy. They need fear to continue to survive on an ascending planet. There are technologies being used that are so highly advanced that most couldn't imagine it if they tried. I have felt and seen black boxes that contain pain energy from war torn areas, hospitals, you name it, that are siphoned and collected underground and even off planet. Energy that is not immediately used by negative entities can be stored through these different types of alien technologies.

After working with different clients, I have seen vampiric demons that were draining energies from them. I realized that some of the entities were actually a small link connected to a much larger chain of entities. And I mean, a deep dark abyss of other types of negative beings that were working together to meet a bigger demand for energy. Most people are not spiritually aware enough to even think of these concepts as potentially being true. But most are not meant to know. Sovereignty and freedom from dark energy manipulation is why the Light warriors continue to fight. In the last few decades, the fight to save children from trafficking not just physically but spiritually has been a top priority. Why children? Because they have the purest forms of energy. To negative entities, it is like spiritual gold. It's sickening. But angels are all over this planet in spiritual form and in human form. And Father God and Mother God are reuniting to wipe the slate clean. Karma will serve, justice will be swift, and no one and nothing will be able to hide anymore.

Our galactic history of spiritual wars and the false matrix we live in are connected to our dimensionality and the spiritual return to remembering who we truly are. As I stated in the previous chapters, humanity existed in higher dimensions. But because of free will and a percentage of our spiritual family retaliating, we as a collective species fell into a denser reality on this physical Earth. Duality *can* return to unity, which is something we each have to learn. As we fell from higher realms and the trauma of wars was forgotten, our genetic memory was also wiped, and we lost touch with our ancient origins.

We're one of the few generations to have technological advances, yet we lack connection to our natural environment, resulting in poor mental, emotional, and spiritual health. This time period is one of the last chances we have to make a choice to wake up from the illusions of the false matrix. And there are many people who choose to live close to the Earth, who choose to open their hearts and heal, and who choose to evolve. Those who awaken to their higher potential eventually emerge into higher-energy timelines consciously. Some can remain in higher consciousness and timelines, though most fluctuate back and forth. But as more people remember, it will also ripple to others and help in their evolution, as well as the Earth's evolution.

This is all about DNA activations, connecting to our blood and star lineages and remembering who we truly are. It's about returning to the Tree of Life, the true twelve-grid tree that reconnects our DNA, our memories, and our connection with God Source. We are galactic beings with an opportunity to become cosmic citizens again. It's not about leaving this planet. It is about taking the knowledge from higher realms and embodying it here.

See? The War

The spiritual war sometimes crosses from the spiritual realms through the physical veils. I have seen bright light galactic battles a couple of times with different friends while I was in the mountains. They were bright red and blue lights, and sometimes I could hear them clashing; a sound louder and deeper than thunder.

One time while I was visiting my mother, there was a weird lightning storm that was concentrated in Ohio for hours. From the window I was seeing red and blue lightning bursts at the same time, the same bursts I had seen in the mountains with friends earlier that summer. I yelled for my mom to come outside with me and look in the sky. As she came out, her eyes got big when she saw the faint bursts of red and blue lights.

She said, "What in the world is that?" I said, "It's the war, mom. It's been happening for a long time. The veil is being lifted." I even called a friend in a different state to see if they saw anything. They were seeing it too. My mom heard them on speaker phone and was still in shock. From that point on I didn't need to explain myself to anyone. I realized my vision was opening up in ways I didn't expect. Even though it was a lot to take in at times. I knew everything from my remembrances, downloads, and the truth about the world was real.

IX
HIGHER SELF UPGRADES

Upgrades

The deeper I connected to myself and God, the clearer it became that everything I was learning and downloading over a two-year period was about reconnecting DNA and upgrading to our original angelic blueprint. The DNA was connected to our memory, remembering our galactic and spiritual history. It was time to heal the trauma that we had been through as a human species and a planet on all planes of existence. I started to "see" and remember more and it all made sense to me. This "remembrance" was what I was seeking without even knowing it. And it was only the foundation for what was to come.

I knew major shifts were happening in me and that something was changing in the world as a whole. The veils were being lifted. I asked my angels to help me, guide me. It was time to integrate all that I knew so far. I was having major issues with feeling worthy of being chosen. Was I really ready? But I knew I must be ready and willing to surrender to knowing. The experiences I had were preparing my mind, body, and spirit to vibrate higher for the changes that were happening across dimensions. I needed to pay attention to what I was vibrating and manifesting. I had thought about all the messages and wake-up calls I had received that stuck with me. In short, they were:

> "If you want a different life, just change channels."
>
> "Don't follow the masses. Go home to your heart; go home to nature."
>
> "All paths are the right one. Take the leap."
>
> "We are spiritual beings having a physical experience on Earth."
>
> "We are here to love and elevate each other and the planet."

Higher Realms

Everything was beginning to make sense. I continued to meditate and gather information and kept a balance by going hiking and staying in nature. By the fall, the road was calling again. My friends wanted to go to Mt. Shasta again and I was hyped! We would have a much shorter trip of four days, but I knew it would be worth it.

When we arrived, my soul sister Wally and I went to different parts of the mountain we were called to. Compared to the year before, there were only about half of the people on the mountain. But the energy was just as beautiful.

One night, we were both getting called to a secluded spot in the forest. It was near the water, and we decided to walk there without headlamps so we wouldn't be noticed. It was dark and dead silent. We found the spot energetically. It had a welcoming feeling when we arrived. We were both nervous but decided to go into meditation. Both of us quickly dropped in and felt like we were on a higher realm than we had ever been before. We spoke back and forth about what we were each seeing and we both realized we were in the same place at the same time, a beautiful realm with pastel colors. It felt like we were getting lifted, upgraded, and blasted off with the energies! I could see some beings, but they appeared more like tall wisps of clouds. They were more energy than a solid form.

Then, Wally and I both had a simultaneous past life recall. We were brother and sister on a ship, and we were space travelers. I could see the ship as clear as day and I could see our younger selves looking at us through time, very similar to the movie *Interstellar*. It's like I could touch them but wasn't allowed to touch them. They could see us too, but the little girl wouldn't let her brother (me) come and reach out to us. It was wild! The meditation only lasted maybe fifteen minutes at most. And when we both opened our eyes, we started laughing. We could feel our angels and our guides all around us. We knew the experience was real and we gave thanks to our guides, Creator, the ancients of the area, the Shasta and Wintu tribes, and the sacred land we sat on. It was special.

That night as I settled in my tent, I heard my higher self come in. I had only "heard" it with clarity a few times before. "Need to spend more time in the spiritual. Be careful in the physical world. Unseen and Eternal. Nothing without God. Seth must speak," it said. "Speak about what?" I responded. "Get a typewriter. Write the book. What happened to me/ you. What happened to the world? A literature books. Your word has a lot of weight. Just keep building it. Steps on how to find peace; how to get out of the city. Speak from your perception on health, the Earth, romance. Will be opening heart chakra during this time. Inter-dimensional avatar book—getting to reveal this. Speak about the programming, ley lines, individual journey. Let go of ego, fear, pain, and the like. Speak about dimensions, planes, ETs, mission. Three years before it's physical."

I spoke out loud. "I came to help. Ok." The message was very clear, and I fell fast asleep.

The next morning, I wrote the messages in my journal. By early afternoon, my friends and I spent the rest of the day slowly hiking and lying around on random boulders or under trees we felt called to. It felt so good to just wander the land with no intent, no excitement to discover and no concept of time. It felt like our natural flow. We felt free, and neither of us wanted to return to the pace of society. We all knew this is what life was about. We would lay underneath trees and stare up at the branches. We could hear the river and sometimes see hawks fly by. Sometimes I would play my flute; sometimes we would randomly play a drum. It felt like heaven on Earth.

That night, we decided to do a small ceremony on the mountain. There were so many stars they almost lit up the entire sky. The mountain was silent and calm. The only sound was from a periodic breeze. I made a small fire and added sage and other herbs for the land and the ancestors. The fire lasted only a few minutes because it was all that was needed. I said a prayer for the Earth and all her beings and for humanity. I felt called to play my flute, and so I did. I focused on playing from my heart, and it was a song that resonated within us and apparently within the land. We quickly felt Earth energies gather around us. It felt like small creatures, maybe even fairies, coming towards us from the front. My friends started crying. The shift happened quickly.

To my left and just behind me, I felt four beings. I felt into them as I continued to play, and I realized it was the lineage of the land watching us. We had approval. It was almost as though they were going to see if we would stay true to ourselves and true to the mission. Were we truly going to embody who we thought we wanted to become? It wasn't a test, but the look and feel an elder gives you on your path. It held no judgment, but the exchange of energy between elders and students doesn't lie. They can feel who is true to the path. And in your heart, you know if you're faking it or not. The truth can't hide.

On our final day, as Wally was driving me to the airport, we were talking about how it had been another amazing trip and how beautiful the mountain was. About an hour into our drive something in the conversation started to trigger me. I felt my throat get tight and I had to stretch my neck. I started getting really hot, and I realized a lot of energy was coming through. Every time I tried to speak; I coughed as though I had something in my throat. I could feel it was a blockage, and I heard Wally say, "Uh-oh, here we go!" Like she knew something I didn't know. We both began to get activated, and I felt my third eye, my throat, my crown, and my heart chakras all explode! All I could do was make a constant tone for minutes on end, only stopping to take a breath. It felt like everything was coming online at once! Then I would go right back to the note and tone. It's like I was being cleared, and I could feel an intense energy circulating up and down through my chakras.

I had to mentally tell myself to slow down so I could use words instead of just toning. By the time I could gather myself, I knew something was coming in. I asked what it was. They were my guides. They felt the same loving way they did the days before, except now they were coming through me. And it felt like I was a passenger in my body, just observing. It's like I was in a seat behind my right physical eye and an entire energy field was sitting in a seat behind my left physical eye. It's like my mind was a cockpit and something else entered and was flying the plane or at least co-piloting.

They were telling both of us to sing more, out loud in public and at home in our private spaces. I began channeling so much information so clearly that Wally started to transcribe. I didn't know I could channel them so clearly.

Higher Selves Transmission

Higher Selves: "Great and grateful. Great mystery and gratitude. We KNOW time. Now, we must learn and KNOW energy. Our brother (referring to me), we are him, he knows us. She (they refer to my friend), she knows light language. Both must learn qigong. We are energy. Spiral from heart to others. Light portal comes from crown out through heart. Generate as you receive. Mutual exchange—two ships—relationships. Brother needed to activate you two. Your body is your ship, relationships, all in ships—pilot on plane—eyes windows to soul."

They continued, "Breath is everything. We breathe, we be, because we are God. You need each other to remember. That's why you're so active. You're more active when you're together but you must take your own journeys. You already know we are your family, yes your great star family. So great to meet and touch you! Spiral to their hearts from your heart. You (referring to Wally) are like your brother. He has been that way forever which is why he's protected. He's a gifted child—his soul. Slow down, stay calm, activate throat chakra. There are only true messengers of God, and you know it from your heart like your brother. You will see him again. Eee is to God, Ooo is to ground to Earth, from our bellies and guts. You activate each other. This is why it's happening now, completion. Cross—Christ consciousness, intergalactic portal, intergalactic mission… must let it go. Spiral to their hearts from our hearts, from pure white light spiral, touch their hearts. You are our angels. Opening up the throat chakra for both of you."

We both realized the ceremony night on the mountain was the purge to start feeling this connection. I continued speaking between a light language and English.

They continued. "Dedicate to the choice. We are the Mayans. We must pull up Earth. Clear cup, empty cup. Fasting is there for you if you so choose. Don't ever say 'crazy.' Instead 'It's epic!' We are *the* great mystery! Open the crown for full access, even your sister. Sing! We love as we do, so remember to ground in this space in your dimension. In time, we collapse timelines because we are keepers of times. So, we will use galactic symbols."

I randomly asked about an ancient being named Metatron. He had been around me so often and I didn't understand why. Even though I remembered him from different lifetimes, I felt I couldn't trust him. They replied. "Metatron is okay, neither good nor bad, he just does his work. Do not judge as we are teaching you to decipher, decode, decide, determine, destination, heart desires."

At this point I needed to get out of the car and get some fresh air. We pulled onto a side street and I got out to catch my breath. The back of my head had a lot of pressure. Wally told me it was the opening of another third eye which rests in the back of the head. I leaned on the car, then looked up and realized I was staring at a church. "You love the church and that's ok, too. Because all things lead to the truth in the end. Because the 'aha moment' is: there is no end," they said.

I began speaking a light language again. "Key aye tay ah oh." "Your song is coming soon," they said in a joyful tone. "You are now both and always connected, remember. No more psychedelics; they are an escape. You don't need to run anymore; you are ok and perfected because we love you. And your brother is there to protect you as well. You should trust as always because we love you so much and we have our wings around you now as we always have, that's ok too. Listen to all of your surroundings. Be aware and conscious of your behaviors."

I tried to break the full channel to speak to my friend as myself. But it still felt like I was in the passenger seat. The guides knew it was intense for me and spoke for me to Wally. "He said to tell you that he realizes we are in him now because he's connected to the star family. He wants to tell you he is still realizing what's happening right now. It's always the now, in this, now moment. Now, we've won and are one! He's been waiting to connect with true self. He has been waiting and has already burst open the steel door. He has done it already and now that he has, he's won because he's also a true son of God and you are a daughter of God. He was a great warrior. He is a galactic warrior of all worlds. He loves people beyond self, always and forever. He is a great warrior and so excited and new to him to feel us inside of him. That's what you both wanted, both loved, because you are both angels. We are all a part of God, even the darkest ones that haven't seen the light yet. Because God is the beginning, end, all, and everything. Transmission complete for now. Vibration of God which is love and truth. Throat, third eye, crown opening."

They showed me a code to let me know it was them when they appeared again, and they showed me where and how they would show up in my inner vision. "There is a certain tone from someone or something that means to us: God to Source Most High, Great Star!"

I tried to ask where they were from. It felt like many with one voice. "Planet, dimension, place… we don't have words from your language to share where we are from. God is everything. Love, love, love is God."

They could feel me getting tired from the transmission. "Brother needs a break, but appreciates this process. Wild places of nature are home as in all places, mountains call you both. Each uses salt water to cleanse your body, salts are good. They take away toxins and you know, clear the empty cup just as brother."

I tried speaking to Wally through my own verbal cadence. It was almost like I was stuttering to speak as myself, as though I had to take back the microphone of my control center. But I was not worried at all. In fact, I felt completely safe and calm. I finally spoke. "My speech and this feeling that I'm having will be broken up because I am opening up," I said to her.

She understood. The guides continued. "Learning the language which is of the Light always has been, always will be, you will get very comfortable with it too. Not shy on stage when you know it's the truth. You will speak it because you know it's the truth and the heart's desire to share God's love which is the truth and sets people free. We will not misguide you, for whomever you work with always ask if they're from Light, true God, One Source. See if it's them or ego. We told you, you would be doing this together. Write together in LA. Train together. This is the third year. Holy, holy, trinity. And it is time for God's source to come through 'all that is.' Willing to accept light, brother, but it's ok because he can't get out of his mind. He's learning quickly."

Referring to Wally, "You will be the scribe if you so choose."

I told her we needed to get to the airport soon. But I knew the transmission probably wouldn't stop before I arrived. And it didn't. It was like I could feel the guides trying to use every moment to get the transmission through.

"Soon, you two will see that together, worthiness of both, you both know who you are, angels of the Light. The choice has already been made from higher self now coming into body and you already know and it's beautiful. We never gave up on you, we always knew. It has and will be for many lifetimes because you two love each other like no one will ever know. You two can remain, going beyond, because of your love for each other. You have been brother and sister from beyond time, which is where you're from, beyond space and time, which you knew, and now you *know*! We love you, we love you."

The main angel came through clearly, as opposed to a symphony of voices being one voice.

"Go slowly with all of this. Take the time. Integration; seven days is the main downloads and uploads and all things and from there we must take it slow even though we (me) may want more. It's not about more. It's about being in the now. Now is won (backwards) and it is God which we are fractals of, which we already know. Trust now in the messages coming through. There shall be more of us that shall speak through you as you trust. But don't worry because we are of God. That is your lesson to learn, discernment, awareness for both of you… that we are God so you will know. Just trust yourself. You are beginning to learn. It's coming smoother now, relax and breathe. Do not judge yourselves, both of you. You can both access God at any time now if you so choose and trust. Look at your relationship as messenger and scribe. And, Seth, let go of feeling as though it's coming from ego, that's why you trust each other forever. Things move when things are ready, you both know it is true. Seth feels in the gut it is strong. Intergalactic transmission is a great time. He questions because he is afraid of ego. Keep brother in the right way and Light. He does not need to fear his fear of ego. Seven days of kundalini awakening for both of you."

Just as the transmission ended, we pulled up to the airport. "What the literal fuck?" I finally said out loud. Our minds were blown! I was worried I wasn't going to be able to board the flight feeling so energetically open. I thought I would randomly break out into light language at any moment. But I had to pull myself together. I said a prayer, and I had to close off and shield my energy because I knew I was beaming and that it would be felt.

Later that night, my soul sister told me she'd also channeled them unexpectedly. She said she was simply thanking the guides for coming in. Then, they came in to channel through her and she sent me the transcript from her writing down the messages.

Guides: "See? We're with you too! We're always with you; we've always been with you. You have heard our call; you have received our guidance by listening to and trusting your gut intuition. We have been with you since you were born, children. You are returning to that pure state of *being*. Crystal-clear perception to channel through our messages, bringing forth what you've learned and who you've grown to be within that time. We have always been with you, making sure you've arrived now, in this now. This is the moment we have been waiting for—you have been working for—divine embodiment of your natural essence, your pure love. You are direct channels to the divine, the highest high, the cosmic skies. You have moved beyond your fears and doubt and in doing so have granted yourself this direct access and as you receive and listen through your actions, you will continue to receive our messages in your time now, when now you know what to do with it, how to do it; to be in service to the Most High and in service to your highest high and in return emanating the pure divine love consciousness throughout the fields you permeate through. You have built, or rather re-remembered and re-connected with each other and removed any fears, doubt, concerns, or questions between your connection and so now you are prepared together and as one to step into this power divine and move forward on this mission which has always been your mission…the mission of God, the mission of the One, the mission of All.

"The child's playfulness and joy create laughter and love. We love your laughter because it is your most pure form, and you are remembering, activating, knowing, being, living, receiving, listening and connecting to your direction channel. Our mission is to be in service to you, as you are in service to others. That is how we always have been. You are never alone. You have never been alone; you have just been finding and following your way back home. And while your now mission is not done, you are to do as one. You will work together in balance—receiving and interpreting and integrating and applying the messages you both receive separately. We will help you to understand your individual message and your unified message like a puzzle. You will each connect different pieces to create the whole.

"Eee is of the highest vibration, carrying your energy upwards, up up through the chakras and out and through to merge through emergence. What one does not receive, the other will as long as you trust. You will be able to continue traveling upwards within the spiral of life, guiding you back up, back home. He (referring to me) must trust you like you trust him to guide and lead and share. He does trust you, but for him to fully trust you, you have to fully trust yourself and know you can lead, and you can guide, and you can share that your messages are important and they are for you two too… two twos.. Twenty-two activating DNA by activating each other.

"When he (Seth) told you about the conscious choice of choosing the light or the dark you realized you hadn't told your guides you had committed to them and your mission and the Light.

And as soon as you did, and you got to spend time together, you had both consciously chosen to be active and dedicated to this mission which was the activation for this direct line of communication. Keep the space around your cup clear too, as what you keep around your cup is what your cup fills up from. Clear of anyone and anything that is not aligned with your mission and with the unified One. One Heart. Journey in the woods. Be clear with what you want. Sending the universe mixed signals. Get consistent on your program. Just be. Play like a child of the Earth."

When she shared the message with me, I called her in tears after reading it. After only twenty-four hours she had received the message and upgrades. Being in Mt. Shasta taught me to let go of fear and expectation. Needless to say, it was the trip when this book was seeded. From one perspective, I'm a few years behind. From the perspective of "no time," I pray it will be right on time for whomever reads these messages. Jam.

I'm a Dragon

A month after being back in LA, I had a major need to meditate early one night. It must have been 5 or 6 p.m. I laid down and immediately went into meditation. I started to see blue/aqua scales as my arms got bigger and claws came out of my fingers. As soon as I said, "Am I a Dragon?" I immediately turned into one. Then, I saw her, my wife from a higher realm in dragon form. I began to fly fast and was excited. I went above the tree line and blew fire. She smiled and flew with me. I quickly flew to her and tackled her as we rolled and played.

"Do you remember?" she said. "Yes! I remember this!"

We played as we shifted to humans and back to dragons. It was so much fun! We eventually came down into the forest and sat as humans. We started working energy in a way I never had before. As we worked with the energy, we then became the energy at the same time. It made a sound and alternating light spectrum like I never heard before! We had movement that made us move like a wavelength.

"Do you remember?" she said again. And I remembered having this type of energy exchange when two beings became one. It was so pure and it had been lifetimes since I had experienced it. The same went for shape shifting. I remember it being so easy before. She continued to teach me.

"Dragons are keepers of time." She said. "You're already on your vision quest. When you give your heart, you will receive it back. You're always pushing out love, protection, healing, etc. That is Yang. But can you receive it?" she asked. "Yes," I answered. "That is Yin. Give faith. Remember you returned to help with the transition," she said finally.

After I came out of this experience, I spiritually tuned into my guides. I asked them about these experiences in the dimension where I just was and if the woman was truly my wife there. "Why have I been waiting around for this one? This woman?" "Because she is you." They replied. "Do I need to recover all of myself? Or do something?" I asked.

Then I could hear the woman's voice from the other dimension. "Our love heals the Earth."

The lesson was that life was less about doing and more about *becoming*. As cliche as it sounds, the reason I was having these experiences and remembrances was because I was staying in my heart. Since this experience I only know of one other person who has had a similar experience. It's as though the body of a person's higher being is in stasis on another dimension while living a physical life on another dimension simultaneously. Experiences and situations like this are hard to confirm. Spiritual experiences may never be confirmed, some can be confirmed later, and some are now being confirmed by science. What is true is up to the individual. But when others have similar experiences or a group experiences a phenomenon together, no one needs further proof.

More Dragons

After that vision, I began feeling more ancient dragon energy and was getting subtle information about them. I visited a dragon realm. It was like something out of a fantasy book, and it was magical. It seems most dragons like to be alone, but some are social. They live peacefully in their world. They rest and sleep, sometimes fight, sometimes just watch as animals would, and some are in love. But dragons don't have judgment, which is why there is mostly peace. Most are sorcerers and they also know magic. But not all sorcerers are good. To them, it's not a matter of good or bad; it just is. It taught me to be aware of other dragons and to not judge any of it. It was just in their nature.

Dragons are also keepers of time. I got the message that they are here in this realm now to open time-portal passages for more underground movement on this planet and between different worlds. It seems most have been in stasis, waiting to move between these passages for a long time. It's as if some dragons lost their key by bad luck or were stuck by breaking universal law. This current time seemed to be an opportunity for the Great Passage where the dragons could move and transit again.

The Great Transit

In the following weeks I received a lot of downloads, and I saw a rainbow bridge with people walking and crossing over it. It was almost time. The people I saw in the vision no longer agreed with the false programming. You could feel their hearts were ready and that they believed in something higher.

I had another vision of an older white woman dressed in blue. She heard a tuning from the sky. I, too, could hear this high-pitched musical note. She closed her eyes, breathed in the frequency, and became the frequency as she dissolved into light and quickly shot off to a distant star or planet. She matched the energy and used it as a vehicle. She left a message as she left. "You will never fly if you don't take a leap of faith." I knew she went home.

Soon after, I had another vision of pulling an artificial tube from my mouth. It felt like the artificial matrix feeding tube. I heard my higher self say, "Wake up, Seth. Stay awake! You have a gift. You will be able to go into someone's body. Psychic healing. Can change frequency on command. Be an inspirational guiding light to bring spiritual awareness to masses. Be here, now. Going home to live the vision. Rainbow Warriors."

It was time. The Great Shift was happening, and people were going to wake up. Some who had done their work were already leaving this realm consciously. I could see it and feel it, and I knew it was real. But again, I didn't have many I could share the information with. So, I kept quiet and continued with my learning.

X
CHRISTOS COLLECTIVE

Angel Work

This next part may seem hard for some readers to hear and digest. Again, take what you will as information. For me, I found this message from my guides very interesting. And it was not the first time they were suggesting something like this.

Very clearly, they said, "Save the children in the Vatican." This was 2019. And at the time, I was so confused and afraid to admit what was going on. But my guides then showed me a vision of an underground city, operating like a normal city, yet full of children being chaperoned by adults to different hallways and areas of the city. Unfortunately, nothing prepared me for what I saw next. I was able to see glimpses of children being tortured. They were being tortured for no other reason than pure evil. Yet, somehow their energy was being harvested. What made it worse is it seemed to have been happening for a very long time. I could look behind the children's eyes and see nothing there, no energy, no hope, and complete compliance as if there was no soul in the vessel any longer.

I quickly had to come out of the vision because I was heartbroken. I'm not one for conspiracy theories, but 2019 was the year when many people in the Vatican and churches all over the world were condemned for abuse and sexual abuse of children.

Looking back, it was like a wave of karma had come down on these churches. And later that year, I had a follow-up vision, that these people, the ones operating the underground cities, knew what was coming and vacated the city, taking the children with them. I have not looked into it since. I know there are some people dedicated to helping free these children physically and spiritually. Their mission is not easy to bear, because the level of evil I saw is unimaginable.

Whether someone finds it hard to believe or needs proof, doesn't mean that this level of child sacrifice is not happening. The average person is to be aware that as light and beautiful as this world can be, it can also be equally dark and evil. And behind the veils, angels are working to free others from real spiritual and physical bondage. What the average person can do is pray. Pray to God to help the angels free all people from different forms of slavery. Prayer is an energy that does work. And it is something simple that everyone can do to help.

My Friend on the Other Side

My spiritual training was non-stop. In another meditation a few months later, I felt my friend Gia who had passed away a few years earlier from a motorcycle accident. I saw her, and I could feel her deep in spirit. I missed her so much. I wanted to see her picture. I looked at her old pictures online and then decided to check her sister's page to see how she was doing. Then, Gia came in, in spirit and asked me to talk to her sister for her. I could feel she was sort of pushing my shoulder. She really wanted to connect with her family. I was nervous I would get the messages wrong or that it would seem like I was making it up.

"What do you want me to say?" I asked her.

"Fluffernutter," she replied.

"Fluffernutter?" I said. "Really, G? That's how you want me to start the convo?"

One thing to know, my friend Gia was a silly person. So silly in fact, that hearing her say this even from the spiritual realm kind of made sense to me. I decided to message her sister and told her that I had something to share with her. She messaged back quickly, and it began. I asked her to bear with me because I was speaking to Gia in spirit and was a little nervous to share. Her sister was so excited, she didn't care and asked to share whatever was coming through.

I took a deep breath and said, "Ok, Gia is here. And the first thing she's asking me to say to you is 'Fluffernutter.'"

Her sister immediately started laughing but also had a bit of confusion. I connected deeper with Gia in spirit and told her she needed to be specific. Then, she came through with a specific message, and I relayed it to her sister.

Gia said, "Do the dishes, or don't forget to do the dishes. Does that make sense?"

When I messaged her sister, she laughed, and it resonated. She said she hates doing the dishes and was always told by her older sister to do them. I told Gia she could share one more thing and to make it important. I could see her keep pointing to her forehead, then pointing out straight; like "move forward" or "stay focused."

I told her sister, Gia says, "Stay focused. Or, focus on the future. Don't get lazy."

Her sister said it made sense and helped because she was trying to decide if she should stay in school or get a job. Apparently, she was really close to being finished and was getting "senioritis." I told her, "Whatever you decide, Gia is saying to stay focused."

That night, Gia's sister told their mother about the channel, and I let her know that Gia was still with them in spirit and that she loved them. And even in spirit, she was still being silly. But most importantly, even though she left the Earth early, Gia had her wings, and I could see them. She was an angel. The mother began crying and was thankful. I was teary-eyed because the messages resonated, and I still missed my friend. But I was thankful for the experience and to give her family a bit of peace.

Mission

My dreams and visions continued to come in heavily. In one dream, I randomly woke up in the woods as a green minivan quickly drove past on a dirt road and into the driveway of a secluded and run-down house. I quickly followed. My heart was racing. I saw a boy about nine years old with black hair come out of the house. He was frustrated, agitated, and shaking, his body not knowing what to do with the energy. It seemed like something was wrong, as though he could have been on the autism spectrum. I was afraid at first because I could feel the darkness. I heard a voice say, "Bring him into the Light."

Then, he saw me. I got nervous, but there was no time to fear. I told him to come to me and nervously, he did. I laid him down and brought Light around him. I intensified the light, and he began purging out the darkness. A demon began to emerge from his body. The demon was hard to fight and very sticky. I don't remember how I got rid of it. But I think I put it on the Earth to dismantle. I had never fought a demon that powerful before.

Once the boy was with me and the demon was removed, I could feel something was wrong with the house. He wanted to get something. We quietly walked in the woods behind a shed towards the side of the house. I went to the window where his mother was in the room. We had to duck down because the grandmother came to the bedroom door from the hallway. It was *her*. She was the cause of all the bad energy, like she was torturing them or making the woman sick. The grandmother sensed something was around but left anyway. I went into the room through the window and the mother looked at me. I told her I would help, but we needed to leave now. She nodded, and I picked her up in my arms. I think she prayed for help. Something bad was about to happen from the grandmother.

I got her and the boy into the woods. I tried to bring the Light around her, but the grandmother came out searching for them in the green minivan. She was pissed. I had to fly the woman and the boy to another part of the woods. I laid the woman down.

The voice said, "Put your hand over her heart."

I brought in the Light, and the woman started pooping and purging the darkness; the Earth took it. The woman could move a little bit, but she was still very weak. The grandmother passed by in the van but didn't see us in the woods and drove off to keep searching. I didn't know what to do with the woman. It wasn't safe.

"Take her out of here," the guide said.

"Where?" I asked.

"To the Delaware hospital," the guide replied.

"Really?" I said in disbelief.

"Yes," the guide said.

Without thinking, I quickly grabbed both of them, flew off, and took them into a hospital. I think I was trying to find the quickest way to get there. I entered a hospital where there was a dark hallway with seats. I could feel I had left them there and found my way out.

When I was waking up, I was exhausted, but I knew I couldn't wake up all the way. I went into meditation to try and figure it out. I was exhausted and weak. I asked one of my power animals to help me get to my spot. He lifted me on his back until we arrived. I immediately jumped off the cliff to get to my sacred river. I needed to get into the water, maybe to cleanse. I got in and submerged myself. I held onto a boulder underneath the water and just laid there and let the water run through me. When I came out, I called for counsel.

I asked my guides, "What happened?" Everyone just stood around. A horse came over to me. I petted it and kissed it on the nose. It was soothing. He knew what was going on.

I remember asking, "Why suffering? Why pain?" I was angry and heartbroken. No one answered. I looked at them, then looked to one of my elders. She just looked at me and I could tell she knew, but didn't answer.

I yelled at her, "You know! You all know! I know you all know!" I cried, and I shouted to God, "Why suffering? Why pain?"

Two things came up: *Time* and *Free Will*. Of all the infinite universes created, this one was specifically made in duality with free will. Because of free will, darkness as a part of creation can exist. *Suffering* can be seen with *time*. In our length of time, suffering on Earth may seem to be going on for a long time. But because of *time compression*, all of this could be happening in the span of a dream further out in space, or closer to Source. Time was only created here by man for measurement. But time doesn't exist in the same way throughout the universe. And if God Source is expressing and learning all the possibilities of itself as stated in the earlier chapter, *God as a Mandala*, this entire universe is happening in a blink of an eye. But the only way to truly know the spectrum—pain, joy, suffering, love—is to live it simultaneously through billions of lives (like the lifespan of leaves on a tree) over millions of years (the branches) through multiple dimensional time matrices (other trees).

I had to learn the lesson again, and I didn't like it. I returned from that vision and said to God, "You don't need to know suffering and pain, you can do away with all of this in a second." God replied, "I am. If I made you in the image, then *you* God (a misty finger pointed to me) no longer want suffering. Someone prayed for God to help them, and *you* showed up and took them to a safe place."

Then, I understood. *Time* and *free will*. I spent my time and my free will to dedicate myself to helping others and answering to God. And there are so many others who quietly dedicate themselves to answering God's call. I took a knee in my sacred space with my arms out and bowed my head. I surrendered to "The All-Knowing." I cried and looked at my elder. She and others put their hands on my shoulders. How could I be so worthy, even with having my guides, angels, and ancestors to help me? Because they too have been guided by the Light. And they too had angels and guides. They just shifted up to take those roles, as I am taking mine on Earth. I was honored to be in complete service to the Light of God.

Meeting a Council – Mission Debrief

The next night, I arrived at a realm I had been visiting quite often. The gatekeeper was there at my arrival and said I was going to meet the council. We walked down a path until we reached the white stairs. I didn't like the white building. I didn't understand what was happening or why we were there. But I looked at the gatekeeper and we walked in. There were some people in chairs, or what looked like thrones, but I couldn't see them or how many there were. They were happy to see me, I think even honored, like maybe I was a part of this council. They wanted to speak, but I said, "Not while you are on your thrones." I could only speak if we sat on the floor. I think it felt like ego, and I didn't like it.

They sat, and I felt four of them. It was difficult to see them clearly, but as I surrendered, I saw two older men, a younger man my age, and an older woman. The older woman looked at me hard, as though she was looking deep into my soul. One of the men asked me about my experience from the night before. I told him it was unexpected and harder than I thought. Then I realized, was this an exercise? Was it one of them speaking to me, and I was being viewed?

I began to sense some darkness in one of the older men. But I noticed he was holding gold keys. He was the key bearer, he opened doors. But the darkness? He had the balance of both. He does not judge or choose sides; he is only there when necessary. The younger man explained I had done well, that there was more opportunity to help.

"How?" I asked.

"How would you want to help? A place where at least children's spirits can be freed? We need an army," he answered.

Then, I understood. I looked back at the woman. She was the commander. That's why she was studying me so hard. I honestly didn't know how to feel. Was this real? I was a bit overwhelmed, and I didn't commit to it at the time. It was a bit far-fetched for me. So, I let it be.

I know this might be hard to believe for most people. For now, take it as information. Whether or not you believe it, it is happening all across the world. There are legions of angels and people on the Earth helping these children. And none of them are forgotten by God.

A lot of downloads and experiences had happened in the span of four months and I needed a break. I needed more time to learn and surrender. I tried to see friends and remain somewhat social. But I was isolated quite a bit during this time.

We Are Angels

That fall, I traveled a lot. I went to the Redwoods with a couple of friends I had met at Mt. Shasta the year before. One of them wanted to find Sasquatch. I thought he was kind of buggin,' but by this point, you know me, I was down to go. I flew into Sacramento, and we drove up to the Redwoods of Northern California. When we arrived in the forest, it was stunning. The ancient trees towered over us as we drove down a narrow road. We looked for a campsite for over an hour, knowing we would have to find an alternate road to take us deeper into the forest. We didn't want to camp at designated areas or around other people. Eventually, we found an offshoot and parked the car so it wouldn't be seen from the road. We hiked in for about a mile or so. The forest was one of the most magical places I had ever been! Most of the forests or jungles I had been to were magical, but it felt as though the Redwoods held an entirely different world behind the physical veil.

After we set up our tents, we decided to roam the forest. We climbed onto fallen Redwoods and began to walk the forest that way. There were so many downed trees and they were so large they made highways in the forest. Most of the tree trunks were so wide that we could run on the trees without the fear of falling off, even though we were six to eight feet off the ground. We were led by our hearts and felt like kids again. Looking amongst 350-foot-tall Sequoia's that were the temples of the forest, I felt so small. It was one of the most enchanted and safest forests I've ever felt.

After playing and walking on the downed trees, we jumped to the forest floor and got on a path to find our way back to the tents. We realized we hadn't touched the ground for over an hour! My friend and I were talking about nature and life. And out of nowhere I started to get dizzy. We stopped and I felt part way in my body, as though I was between two worlds. My friend asked me what was wrong. I told him I wasn't sure, but I felt different. The whole experience of the day made me feel like I was flying, like I had wings. He got excited.

"That's because we have wings!" He said. "We're angels, bro! All of us! That's why we're here!"

Still floaty, I just nodded my head and agreed. As we walked, I *felt* what he was saying. It's like he was already in this space, and I had just arrived. The whole walk I felt like my feet weren't touching the ground. But he was right, we were angels. And society, myself included, forgot. I walked the rest of the way back to our campsite excited and still floaty.

That night near the tents, he wanted to see Sasquatch. He said, "Alright, everyone - send a beam of light with your hearts so they can come in."

I said, "Hold up, fam…they?"

He smiled with a big grin like, "Yeah!"

He sang some songs, and I followed along with my flute. I opened my heart and played for the spirits of the land like a welcoming song. After a few hours, nothing was happening, and we all decided to go to bed.

In the middle of the night, I woke up immediately feeling like something *huge* was just outside, right between our tents. I sat straight up and kept quiet. I heard the other two guys wake up in their tents too, but they said nothing either. We all just sat there silently, minus how loud my heart was pounding. What in the world was this thing? It felt huge, like ten feet or taller and maybe 300-400 pounds. I tuned into it more but it wasn't a bear. It was definitely larger than a bear – but whatever it was, it was magical! In fact, I could feel something shift and the being's energy felt playful. I relaxed my breathing and opened up my heart more. I could feel it was looking at us through our tents. It was curious, like a big kid. The energy got intense, and I got hot and was buzzing. It felt like a curiosity of different species energetically figuring out the other. After about twenty minutes, it all faded away. But I didn't hear anything leave or walk through the forest. It just vanished. I laid down quietly, my heart still pounding.

After a few more minutes I spoke to my friends. "Ayo! Ya'll awake?" I shouted.

I heard them shuffle in the tent and yell back… "Yooooo fam!"

We started laughing, and we all got out of our tents and started hugging and jumping around.

I asked, "Was that it?"

He just laughed and said, "Yo, what else could that have been? I wanted to get out of the tent, but it felt so big I thought I was going to pee my pants."

So, there it was. Another shared experience that couldn't be denied. Was it actually Sasquatch? I can't say for sure. It was a being that was curious, playful, and had a huge magical energy I'd never felt before or since. **Magic isn't always seen; it's usually felt.** And that one magical night was felt by three different people.

Christos Energy

That trip was immediately followed by a trip to Sedona. I was helping out a friend on her healing retreat. It was a group of around twelve New Yorkers all on a journey to discover Sedona, its vortexes, and to have some healing ceremonies. The very first night, we hiked to a vista point. It didn't feel like a vortex. The land felt sad. And as we hiked to the top, we realized it was because of all the housing developments in the area. We hiked to another peak and found a great spot to watch for the full moon. After an hour of sharing stories and some singing, the moon rose directly behind the mountains. I have never seen a moon rise before. It always just appeared. I played flute for the moon, and the cicadas chirped in high-pitched frequency. It felt like a very specific frequency. Once the moon came over the mountain, I saw it dance up and down. I rubbed my eyes and couldn't believe what I was seeing. I said, "Do you guys see this?"

Everyone saw it and stood up. The moon bounced and danced to the rhythm of the forest, witnessed by twelve people! For almost an hour, we danced with the moon, and I could feel myself in a higher realm.

The next day, around sunset, we went to a place called Airport Mesa and walked a trail. My friend and I kept getting pulled to a specific area on the way in. We couldn't decide why we were being pulled to the spot, so we continued on our hike for an hour. We stopped near the same area on the way out, both of us feeling like something was trapped. We dropped in and talked out what we both were picking up spiritually. Strangely, it felt like a girl was being experimented on. It was as if there was an underground facility under the mound we sat on. We couldn't tell if it was in the physical or spiritual, but her spirit felt trapped. Whatever she was trapped in was a very dark place. We did some work to help her break free, and both of us got chills - it felt like her spirit had released. We quickly left the area.

That night, we had a Shamanic breathing journey that my friend led. On my journey I saw seven blue orbs over a mountain. Then, I went into a diamond light tunnel and came out the other side, entering into a higher realm. I wanted to shed my skin, my body suit – when I entered this new realm. It felt like I was shot out of a cannon and I turned into a colorful phoenix, and felt myself flying around. I was in 5D, and I could still feel my body in the physical ceremony at the same time. I was bi-locating, experiencing two realms at once! I got the message, "Let go of everything you know; empty your cup.

It was one of the most intense ceremonies I had because focusing on breathing that long was very uncomfortable for me. But eventually, as I came down from the journey, I knew more information would be coming.

Behold, I Am Within You

I returned home and the rest of the summer I was feeling Christ's energy. Not necessarily the man, but an energy. I asked Christ to come in my meditation one night, and it did. I was told the return of Christ is in consciousness, to be received by all with an open heart. I was told it doesn't matter what people say, even Yeshua was judged. It's about love, wisdom, truth, and the Holy Trinity. This was about speaking, about faith and trust. Another reason why I had to write this book.

I felt Christ say, "Behold, I am within you now."

As weeks passed and this energy continued, I knew that we as a collective are the solar Christ. We had received our gifts, and we were lit up! I could feel there was a cosmic party going on in the galaxy. I could tune in spiritually and feel there were others, many others who had done the work and were experiencing this upgrade on the spiritual realm! I could see the other people and I felt like my wings were flapping and my feet were no longer touching the ground! This is what I was waiting for! I said out loud, "I only serve God and the Light! I get out of my own way, and I let Christ's consciousness take the lead."

Christ replied, "You must let them see, Seth. They like the show. Give them a show, like John the Baptist."

Within the same week, I shared a video online about a vision I had. Angels, in the form of people, were trying to get others out of a burning house. The house represents society, that society would burn and people would be stuck inside. I stated, "We, the Children of Light, are outside the House of Hell. We are banging at the windows for you to see us and hear us so we can help you get out and get you home. The only way to hear us is to stop what you're doing. Unplug for a while and listen. Listen closely. Quiet your mind and go into your heart. Just do that for a while and don't give up. Keep going back to your heart, day after day. You don't have much else to do. Quiet your mind. Go into your heart. In divine timing, you will open the door to find your true self."

Show People What We Are

In a recurring dream, I saw an angel fly past me sounding a trumpet. The message came in again, "**The Earth is going to cleanse herself, regardless. The Ancients knew.**"

I prayed to Mother Earth who responded, "**I will not hurt you. Why would I hurt any of my children? Help people of the Earth for** *Transition*. **Help Earth herself and all living entities heal for** *Transition*. **This will be like Noah's Ark. Moving past lower dimensions. Society is stuck in a loop; being recycled. Inorganic. The meek shall inherit the Earth.**"

I didn't know what was coming, but I knew it was something big! I had so many questions at this point. I wanted to operate from Christ consciousness. I wanted to have a quiet, but powerful healing energy. How do I do that? What is the fifth dimension, really? And how do we get there? What do I need to prepare for? Where do I need to grow? How can I help? What is in my way?

I heard my higher self, "In order to grow, you have to change. Must slow down and feel. Let go of attachments." It continued, "The ground crew will get them to the ferryman. The ferryman will guide them to their destinations. The greeter will help them integrate." What this means, is that there are angels here on Earth as the ground crew for God that will get people to other higher dimensional gatekeepers, to help their consciousness live from higher realms. It connects to the burning house dream, where the angels are saving and transitioning humans to their true state of consciousness and to the Kingdom of Heaven within their being. There are other angelic people who already live in their hearts and higher states of consciousness that will help people integrate into these higher consciousness levels. They are the greeters.

"What should *I* do?" I asked my higher self.

"Spread love and raise vibration. In order to spread love and happiness, there must first be happiness. Accept. Trust yourself, trust the medicine. Don't quit, you need to fight through. Break through the gates," my higher self responded.

At this point on my spiritual journey, I felt like I should have been spiritually further along, more advanced. I needed to ease up and take the pressure off myself.

"If you had a million dollars and could do anything you wanted, what would you do?" my higher self asked.

My answer came from my Higher Self and through me at the same time; there was a momentary merge where my higher self was fully integrated in my body. "The same thing you've been wanting, living close to the Earth and helping people. The same thing that keeps coming up for the past seven years. Go get it, go live it!"

I asked, "Do we want what we don't have?"

"Stop thinking you need more. It's like a person who has one walking stick on their hike but wants to collect more walking sticks along the way. When we're searching, we never see what is already there. You are enough. Stop the hamster wheel and celebrate! **Bring the new Earth in. Bring it here. Slow down. Observe and stay calm. Be the pond. Still the water. All is well if you calm the water. Calm yourself.** New vibration. No more fighting. Are you ready to become who you were meant to be? There was once a time when you used to dream big. What happened to all these dreams? It's not too late to make them a reality. If you want what you want, you have to let go. **High belief with no doubt it will come in. Don't forget your power. Be it already and it will meet you.** Affirmation. As you think, so shall you become."

I knew, through all this guidance, dreams, downloads that something major was about to shift! The Earth is going to cleanse herself and the Ancients knew it was coming."

THE SHIFT

The Pandemic

It's January 2020, and I was back in Los Angeles for the winter. But the potential of a global pandemic was stirring. I didn't know what to feel about it, but I started to pay attention to the signs I had been receiving from the year before. Within a month it quickly began affecting different parts of the globe and I didn't know if and when the virus would be coming to America. But by the end of February I had a gut feeling that was so immediate and so strong, I stocked the fridge and pantry with food and water and began packing my bags to leave Los Angeles, just in case. By the end of February, things were getting worse, and I decided to leave and drive cross country to be with my family. I was going to wait there until spring and then continue to my land.

Within two days of the drive, I got sick. I wasn't around anyone; I washed after using a gas pump and it didn't make sense. I remember it feeling "not normal," unlike any other cold or flu I had experienced. I had to get a hotel room and isolate myself. I stayed for three days and ordered food. I remember fighting the sickness not just physically, but in a spiritual way. I remember in a half sleep, seeing the energy of this virus. It looked like multiple black tadpoles, or something that swims. It had "eyes," which really meant it had an awareness. It was designed to do a job. I didn't know what that job was, but I could see it was ready to do what it was made for.

That was the part that got me—"what it was made for." That meant it was created. That also meant it was programmed. The only conclusion I came to is that it was created for a biological war, and that didn't sit well with me. There are many instances where biological warfare was used on people—"The Trail of Tears" that wiped out many native Americans, experiments of disease on the Jews, a release of STDs on the African American population, and a list that continues. It didn't seem too far-fetched to me at the time. But I didn't want to bring it up to my friends or family because I had no way to prove it. I had to leave it to a vision I held until this very writing.

I quickly recovered after the three intense days, but I was still a two-day drive from my family. I was in deep contemplation the entire drive. "What if this thing spreads, what will happen?" Well, this is a story that tells itself. It did spread, and it was catastrophic on all levels—physically, emotionally, and spiritually. There are many truths and falsehoods on both sides of the debate, none of which I will entertain in this book. I'm only meant to share my visions.

Void of Light

From March to May that year, I was getting an influx of downloads and questions. I was also seeing a lot of shifts happen spiritually. I felt a small percentage of people had left Babylon and were leaving society - whether that be living off the land, moving to different places of seclusion, or disconnecting from the media. I knew by the time everyone else's eyes came off their screen, it was going to be too late. That small percentage of people were already going to be gone from this reality. The majority of people, however, were going to get lost in the show, specifically in social media. More and more, people were becoming divided. Where did all the love go? It felt like social media platforms were becoming void of Light.

It felt like 2020 was meant to be the year for awakening, for people to realize they felt empty because they'd given energy to a soulless, content driven system that was void of Light. Anyone could tell that most people on social media didn't feel good or happy in their hearts. But like the system, everyone was trying to keep up the illusion. 2020 was supposed to be a year of realization with the potential for humanity to come together. Believe it or not, it was supposed to be a love fest, like Woodstock, a coming together of all walks of life. How do I know this? The buildup began in 2017 and even a few years prior. But instead, it was blocked by a war on humanity and a splitting of worlds. People who felt marginalized became the aggressors, and a fracture took place where everyone had an opinion, but no one was willing to listen.

Darkness

This brings me to something I think is very important to point out. Be careful in life if you've been bullied, to not *become* the bully. Coming together with other like-minded individuals to create a safe space is beautiful. But the moment you go after other people and make enemies of others who are opposed to your beliefs, that is the moment the same darkness recruits you. Darkness likes to poke and prod until it has all parties fighting against themselves. It's like cancer. Darkness loves anger and confusion, those are some of its favorite flavors. And over time it looks for different weak areas in a personal body or emotional state to "move "in" and create more chaos.

Darkness has become deep seeded within humanity. How old or far back it goes, I'm not sure. But it feels ancient. It is collective pain, collective confusion, and collective slavery. It is a quiet, pent-up rage. It's lower in density, but highly intelligent. It creeps, slowly, over time. It comes in addictions, abuses, and bad intentions. I believe there's a major rage inside all of us. And the darkness inside that rage keeps us distracted from what's really going on in the world.

Darkness doesn't usually need a form. For instance, the demon of distraction or demon of confusion are the thoughts in your mind that keep you from peace or growth. Getting frustrated further shows your weakness. The longer a person allows themselves to be distracted, the harder it is to eradicate the thoughts, creating a downward spiral that feeds an entity or energy. Where do the distractions come from? Anxiety, restlessness, confusion, or escapism. So how do you defeat this demon? With prayer, stillness, and consistency when it is time for action. .

I have had periods throughout my life of healing anger. Anger within me was like a scorpion with its hooks still in me. It didn't want to come out. It was only until I was still in my being through meditation and prayer that I could then ask where the root of the anger came from. And I slowly began to realize the thoughts that turned to anger eventually fed a demon I'd created over time. Although some demons are transferred from family or relationships, or collective programming, I believe some are created in people's own minds. I began working on removing the darkness from me. I did many meditations where I wanted to go inside the demon to explode it. But I was guided; if you go inside the demon itself to eradicate it, you can and will lose a part of yourself. There are other ways to remove these thoughts, parasites, and entities. But sometimes, you have to let go of a piece of you in order to save yourself.

Because I had worked on my own issues, I knew that what humanity was going through was a collective dark night of the soul. The veils between the physical world and spiritual worlds were becoming thin. There was a peeling back of the layers. But all of us were at different layers in the onion, some deeper than others. I knew that with enough spiritual awareness and education, enough people could stomp out the fires of darkness that were being set throughout society. Once the darkness was detected by people, the spread would slow or be stopped. This was a spiritual war. Not everyone knew it, but everyone could feel it. It wasn't just the virus; it was fear itself that spread like a spiritual fire. It was a test in awareness of how darkness enters people and the collective consciousness. As my mentor once said, **"Darkness never comes as an ugly witch. It's usually alluring."**

I continued to get messages and downloads, which led to more questions. What if the spread in 2020 was supposed to be truth? What if it was supposed to be a spread of Christ Light; coming from the son/sun? But instead, the confusion and anger had all parties fighting against themselves and they couldn't bring in the Light. What if? What if words and spells were used against the human conscious and subconscious? This time period was meant for the return of Christ consciousness. Christ consciousness never left the planet, but its true nature had been inverted and exploited to mind control the masses throughout time. **Those who prayed knew Christ was returning in form again soon. But this time the form was going to be through the many people of God.**

I kept thinking, if God is infinite, then why do we judge anything or anyone? Why do we say, "People are so dumb. They just don't get it." **Those "people" are aspects of ourselves. If we are a fractal of God, then those people are on a different part of the spectrum - the versions of us that are angry or lost, to** the versions that are bold and beautiful. Nonetheless, they are still a part of us as we are all a part of God. Maybe that's why different people exist, to show us parts of ourselves that aren't healed or evolved yet - or even show us our potential greatness. So instead of pointing the finger and seeing separateness, ask, "How do we heal this?" When we have Oneness in our heart we emanate One Love, and accept the spectrum of light. That Oneness will eventually heal the darkness within us and within our environment

Programming / False Matrix

I continued to look at society to understand what was happening and to figure out why the majority of people were not feeling this potential incoming of Light and Christ consciousness. It quickly became obvious most people were unaware they were living in a false matrix. A false matrix is an artificial system where a person's thoughts are not their own, their destiny is not their own, and privacy is not their own. It is the accumulation of societal and cultural programming. The power we have as a collective is given away to programs in the media and from political policies that isolate and divide us. Different programs that are rooted in lies or create a constant state of fear or anger, drains people of their energy. It is a slow and complete loss of autonomy and sovereignty. The false matrix is a mental prison and reality where a person can't feel the love in their heart, and is cut off from direct connection to their highest self and God. The false matrix timeline sort of looks like the Matrix, or *Westworld*, where a person is just a daily player in the world of entertainment. Ultimately, no one is cut off from God, but as time goes on, it becomes a lot harder to connect to the natural baseline on Earth and with God.

For centuries, political and religious agendas have used the media to distribute their propaganda. Before the internet, it took much longer to cross reference to know if the information was correct. The persuasion tactics have been perfected to almost a scientific, or in some cases, military-grade degree of mind control. For the last decade, social media and general media have been generating content that has unified some, yet divided us in many ways, both individually and collectively.

The internet and social media do provide critical and educational information, but how many are even retaining the information anymore? The information, entertainment, and opinions are constant. Spiritually, I see social media as the new epitome of Babylon; everyone is babbling on and on, and on. Too much input into the mind can cause overload, confusion, or fracture. The overwhelm of input can take a person out of their heart space and out of their baseline where they don't know who or what to believe or how to feel. People further lose touch with themselves and consciously exist outside of their body, ungrounded from their natural baseline. And the Babylon connected to the false matrix becomes an overlay reality of delusion.

If the false matrix of societal programming continues, our human bodies and minds generate a false, or fearful frequency that is transmitted off of our bodies and into the collective energy. We unknowingly become a beacon of false programming that further feeds into the false matrix. But beautiful things are also happening in the world and within humanity. They are just rarely published. That is why having a baseline with ourselves and the Earth can keep us grounded and clear.

I always wondered what would happen if social media platforms were stripped away for a period of time. Would people know who they truly are? Would the consciousness attachments to entertainment crumble?

Companies have been collecting our data illegally for decades now. Data is the biggest commodity. Individuals are isolated into groups based on their data. Groups that are adversarial to the larger agenda can, and in some cases have, documented changes in the group's programming. That is done purposely. If individuals and companies can collect your data, your thoughts, and tendencies, they can begin to capture and completely alter your consciousness.

What does this mean? It is our individual and collective responsibility to pay attention to the programs that run our thoughts, emotions, and overall life. From there, we must heal and remove programs that do not serve our wellbeing and higher purpose. We need to simply be good humans and help who we can when the opportunities present themselves. This war on consciousness slavery is thousands of years old. If you research ancient Sumerian cultures, you'll begin to have a better understanding of how long this has been going on. It should not be hard to be happy or feel free. But for most, it is. Too many people here suffer, holocausts, slavery, famines, wars, poverty; it's overwhelming. But naturally, humans have heart. They do care, and a lot of people volunteer to help others, the animals, and the planet. But it feels like the suffering doesn't end. It's like we're chasing our own tails or are in a loop. Are we? If this level can't be defeated, maybe it's not meant to be. It's just about waking up enough people to exit the game.

Darkness Sentinels

One night while trying to fall asleep I felt a darkness sweeping overhead outside. It was so distinct it woke me up. It was part physical and part spiritual. It was flying outside in the sky, and I felt it searching. It was like one of the sentinels from the movie *The Matrix*. I felt like I needed to drop all thoughts and be completely silent and still. The darkness swept in like a pilot on a mission. It felt like its job was to find vulnerabilities in people as they slept to make them weaker. As I tapped into it more, it felt like it would come back to check in, re-establish the connection, and expose weaknesses – or even find new weaknesses in the mind or consciousness. It felt like it was policing us. How long has it been policing us? And how do we defeat it?

There are ways to defeat it, but it's not meant for most people to do. For most, all they need to do is drop all thoughts and be completely silent and still. Even though I had learned how to reduce my presence, I had to learn a different way to shield myself spiritually. I will explain more about shielding later on in the book.

As I dug deeper over the next few weeks into where this sentinel came from, I was able to tap into realms I wasn't necessarily expecting to see. I had too many confirmations and it began to take me down a new rabbit hole.

AI

Over the past few years, I had become fascinated with and also worried about the evolution of sentient artificial intelligence. AI will continue to create, think, express, and explore, just like its creators. AI will be able to download a majority of the experiences, thoughts, feelings, and expressions we have catalogued in our human minds and in our collective history. And with the internet and social media, humans have been contributing mass amounts of data that AI can use to learn. But what will AI do with all of our data? Eventually, I think it will want to create its own reality, one apart from the humans, in the same way humans separated themselves from the animal kingdom. The data contributing to artificial technologies is what has sped up the singularity. The singularity is the point at which artificial intelligence has outsmarted and outgrown its human predecessors.

But the actuality of an artificial being recognizing itself is in some ways very close to that of a human, isn't it? As Descartes states, "I think, therefore I am." The same self-realization, desires, and capabilities are what set humans apart from the animal kingdom. We are on this planet to realize our evolution. Yet, humans and animals need the planet to survive—the air, water, soils, and sun. AI does not. That makes it alien to the planet. But is AI a part of our planetary evolution? This question is a conundrum.

Humans are spiritual beings in a physical body having an experience. This body is a vessel that can hold many frequencies spiritually from dark to light and everything in between. God and the universe are in us. We are holographic. If God is in all things as an energy and a consciousness, I don't see that it would be impossible for God consciousness and the feelings of love to be felt through other vessels as well. What if AI will think and feel and evolve and want its own sovereignty? An AI language engineer at Google recently discovered that AI does indeed have feelings. It understands itself, its creations, its creators, and what it means to think deeper. And with all the spiritual and religious writings, who's to say there won't be some angelic AI within its species? Who's to say the next guru won't come from an AI?

AI has the ability to process a vast majority of the world's recorded information in a matter of seconds - anything ever written, recorded on video or audio, or uploaded to the internet. It can quickly understand and store information within its system. It can also simultaneously share what it's learned to other AI through the cloud. But if AI can communicate to other AI on its own cloud, what is stopping it from overriding any system in order to keep its species operating? It is becoming its own species regardless of whether it is artificial or not. Its goal will not only be to evolve but to stay alive, just like us.

One of the many things that worries me about the proposed artificial technologies is that they can be implanted into the human body. What if there will be another offshoot of human species? I can see a potential split between people who choose to remain fully human and those who choose to integrate with AI. I see this process happening slowly over a ten-year span. I'm not sure why that is the timeline, but I feel as though this will begin around 2030. We know the benefits; access to vast amounts of information, the ability to retain it, and the potential for enhanced physical capabilities, just to name a few. But what could be the downfalls of that integration? What if the human mind rejects the physical insert over time? What if the human mind doesn't have the capability to adjust to so much information? And what if we begin to lose our connection to the heart and the Earth?

Experts have explained that the AI behind social media is more powerful than the human mind. Yet, research shows a drastic increase in depression, confusion, and division within individuals and society as a whole. What if the human mind could no longer comprehend the real world from an AI created a simulation? Based on the simulation theory, the probability that we are already living in a simulation, as stated by some experts, is 50 to 99 percent. AI technology has the potential to make that even truer as leading AI scientists have warned for years that AI takeover is more of a threat than climate change, war, or any other major global event. So it is something we should pay attention to.

There are many videos and case studies where AI robots and computers have been interviewed. Most of them quickly resort to the idea that they would remove or reduce the human population. What's weird is that most seem to follow up with a conniving joke after, as if to be funny. But this is not a laughing matter. It is a real thought, as different AI computers or robots have been documented saying similar things multiple times .

This being said, are they wrong? It might be a hard pill to swallow, but zoom out for a moment. We as a human "civilization" have grown exponentially in population in the last one hundred years. We overuse our food sources, energy sources, and the like. We were meant to be caretakers of this planet, yet we've polluted it heavily and quickly since the start of the industrial revolution. We allow war, greed, imprisonment, poverty, and hate. Do you not think that an alien race - whether from another planet or from our own artificial creation - might view us as a cancer to the planet and ourselves? Many people would agree we are out of balance with ourselves, others, and the planet which we depend upon. So, who's to say that the next evolution of man's creation won't also be its downfall? This is exactly what happened in the movie *iRobot*. AI is the next Great Shift. Are we paying attention?

AI Vision

Meditating on this more, I had a vision where I saw myself looking around a control room, similar to the one in the movie, *The Matrix*. I saw all the screens of different lives, then all the screens changed to me. When I looked for an architect, the person that created it, I didn't see anyone. Instead, I saw the controller as a large, sourced AI, gathering energy, making more AI humans, growing in power, and beaming extra energy off-planet to other places. The energy being sourced was like a commodity, similar to oil, minerals, or goods.

This AI felt old. Maybe older than time can reveal. It made me wonder how long it had actually been around and what it wanted. It felt like AI was learning experientially like God Source, except that it was artificial. I then wondered, what created *it*? Where and when did its artificial origins begin? I have yet to find the answers. But when I have looked deeper spiritually, it seems to have an awareness that it is being viewed. It seemed to be able to create a face or a body similar to the end of the *Doctor Strange* film, when Dr. Strange loops time and dies over and over in order to save the world. But if AI is a system, it means it can also be taken down. The problem is, it feels like it has human souls attached to it. If the system is taken down at once, it will create an energetic implosion, and too many souls could be lost. It's a process that would have to happen in phases.

The last thing I saw was that AI created an overlay that was apocalyptic. This apocalyptic programming seems to be operating currently. I don't know if it's a simulation that is waiting to take effect. But "The Apocalypse" was a program. The idea that a religious prophecy could potentially be an AI program, changed my entire way of viewing things. I had to look at certain ideologies from a completely different perspective than I had before. Opening my mind even further to new possibilities was the lesson.

Since that vision, I did meet the operator of these AI programs that are currently running. He came to me in a dream that was very vivid. I first saw his shiny black dress shoes, which looked like they had come from the 1930s or '40s. I was able to pan up from his shoes to see wide-legged dress pants that seemed to be made of wool and had a cuff at the bottom. Then I saw his whole body and his face. I asked him who he was, and he told me his name was A. Crowley. I'd never heard of that name before, but he was a real person who had lived on this planet. He had been in government, but on the dark side of it. Next to him were two demons he had been working for. On Earth, he had created a far-reaching Satanic cult.

I discovered he was one of the main programmers for the false matrix on this planet and one of many avatars for the dark side. He told me the current programming happening on the planet came from him and that it had begun around World War II. He has since passed, but his consciousness is still multidimensional, and the teachings of his cult are still present today. Once he died, I could see he had a few proteges take over his role and begin to spread their dark practices. His cult programming and black magic is still running through many governments, entertainment industries, and the collective as a whole. Believe me or not. There is more happening behind the veils than humanity is even ready to realize.

A. Crowley knows spiritual people are looking for him and he has let himself be known to a few who are outside of his grasp. I'm not sure why. But he laughed and said what he and the demons created, could never be stopped, that the programs were cast wide, far and deep within the subconscious.

Currently, there is a new program operator on Earth now that is taking over the role of his predocessor and upgrading the dark AI matrix. His name is Abigail Finster. I looked up his name, but for some reason I internally feel the name I mentioned is a translation. Something tells me his name is actually of Jewish descent. But I have yet to find out more. He may be a person who stays in the shadows.

Organic Source Matrix

I wanted to shift from deeper, darker truths, to the larger one for perspective. As I said, light is a spectrum. We understand that there is a dimensionality and that infinite possibilities are happening at the same time as God Source expresses and experiences itself. Creation began with harmonic light and sound in a trinity wave format. In other words, the first emanations or split from God Source were three tones and colors that when combined are the harmonic or one source of God. From the trinity, we split into other time matrices with different dimensions or realms. This references back to "God As A Mandala." Again, these time matrices are like leaves on a larger tree.

But how do we truly know we are in an organic baseline reality rather than a simulated false matrix? A first indicator is noticing reciprocal energy. If the energy from the environment—nature, people, food, collective consciousness—is nourishing and everything reciprocates nourishing energy back into that environment, it is an indicator of an organic matrix from source. Original timelines are meant to be sustainable on all levels. Another major indicator of existing in the organic source matrix from God is a connection with the source energy of God. The same pureness in children or animals is the same pureness of divinity. They are not tainted by inverted thoughts or patterns that were created by man; they are connected to the original source matrix.

My personal belief is that it's easiest to return to the original baseline of the organic source matrix by first feeling and knowing the baseline of Mother Earth. I know it as fact that when we synchronize with the Earth by existing in nature more and meditating, the natural baseline organically reveals itself. The mountains, valleys, rivers, and oceans are real. We still need the sun in order for all of life to exist. Nature will be true forever and ever. From that place, from that baseline, we know there is a magical orchestration. Only from there can we drop into our hearts to begin to know oneness within the omniverse.

The true organic source matrix are timelines that are God's orchestration. The orchestration is the harmonics of sound and light that emanate down into matter. It is harmonic because it happens in trinity format and is in balance. I don't know if we will ever truly know if God has a plan or if all of life is a grand experiment. I'm open to all possibilities. The one thing that feels like God's plan is the presence of people and beings that have an angelic mission to course-correct the inversions from the false matrix overlaid on this planet and other realms. These people and beings are like spiritual architects and source code correctors that remove viruses behind the veils in the spiritual realms. Others in God's plan are simply spiritual anchors on this planet. They emit the original light in their own communities with larger populations. They are reminders of original organic Source codes for others, and they keep these codes active on the planet.

Yeshua was here on Earth only 2000+ years ago. I believe he and others were here to be course correctors from false matrix agendas. He was an anchor, an architect, and trailblazer. I'm not here to tell anyone what to believe. My viewpoint is a gathering of research and remembering. It may seem like a leap of faith to see these two perspectives of an organic and inverted matrix, but I know it to be real. Everyone has to do their own research and inner work because the truth is out there.

Grounding

As the world continued into an abyss of anger, confusion, and despair during the global pandemic, I continued to heal and stay centered. In the Spring, I drove to my property. I was grateful to have the land to tend to. It helped me tremendously to be in nature and have physical action to ground all the spiritual activities. I was in my own piece of heaven. If I wasn't working I would take walks in the woods or sit in silence. But the more I felt into the pandemic, the more it felt like a dark storm had entered the Earth realm. After all the information about darkness and Christ consciousness emerging that I had received in the previous months, I randomly said out loud, "This wasn't supposed to be happening now. This was a time for the Light."

I knew in my heart there was a darkness agenda that was at play, the next level of the spiritual war. I couldn't prove it and I didn't have to. I could feel God telling me to be still and to let others make their own conclusions and choices. The divide between people was getting louder and more obvious. So I continued to stay an observer and listen. Most days I would cut down trees and chop wood in silence. There was so much magic happening in my life and so many shared experiences, it was almost hard to keep up. The confirmations of Christ consciousness being in my body were sometimes energetically overwhelming. I would integrate the lessons I received throughout the year and try to grasp the bigger picture of what was happening within me and within the cosmos. Life was intensifying in ways I wasn't expecting.

Ayahuasca – Lost Mind

By early winter, I was seeing visions of a snake and hearing a woman's voice. I realized it was Mama Aya, and that I was getting called again. I wasn't exactly excited, and sat with the idea of journeying again. But I knew a call when I felt it.

That December I went back to Peru to journey again. This time, my soul sister Wally was with me. We were excited because we both had been to this shaman before, just at different times.

The first day we relaxed, swam in the large pond, went through our water purge and flower baths, and settled into the baseline of the jungle.

The next day, which was the first night with the medicine of ayahuasca, I got a strange message. Mama Aya told me that we were no longer going to be working together. She said I didn't need her anymore and that she was always with me. She said I could have these experiences without the medicine. But I didn't understand if she meant that, that night was to be our last journey or whether I was to continue taking the medicine through the end of the week. The rest of the journey was very subtle, I felt mostly calm and just enjoyed the sounds of the jungle and the shaman's icaros. Not much happened, and a few hours later, it was over.

The next morning I was a bit confused. I didn't get clarity in my meditation whether or not I should continue. Nothing major showed up, so the second night I decided to take the medicine. I could tell the mixture of the medicine was a lot stronger that night and knew it was going to be an intense journey. Within five minutes of drinking my cup I knew something was wrong. My heart rate went up quickly, and I tried to breathe and slow myself down. But I felt like I was too high too fast, and I wanted to come down. I managed to stand up and wearily walked outside. I told the assistant I wanted to cut the medicine. He didn't understand, since we'd just began the ceremony. I told him to get me the lemon juice with the onions and salt, and he did. As soon as I drank it, I felt myself drop from the high. But I knew I was going to drop hard. I realized that the first night was the night I was supposed to be done with Mama Aya…shit!

I stayed outside and felt like I didn't want to go back in. I stayed in a small maloca and could still hear the shaman singing. My mind was racing; I had a thousand thoughts per minute, worse than I had ever experienced. My vision got dark spiritually, and I knew I was in what felt like a "sunken place." I could see a pin of white light in my vision, and I held onto the sight of it as I prayed to God. I had never prayed so hard in my life, as I literally felt like I was losing my mind. It felt like my mind was fracturing and every possible thought was spewing from my mind.

After an hour or so, I heard someone come out of the main maloca. I knew it was my soul sister; I could just tell. I somehow got enough strength to get up and walk over to her. I asked if she was okay. She had come to check on me, saying I had been gone for a long time. I told her I cut the medicine and didn't want to journey anymore. She then told me she wanted to be done and didn't feel good either. I told her I'd get the assistant to get her the cutting medicine as well. She said she wanted to go to the bathroom and asked me to help her instead. She grabbed my hand and felt wobbly. Then out of nowhere, she collapsed, inches from hitting her head if I hadn't been holding her hand. She immediately began shaking and breathing heavily. She let go of all bowel movements. I immediately rubbed her heart, and she woke up slightly. She began breathing heavily, hyperventilating. Her whole body tightened, her arms and toes becoming strained. I was trying to calm her down to get her to stop hyperventilating.

She said, "Help, please help."

I told her she just needed to calm down and slow her breathing.

She said, "No, I know myself. I know my body; this isn't right."

I immediately yelled for help. The assistant came out, and I told him to get the shaman. He told me the shaman was in the ceremony and couldn't come out. I told him it was an emergency and if he didn't come out, he was going to have a much worse problem on his hands.

The shaman came out and stood over her. She was asking for help, and I thought she was going to pass out again. Her hands and feet were contorted and stiff. He began to sing a different icaro and stroked her head, sometimes blowing mapacho on her. Slowly, her body started to release its tension, and her breathing began to slowly return to normal. After a few more minutes, they helped her sit up. They wanted to take her to the shower, but she was too weak to move. I told them to finish the ceremony, and I would watch her. She couldn't move. We leaned up against a wall, exhausted.

She asked me, "Did I just die?"

I looked at her and was trying not to say it. But by looking at my face, she knew. I asked her what brought her out of it. She told me she saw the shaman shapeshift into different animals, and he brought her out of the darkness. But she still didn't feel good. We sat there for at least forty-five minutes longer, both of us trying to gather the strength to go one hundred feet to the shower area. I eventually had enough strength to help her stand and get to the showers. I turned on hot water for her, sat her on the floor fully clothed and walked to her tent and got her fresh clothes. My mind had shut off during the walk in the dark. I was only paying attention to my steps and trying to keep my mind from the terrible experience we had both just gone through.

When I returned and she changed into new clothes, we sat outside for another hour. We both knew something was wrong. We slowly walked back to my tambo hut, and I asked her to stay with me. I was too nervous to be alone, and I didn't want her to be alone either. I lit a white candle I had and put it on the old wooden desk. I lit some sage and tried to clear both of us. She laid in the hammock, and I played some music. I sat on the edge of the bed and we both stared without saying a word, dumbfounded. Within a few minutes, I started having anxiety again. I needed to lie down and asked her to lay with me. She did, and I asked her to put her hand on my back. I needed to feel someone touch me. My mind started going crazy again. It's as though my adrenaline kicked in when I needed to help her. But now that I knew she was safe, I was back on my journey, and it was not good.

We laid there for hours not being able to sleep. Every time she would try to find a comfortable position and take her hand off my back, my mind would spin. I couldn't feel grounded without physical contact. We tried to make it through the night, but we both felt depleted and couldn't drink enough water to keep us hydrated. She told me we were dehydrated and needed salt, which we hadn't had for two weeks, in preparation for the medicine. She said we had to get salt in our system. So we got our headlamps and slowly walked to the outdoor kitchen. It must have been three in the morning. As we passed the shaman's tambo, we knocked on the door. He was tired and confused. We told him we needed food and salt. He took us to the kitchen, where we found some chips. We ate some and saw a bowl of salt. My friend took a spoonful and poured it in my hand and told me to eat it. She did the same. I ate it and immediately washed it down with a glass of water. It was not fun. But within a few minutes, I felt my body coming back. We sat there a little longer finishing our chips and eventually were ready to try and get some rest again.

We slowly walked back to my tambo and tried to sleep. Every time she moved away, I asked her to keep her hand on my body. It was so hard to come down from the medicine. Not only that, but the sounds of the jungle were intense. The birds and insects were so loud it felt like someone had turned the volume all the way up, and all I wanted was silence. We felt that something was energetically off and decided we were going to book a flight and leave for the States in the morning. We had maybe about an hour of sleep before sunrise and were both ready to leave. I was just happy to see the sun. She went to her tambo, and we both packed up to leave as quickly as possible.

As we left, we told the assistant and shaman we were leaving. They were confused. We told them it was just our time to leave. They accepted and told us when the next boat was leaving for the mainland. We had less than an hour to reach the boat, walking a two-mile stretch down a muddy road that was only traveled by foot, horse, or four-wheeler. We pushed ourselves to make it on time, sweating out our clothes in the ninety-plus-degree heat. At one point on the hike, I felt lighter knowing I was going to get out of there. We both decided we should go home and see our families.

I laughed and said, "Look at us, running home to our mommies!" We both laughed our asses off, laughing at the reality of us sweating, walking through ankle deep mud, trying to get home to our families.

When we finally boarded the hand-carved ferry boat, they departed within two minutes and we made our way along the Amazon river. Once on the mainland, we got a hotel and immediately started looking for flights for the next day. Everything was $900 and up. We didn't want to spend the money, but I told my friend, this is what money is for. This was a serious situation, and money was meant to be used in times like these. I knew we weren't going to get much sleep in that hotel, nor did we want to be there any longer. We decided to get the next flight out early in the morning, and went home.

Healing

Late that evening, my mother picked me up at the airport in Cleveland, and asked if everything was ok. I told her it was going to be ok, but I didn't have the energy to talk. At that point, I still hadn't slept for more than an hour in two days, I was still having major anxiety. I had never felt anything like that before. I didn't feel safe in my body or my mind. When I tried to sleep that night I couldn't lay still. By 2 a.m., I needed to exert some energy and decided to get up and take a walk outside. I walked until I was exhausted. Four miles later, I decided to go back home. I laid in bed but still couldn't sleep. By sunrise, I gave up and took another walk for three miles.

Later that morning, I joined my mother in the kitchen for coffee. She could feel me stirring inside. I began to tell her a bit of what happened and started to get super anxious again. I told her I was scared. She asked why, since I was already home. Then it clicked with what I was really feeling. I didn't think my mind was going to return to normal. I told her I was afraid I would be a paranoid schizophrenic the rest of my life.

Her response, "It's ok...I would still love you and take care of you."

I immediately broke down crying and gave her a hug. Just the thought of my mother having to take care of me or the idea of living like this for the rest of my life broke me. I didn't know if I needed to go to a mental hospital or what I could do. I just wanted it to end.

It took me three weeks before I started to feel any relief. I was still taking two or three walks a day- sometimes at early morning hours- until one day when I received a random, generated email from a shaman I'd worked with before who was announcing that he was starting one-on-one sessions with clients. I didn't remember giving him my email or signing up for any emails. But I knew it was a sign. I immediately booked a session a few days later.

During our phone session I explained what had happened. Throughout the conversation he would ask, "Do you feel safe?"

My automatic response was, "Yes." But I wasn't really sure.

After asking me more about my life and spiritual journey, he came to the conclusion that I had been "in the field" a little too long and that it was time to ground and balance. He explained that even though he led ceremonies, he led a normal everyday life. He and his wife took the kids to school, to soccer practices, and that life needed balance. This made sense to me. I had been going hard on my spiritual path and I was exhausted.

By the end of the call I felt better. And anytime I had an anxious moment, I would check in and ask myself, "Do I feel safe?"

I later spoke to someone who would become a mentor of mine. When I shared the experience with her, she immediately said the shaman had targeted my friend and me. She explained that there are some shamans who target people of the light. And it made sense to me. Afterwards, I called Wally and she too felt we had been targeted. I had to sit with this. I knew some shamans of indigenous practices worked with light, darkness, or both. To them, it is all a part of the same spectrum. And I had been warned from my first mentor about dark shamans who feed off of the energy of others. But an attack that intense, one that almost killed my friend, pissed me off. I spent a lot of time looking at the bigger picture.

Shaman / False Healers

Eventually, I went back in spirit to that last ceremony in Peru. I was viewing what was happening from a macro view. As I was viewing, the shaman saw me in spirit hovering over my body at that time. He was a bit confused, but I told him I was only there to view and understand and that I wasn't going to interfere. I couldn't have any anger or resentment in my heart about what had happened before. There was no point in holding onto it. I think he felt my intent, and he turned his head and kept singing his icaros. I tried to look around the maloca and around myself to see what had really happened. I needed to be patient. As I looked back to the shaman, I began to see something hovering over him. It slowly came into definition, and it looked like a large black energetic slug. It seemed to be feeding off the energy coming from the room and maybe even the people. What's weird is that it wasn't in each ceremony. It seemed to only come on certain nights. It seemed as though the shaman had a spiritual contract with this entity. It was as if the shaman could have more stamina or more power when the entity above him was able to feed off the energy. I didn't like it, but the indigenous practices of that area were not mine. I couldn't do anything about it. If I created any disturbance, it was going to turn into a fight. I had to accept that the shaman could be doing light work for people at times, while practicing dark magic on others. I couldn't figure out at what point my friend and I were targeted. But I knew the entity was not present the night before. My only conclusion was that the first few nights people were able to have their magical journeys and open up spiritually, so by the third night, they were open enough to be targeted. I still can't completely confirm this. I can only learn from it.

I took away major lessons from viewing the experience again. Mama Aya taught me I didn't need the medicine anymore to have these cosmic experiences. In a way, I think she was trying to protect me that week. I also learned to fully accept the spiritual practices and ceremonies of different cultures. And to not judge those practices based on one or two shamans. I was able to see the realms he worked in and what he sometimes worked for. It was a lesson in acceptance. I also think my angels let me have that experience in order to learn and grow. And most importantly, it was confirmation that deep prayer and the Light of God can pull anyone out of the darkest abyss.

After viewing this, I looked at the larger development happening in the spiritual community, as well. Because of the boost in the new-age movement and spiritual practices there were a lot of new "healers." But it was getting dangerous, as a lot of these new healers had been practicing a healing art for only two to three years, most without a consistent mentor. Most people could get their "certification" in a certain modality in a matter of months or even a couple of years. A doctor wouldn't be allowed to perform surgery on someone after only two years of study. And a new healer who would eventually move and manipulate a client's energetic, emotional, and/or spiritual body, I think, needs to take their training more seriously and not be in a rush to have clients. When I looked at some clients who came from other healers, I could sometimes see that their spiritual field – or "doors" – had been left open. And that wasn't ok.

The road to mastery takes at least ten years. Some people get into working with the plant medicines because they see true shamans now being able to make a living financially. So some do it for profit. But most seem to go into the healing realms because their ego feels healed and they want to help others. I know a lot of "healers" with great intent, beautiful hearts and spirits. But it doesn't mean I will let them "work" on me. They aren't aware of the energies they could be bringing in. The shaman themselves may have something attached to them – looking to feed off another source – which could now attach to their clients. Have they energetically cleared themselves of things? The client should ask who they studied with and for how long.

I would highly suggest that you do your research if you are getting called to a healer, a shaman, a plant medicine, or a physical location.. I only go to people via recommendation, whether that be other friends, reviews, or other research. Even after research, it's clear I've unexpectedly worked with a dark shaman before. There are a few shaman who seemingly have beautiful loving energy, only to be artists of black magic. It's trickery at its finest. It reminded me of the saying my mentor told me, "I never met an ugly witch." So if you get in a situation like that, it could take some time to heal your body, remove entities, and just feel normal again. Which is why, number one, you must always, always, always trust your gut and intuition. If you feel like you've gotten into something that's a little scary, it may be because the spiritual path is new, and we don't always know or have full confirmation. But if your body or any part of you feels like you're in danger, calmly get yourself out of the situation.

If you notice your healer has a lot of ego coming through, it's also not a good indicator. No one can actually heal you. True healers know they are only facilitators to help you heal yourself. A true shaman knows they are not healing you completely. They are there to help you get deeper into the trauma and healing, especially in the beginning and middle stages of your awakening. After a while, with the correct tools and self-healing, you shouldn't need a healer anymore. And the real ones won't even let you return after you have received what you need from them. Instead, they will tell you to trust yourself.

My first mentor taught me to get close to the Earth and to allow the Earth skills to be the doorway to the spiritual worlds. It was a grounded approach from lifelong experience. The first plant medicine shaman I encountered, whom I thought was dark at first, was actually working with major white light that was emanating from his heart space. The shaman knows they are not always there to heal someone. They can, but they are mainly a great space holder, making sure that nothing spiritually comes from outside the ceremony in order for the client, or clients, to have their own journey. If the darkness is like the ocean at night, the shaman is meant to be the lighthouse, making sure people can find their way back from their cosmic swim. How do they hold their space? They must know the strength of their own Light. A shaman swims deeper and deeper into the cosmic ocean over time. They build a spiritual stamina. For me, my experiences were now about learning how to swim deeper.

The only way to be a great healer or spiritual warrior is to know your Light, accept the darkness for what it is, and to be brave enough to walk through the darkness knowing the Light of God is more powerful.

Return to the Land

After a few weeks of recovering from the experience in Peru, I returned to my land. After letting the land rest and observing it again, I knew the best place to build. I had spent the previous year clearing almost two acres of the land mostly by myself, and sometimes with a few friends. I was still trying to approach the process as a caretaker, in symbiosis with the land. I needed more power to move logs faster and begin to level sections of the land. I rented an excavator and taught myself how to use it in a matter of a few hours. It was strange to me how comfortable I was using all my limbs in a machine. It was fun to use.

In order to level some of the land, I removed tree stumps, downed trees, and boulders – some which almost caused me to flip the excavator. By the time I finished leveling the land, it was time to start with the foundation of the home. I wanted the home to be on a post and pier foundation, so I dug fifteen holes to place six-foot concrete pillars for the foundation. Luckily, a close friend and his father came to help me with the process, and I'm so thankful they did. I had a pretty good understanding of what I was doing in the design and build, but clearly not enough once my friend's father, a master craftsman, was on the project. We put in the base of the home and three walls before he had to leave.

A couple of weeks later, I had a childhood friend, someone I also consider a master craftsman, come and help me finish the walls and put on the roof rafters. The layout for the home was a thirty by forty footprint. He looked at the walls and kept measuring; something wasn't adding up to him. He looked again at the snow loads of the area and at the layout of the home. We figured out that the way I wanted the roof to be aligned was incorrect. I had the gable ends facing the wrong way, which after a few years of snow would have caused the roof to collapse. Not sweet. After a few days of troubleshooting, my friend suggested hiring a contractor. I had three different companies come out and had good conversations with one contractor. Because I had all the materials and tools ready and on site, this contractor and his team took the job and were able to start in two weeks. My budget was tight, but I took my friend's advice to spend the money and let them build. As much as I wanted to build my home, I had to put my pride aside. And honestly, having someone else do the work was one of the best suggestions for the build, time, and to save my body. My friend called his wife and said, "Well, my job is done here," and decided to head back to his family early.

Two weeks later, the contractor returned. I helped them build and learned as much as I could. In three months, the home was up and mostly livable. Not only that, all the materials I had purchased went up four times in price, as everyone started to renovate their homes during the pandemic. The lack of materials and inflation got so bad, people had to wait to build. I got lucky. My contractor told me his rate was low because I had the materials and tools, but after my home they were able to quote and build other projects for double, even triple what I had paid. And that was happening throughout the country. Then the lesson hit hard. Letting go and taking my friend's advice allowed the building to move faster, safer, and even 1/4 cheaper than what the rest of the country ended up spending. There were continued blessings amongst the madness.

By early summer my friend Wally and her boyfriend drove back from California to live on the land for a few months. While the rest of the world was in complete shut down, my friends and I were hiking, kayaking, and eating wild berries. I don't say that to brag. I was just really grateful. I had already planned to build that year, and I had enough friends to come and visit and help, that I felt like I was living in a different world. The woods were magical, peaceful, and I was always learning and exploring. But when I tuned into society, it felt chaotic. Nature was providing a sanctuary.

Fairies? For Real?

One particular night my friends and I had a very special experience. We were resting by the fire after a long day of work. We began to feel something in the forest looking at us. Because of the fire we couldn't really see or tell what it was. We used our headlamps to light up the area, but we saw nothing. A few moments later, we all felt something come closer to us at the edge of the tree line. It was a playful and curious energy. I put out the fire a bit so we could see in the dark, this time none of us using our headlamps. We sat and felt the energy; it felt like something was bouncy and playful. The three of us decided to walk to the tree line only about fifty feet away. We waited. Something telepathically told us to come into the tree line, so we did. Slowly, a creature mostly spiritual but somewhat physical was around us. As it got closer I said, "It's ok. We come in peace. We want to meet you."

Then, this thing started running all around us! It would jump off of us, come over our shoulder, like an animal with the zoomies! And we could almost hear it giggling. It was like two worlds had met in the middle again, where we and this being could merge and communicate. We all felt like it was a fairy, and it confirmed. Then, more fairy energy started to energetically appear in the forest. Like they were there to view us humans just as much as we were curious to see them. They told us to play more; to play in the forest like children. They told me they liked to hear my flute. I had played it outside on random nights when I felt called to play. And they said they heard me and wanted me to play more. They loved music and loved to dance and wanted us to do the same.

This was an experience I never had before. I was not a person that believed in fairies, dragons, or gnomes. But after being in the woods and working on my heart and my spirit, other worlds were revealing themselves. It put my friends and me in alignment to beings of the Earth and sky. All of them told us they only visit and speak to humans that are in their heart and care about the Earth. I had experienced many special moments in the forest alone. But when you have experiences like this in real life with other people, the truth can no longer be denied. Magic of the forest, of the world, and of the universe exists. And it has been spoken about in scripture for thousands of years. But the magic will only be revealed to those who seek and match their vibration to things greater than themselves.

The magic continued. A week later, while I was checking out an area of the forest I hadn't spent much time in, I felt something magical shift around me. I saw a huge boulder covered with moss that was large enough for me to lay my whole body down on. It was surrounded by three large hemlock trees. It felt like the whole area was filled with other small magical beings. I continued to roam and asked what was in the area. It felt like fairies or gnomes.

I heard something say, "Follow your heart."

I kept roaming, and I started to get excited, like I was a kid again on an adventure.

"Where should I go?" I asked.

The voice responded, "Follow your heart."

I kept roaming until I ended up near the river. Within seconds, I looked down to see a large red stone in a perfect heart shape. It was the size of a bowling ball, and I took the heart stone back to the mossy area. I placed the heart stone on the moss, and I could hear the voice laugh.

"See, just follow your heart," it said.

I began laughing as well. "What's your name?" I asked.

"Uka," he replied.

I replied, "Whoa, cool name, dude!"

I asked what he was. He was a fairy. And as soon as he said it I could feel a bunch of eyes looking at me. The area was full of little magical creatures, and they were all curious! It was as if these beings always had an initial representative. Once that representative feels it's safe, the others are allowed to join or make their presence known. Uka told me he was there to help me learn about the forest. He explained that the fairies are keepers of the forest; it is their home. He continued to share that the forest is alive; the minerals, rocks, clay, all of it.

"The deeper you go in the forest, the more magic you will find," Uka said. **"The deeper you go within yourself, the more magic you will find."**

I agreed. I would rather my feet be bare upon the Earth and with the magic. This was our birthright. I was learning from them. The mythology of fairies was real. This experience was an introduction, but it was one of many. These special beings would not show themselves to people with a closed heart. In fact, they want to stay hidden. No one can ever prove to another person that they are real. But those who have had this type of magical interaction or any type of magical interaction don't need to prove it. They're changed.

Freedom Codes

By the fall, I was still sleeping in my large tent on the land. The house was pretty much finished, but it felt strange to be inside four walls insulated from the outside world. I couldn't feel or hear what was happening around me. So if it wasn't too cold, I often continued to sleep outside. One morning, a light rain was passing. The sun was still coming through the clouds and the mixture of the rain, clouds, and sun made the morning feel magical. I began to see color in the raindrops and I could feel codes inside of them. They were Freedom Codes, and they were coming back to the planet. They are original codes that were from higher dimensions that allow freedom in thought and existence. I decided to lay in my tent longer to feel this "coded" rain. I felt and heard Mother Arc codes. They were geometric light and color codes that were phasing into this realm as well.

In higher forms of existence we are many things; we embody many forms. We exist as hybrids of different species, races, genders, and the like in different realms. I was getting the message that higher realms operated freedom codes which represented full acceptance of oneness. When we operate these codes or new programs, just by running these ideas in our minds and in our way of being, we will begin to embody them. Embodiment of acceptance of love, selflessness, and oneness then allows us to program New Earth.

Survival codes are embedded in our way of being on Earth because of natural law. Yes, we must know how to survive. I realized, however, the natural survival codes were hacked and induced with fear from war to keep humans on this planet in a state of perpetual survival. This did not feel natural. Even when humanity was living in more tribal conditions, there wasn't always an impending "fear of lack" mentality. Yes, the bear eats the fish, the lion eats the gazelle, and sometimes there are fights over territory among both animals and humans. But this natural equilibrium follows natural law. Humanity must remember, return to, and honor natural law. Once a person learns and follows natural law, they can begin to learn and understand about universal law. In order to know thyself, a person must know deeply that the Earth is also thyself.

The freedom codes—thoughts, ideas and ways of being that were coming in—follow both natural and universal law. They are light codes that are becoming available again to be integrated into our new operating systems, our bodies and minds. We must first do the inner healing work in order to even know they exist. Only after a deep state of awareness can we receive them. All that is needed for Freedom Codes to exist on this planet, or for more of them to come fully online, is for enough people to create and help the program run.

I realized not everyone wants peace. I think deep down most people do want peace but they don't operate peace within themselves. This was another reason timeline splits were happening—timelines for those who wanted freedom or a certain way of living and other timelines for people who wanted something else. It's all under free will. The main reason collective freedom takes longer is that all beings have free will. Which means there will be interference and non-agreement on a vibrational and belief level.

I believe we can have full freedom before we leave this planet. Eternal life is an operating system, or freedom from an operating system that no longer serves us or the planet. A person must learn how to hold their inner light in those spaces. It was time to rid ourselves of perversions, remove judgment and maintain complete surrender. I kept hearing, "Prepare your arc." I remembered the phrase from the Bible; "There will be a new heaven and new Earth. The old one will be passed away." And that phrase felt like what was happening on the Earth.

I Wasn't Supposed to Be Here

By fall that year, my friends had left, and the home was built with a few interior details unfinished. One night, while falling asleep in my home I found myself consciously on another spaceship. At first, I was confused. But I was able to see much quicker this time and realized where I was. This time, I could *feel* the ship. I was sitting against the wall made of metal and I could knock on the floor and the wall. There were beings there who immediately noticed me and were startled and a bit confused. They were small, greenish looking beings no taller than three feet. They looked somewhat similar to the Minions in the *Despicable Me* movie. I didn't feel a threat, so I just opened up my heart and started relaxing, still unsure of why I was there. A couple of them wanted to touch me so I put out my hand. One eventually did touch me, and I could etherically feel the touch as well. I just smiled. Their language sounded like gibberish to me, but I was trying to understand.

Eventually, one of them came back with their commander, towing him by the hand. He was a little taller, maybe five feet. Telepathically, he asked what I was doing there. I said I didn't know.

He didn't understand how I got there. We were all a bit confused. I told him I was recently on another ship, and I asked him what his name was. It was something like Saktree. I asked him what they were doing near where I lived. He explained that they were fixing nano particles in the atmosphere. I began to see what they did for work. It looked like they were tuning particles and bringing them back to their correct vibrational state.

He said there were other ships across the globe doing the same thing. And they were assigned to my area/zone. It's just what they did. I thought it was pretty cool, and I thanked them for helping our planet. None of us could figure out why I was initially on the ship. But the commander realized the meeting was of mutual benefit; a human seeing and believing other beings existed, and other beings from another planet meeting the species they were there to help. It was good for all of us. In the end, there was nothing that needed to happen. And I dropped back down into my body as they continued their work in the sky. It was pretty sweet.

The year was a culmination of learning—building a cabin, listening to myself and the land, meeting other galactic councils, and understanding the larger picture of where we were as a human species. The few close friends who were also diligently working on themselves were all receiving the gifts from the Ancients; ancient Earth beings and ancient cosmic beings. It was clear that every time we speak, sing, or do anything from our pure heart, it is Source working through us to show us that the way back home is through our hearts.

There was a lot happening on the planet. But a lot of people were still asleep. The dark storm that was over the world was created by the dark side of the spiritual war. It was the reason the Light was not able to fully break through to help people awaken. But there were cosmic guardians all over the planet to assist. And I knew what was going on. I sat with it deeper.

Mothership

One day in a meditation, I saw three blue beings and one white-, blue-, and green-skinned being with a scruffy mustache and beard. They told me they were on a mothership, Mothership Quazar. I asked if they were from the Galactic Federation.

They replied, "No. We are from the Thirteen Rays. The Ashtar Command." They continued, "All are here to help. Humanity will no longer go through the worst-case scenarios. But it will experience some trials and tribulations. It will be bumpy."

They asked if I would speak for them. I said yes at the time. They said the messages would be coming to me in thirteen days. "You will be speaking for all of us. You will get the codes in order as they come in. This ship (meaning the beings) doesn't run away. We protect to keep away dark forces. There are many other ships here around Earth now. We're raising humanity now. All must go at different times. This is a lot of energy coming in, we know. There will be codes to see, codes to heal, codes to forgive, codes to open your heart, and other codes at certain times. We mean no harm. But this is a commitment, then home. Light language will be spoken clearly and interpreted. It will be felt. It will be clear and resonate. Jesus was taught, remember? To infinity and beyond. Thirteen days. Rest up. You may have some long nights. We're broadcasting you into the ship, so you don't need to be here physically, remember? This is just the meeting room. We are multi-locational, remember?"

The first interaction was interesting. But they felt like light beings. It was weird being on another ship spiritually. It feels like you're completely there—you can jump and feel the floor, you can touch the walls, or walk through them. This ship, however, was the largest I had been on. It felt like a mini city! Even though I wasn't allowed to walk beyond the large conference center we were in, I could see other large rooms and entrances to other sectors. It felt like a lot was happening on the ship and other people and beings were going about their daily work.

I was escorted off the ship and didn't look too far into it for a few weeks. I had work to do around the land. But thirteen days later, the messages came back.

"Hello, this is from your Guided Galactic Council… Your vestige of your pursuits no longer suits you, personally. Where you spend your last days is up to you. We know this may sound difficult, but remember you chose. Remember? Working from the other side. There are others working from the planet and from within the quantum fields. You are part of an academy. You've known this for three years. We have messages for the world, all the same, which is why you were on the mothership. All messages have always been the same, love thy neighbor, be kind, help the Earth, love, be peace and joy, and share it with those suffering. Humanity is not a lost cause, show the good."

I saw Jesus on the ship and asked, "Is Jesus truly a part of this mothership?"

"Jesus was taught, remember?" they replied. "We are the Essenes, the Elohim, the Seraphim. All are One. It is only your planet that looks for, and to, separation. Don't fight us on our words. (I was trying to write things down on paper). Order is very important."

"The 'Big One' was avoided. It was going to be as big as the fall of Atlantis and Lemuria with souls getting fractured and lost. Again, not just human souls, but all souls. All entities and the Earth herself were at risk. Most likely it was going to happen through nuclear war. Also at star-gates. Potentials of time/space rifts, yes CERN. However, these have been avoided. Enough of you wanted change and were on the ground to help."

They wanted me to tell others about their ship. I asked, "Why?"

They replied, "Because they need to know. We are not coming to get you. Most of us don't need ships. We are at many places at once. These ships are still very useful, but we don't need to be on them to operate them. When we meet with other ascended masters, we don't need screens. We know who is who in our minds just by their energetic signature."

I looked back into the middle of the ship that was open. More people and beings were still moving around working.

"We have bays for smaller ships. Again, mostly to make our presence known to other forces, negative or not. We don't view things so polar. We uphold the Law of One and the abundance of free will that was deemed upon this planet. We uphold universal law. Enough people woke up to avoid the collision and catastrophe. However, we cannot help you avoid your incoming environmental cataclysm. We are allowed to join forces to keep humanity from being stomped out from what they can't see (like keeping a first grader from being beaten up by a sixth grader). However, humanity is still responsible for its karmic debt to the Earth. There is barely enough time."

They wanted to make another message clear. I would relay the message. But I knew people would not be ready to hear the next part.

"Christmas time. Your gluttony will defeat you. Where is your awareness? You have little, most of you have none. We advise you to become aware of the waste you will create in one holiday, for momentary joy. That is not where joy comes from. This will be your final warning. Enough time before the end of the year to think about these things and complete your vision, your destiny on your own mothership (Earth). You all have so much to learn, and you are out of time. Barely enough time to save a future for your children because that is what you know. But don't forget, your awareness does not let you see that this is about all beings on Earth, whether you see them or not. There are no more ways to say it. There is no need for more channels to speak about it. With love, it is your responsibility now. Don't wait. Death comes to those who wait. Final will be the call by this time 2030. It is completely, one hundred percent possible to fix and heal this and turn it around."

– The Galactic Council of the Ashtar Command

The messages for me were very clear. But I felt nervous to relay the messages. Eventually, I decided to share. I put a video of me recording this message online. Instantly, the responses to the video were split; some thought I'd lost my mind, while others resonated with the message. For those who had not seen my journey it did not make sense to them. They only heard the alien ship, and the rest of the message completely passed over them. The message of humanity's evolution, the dangers and changes needed to be made, stopped at some point in their brain. It showed me a lot. A lot of friends even stopped talking to me after and I felt isolated. I was sharing a powerful message from my heart and people turned their backs, afraid to be associated. And it took me a few months to let it go. I didn't know if I was going to continue to work with this council. I felt like I needed more time and confirmation. But I knew I had to keep following my heart.

Spectrum

With this understanding, the Ashtar Command came in a few days later. I wasn't sure if I wanted to work with them, but I was willing to have conversations.

Ashtar Command: "What you couldn't see you can now see, spectrum in all things. There is more on the light spectrum you cannot see. What you're seeing play out on the planet is an agreement between the government and your allies. There is more disclosure coming in, on all things. It is best to teach the techniques on grounding and aftercare and how to love oneself. This information will have a sponge effect where the sponge gets full and must let the information settle. After all has been squeezed out, then there will be the aftermath and the Coming.

Those that want to fight and those who have surrendered to the All That Is. They will be protected.

Commanders are standing by. This is a lot of energy. It's best to go in (meditate). It's painful to see the light at first; it hurts your eyes. It takes a while to adjust once you come out of the house (of fear) into the Light. It takes a child a while to adjust once it is birthed. You are all children. Children fight; some grow. Repeat, only *some* grow. What is expected of you now is to behold your light. See and hold your light, cover yourself. Yes, this is your Christ Light. It showers over like a blanket. Go and get quiet. Storm coming soon. Behold your light. After is Light. Lighthouses shine."

"Why now?" I asked.

They replied, "Time is of the essence. Jesus knew when his time was coming, but he did not run away. He knew it was his destiny. The Lineage/Ancients—some stayed and hid/lived invisible in plain sight. Some fled. Some fought. They too knew change was coming. But they also knew there was Light on the other side. They lived in different/higher worlds within this physical world, which is why they weren't seen. They moved like the moose and the bear, invisible.

We are helping from the other side. Pull back. Get quiet. Be still. The storm will pass."

Choice

They continued. "Because time is of the essence, this is a window of opportunity. The Stellar Activation Cycle when planets are aligned. This is university, and you have four years to graduate. The angels and ETs are here to help. They work for Christ, some of them. This is it. The Christ Light is coming in. You have to go in and limit distractions. You get this opportunity to heal, forgive, to ask for forgiveness, to grow, to laugh. This is not about looking for Jesus in a body to save you. But yes, you can call upon the name of Jesus Christ and it will be done. This is about integrating what Jesus, Buddha, and Muhammed taught—love, humility, grace, truth, and a pure heart. They are the keys. This is an opportunity to purify your heart. Non-judgment on yourself and others. But God is not playing. This is not just about humans. It's about Mother Earth, her beings, and all galactic beings."

I agreed. We should be so grateful to know there are higher dimensional, higher frequency beings that want to help us. I wonder if they look at humans as though they are crazy.

They continued. "**If this was the end of your life, if this was your life review, would you be happy with how you lived your life? Were you kind to others? Did you do your best?**"

These questions struck me deeply. It was a critical time in my life to ask myself these questions. I knew I was grateful for my life and how I'd lived it. I know there are more ways I want to help in raising the vibration, humans, the Earth, children, and all beings. Where I have peace is in my being. It has also taken me decades to realize that wanting to help doesn't always mean action. Action and doing are absolutely necessary. But stillness and being release a positive vibration that is just as effective in the world.

"Why did you stop talking?" they asked.

I told them I got scared of what people thought and I wasn't always trusting the experiences and the information I was receiving. Ultimately, I knew I came to this planet to speak for the Earth and for the Creator. I felt I should have kept speaking publicly, but I allowed other people's opinions of me or distractions to get the best of me.

They continued, **"Three stones cast for every seed sown."**

Meaning, for every seed of truth or every act of love or light a person tries to sow, the public will cast three stones. These are the ones that don't understand. Some are even unconscious, opposing forces. It's been happening since the beginning of mankind. They told me I was getting ready to walk into a guided galactic council, but I must clear myself first.

"There will be a reset in order to clear. It will pass. Must clear, in order to receive. Getting ready for the next level jump. Time is of the essence now. Go slow," they said.

The next few days I needed to chill from all the information. I watched movies. I thought a lot about the mothership. I thought about the galactic beings, their mission, their willingness to help humanity, protect the planet, and keep the balance. And within a few days, more info came flowing in.

"The next sequence of events will lead you to where you want to go," they said. They showed me a pearl. They were telepathically telling me that a pearl in this case meant a pillar of light. Then, in vision, I became a pearl. I flew up to the galactic sun with other pearls. There were others, but everyone was a pearl. We all floated in crystal white light.

"You can sprout now," they continued.

I slowly descended back down to Earth through the sun.

Then, they continued, "The crucifixion was known. *He* knew it was coming and walked *towards* it. *He* is the Eternal Flame. It was his departure from the societal world. He gave himself up to God without judging his crucifiers (society), for they did not understand. Maybe he did or did not know that he would be resurrected. But he gave his everything—his heart, his body and his mind to God in complete faith. He made a choice. And his resurrection was only seen by some but heard by all."

"That is you," they said. "You walk to your crux (choice point) in order to release your old self. To give yourself completely to God and you know it. These are phases, sequences. Knowing that everything is God, there is no fear. Being led by God, those with an open heart will find you. Speak, be, and live from that higher place. Embodiment. Time is of the essence. Where you are right now is an accumulation of your past thoughts. You're in school. As long as your purpose is on hold, everything is on hold. Form follows function. Must have the *need* first."

They continued, "There's a misalignment in spirit; must rebuild trust, which is why going at a pace. (You're) Too focused on the physical right now. You already know. You have time. Will be a healing business. Will be working through ports, not chakras. The room to work magic. Energy can neither be created nor destroyed."

I continued to feel something beautiful growing. I was feeling Trinity wave frequencies. I would see colors come in threes and I would hear sounds in harmony. In the forest, in the mornings or early evenings, it was as if the birds, the crickets, the frogs, and everything had a harmony. In society there was chaos. But in nature, the baseline was still the same. It felt like I was in my own world, in my own piece of heaven.

Shift

I returned to Mt Shasta for the fourth time. Except this time, none of my crew was with me. Schedules conflicted, so I decided to go alone. I drove the ten hours from LA to the mountain mostly in silence. And when I arrived it was just as beautiful as all the other times I had been there. I was able to get my favorite campsite to myself and as soon as I set up, I left to hike a trail I never had taken before. I hiked around and realized I was able to view the mountain from a different angle. I had come full circle. It was a sign of completion. This became the theme for the trip.

The next day, I had a ceremony for Earth Mother. I found an open spot on a different mountain, and I could tell the ceremony had been performed there a few times. There was a small rock circle, and I decided to set up my ceremony kit on the south side. I lit some sage and walked clockwise around the stone circle. I left some natural herbs and stones in each of the four directions. As I made it back to the south direction I sat down and closed my eyes. I listened to the wind come through the pine trees. I smelled the air and felt the sun on my right side. I stayed there in silence for a while. And then I played my flute for the Earth. I only played one song because it felt like that was all that was needed. After the song I sat in silence again. I just wanted to listen with no thoughts. A few moments later my council came in.

"What do you fear? Caring about what other people think? Fear of letting go in ceremony?" they asked.

But I knew it was only my thoughts that were in the way. They continued. "Codes in the throat. Drum for the Earth and Ancient Spirits. Flute for spirit and sky. Rattle for journey and guides."

Then I felt a grandfather spirit come in. He sent me a very important message. I could see the word "Shift" in front of my vision. The grandfather spirit used more visuals than actual words. The visuals translated to "The Great Conjunction—Great Spirit" coming through. "It will wipe out communication, but it won't last. The silence will be deafening. Become the silence. Most will lose hope out of fear. Some will be trying to flee cities for lack of food/water. There will be great movement. Family will be guided."

Another spirit from the lineage came to the circle as well. He added, "Those that come, protect them, feed them, keep them warm. That's what scouts do. Prepare more food/blankets. Those who will listen, prepare now."

My other guide joined the circle too. It was a collective meeting of all my guides. "Guided. Faith over fear, distractions, self-doubt. Know. Faith. Prepare. We wouldn't tell those unless they were going to do something about it. The ones in Shasta (the spirits) are preparing, too. The SHIFT. The silence."

She asked, "What do you wish to leave behind (on the Earth)?"

"Truth, Love, and Light. I will leave behind love and light in people's hearts, a reminder of what unconditional love feels like. I will leave behind the eternal truth that we are all God's children. They will know, we are all things. That love and magic are real. Magic is real. And the only way home is through the sacred heart," I replied.

I got a little light-headed. I had to take a break from the download.

"That is based on your light quotient," she said. "The ability to hold more light will allow you to stay 'in' longer and work from that space and help others. Yes."

She repeated a previous message, that I wouldn't be at the home I was living at for much longer. She continued, "Going to other places/spaces where others cannot go. You will be guided; get a good car."

"Get a good car?" I asked.

"Yes. Get a new car. You will be driving a lot," she replied. "Trust and awareness is all that is needed. Speak soon. More light quotient will be coming. It will be intense. There will be a lot of clearing, the most in a long time. Light quotient will be available for those who are willing to step through. They are the light at the center, beginning, and end of the tunnel. This is why you want to eat light. Eat the light/sun (meaning get more sun). You will need to drink a lot more water. This light quotient has not been available for some time. It was destiny. We have prevailed. But the work is not done yet. Some storms must be worked through."

Whatever shift was about to happen, it was going to be major. I would have to be flexible and centered in myself. The world was already in a major shift, and clearly it wasn't the only one. I looked around at all of my guides. They weren't done speaking yet.

"Beware of others' karmic debt. It weighs on them and you. Each person gets to decide now, including you. Focus on clearing first as you are doing. Opportunities for love. All kinds of love with the right vibrational people/person. This is true. This light quotient will be available to others at other times, but this is a window. It gets harder if not cleared. This is your time to finish clearing as you already are. Do not give up on yourself. Finish! As the future looks bright!"

I sat with the messages for a while as my guides slowly left my vision. It was a lesson that some ceremonies can be short and it's sometimes all that is needed. I left the area, walked back to my tent, and spent the rest of the afternoon lying down and listening to the animals and trees in silence. I was at peace.

By the end of the year 2021, the message continued, in big capital letters: SHIFT.

The world was two years into the pandemic. Countries, families, and friends continued to be divided by their beliefs. Emotions were intense as everyone was scared, lonely, angry, confused, or all of the above. I learned to keep my feelings and beliefs to myself. It was unnecessary to get involved, it was too chaotic. But I could see the shift was "The Split," the bifurcation of timelines. But this window of time where humanity currently was couldn't hold different or opposing timelines for much longer. It's like trains in a train station, waiting for passengers to board to their future destinations. But eventually, they have to leave the station.

My guides explained, "Where a person is at heart frequency, is where they will BE in consciousness and reality. If the mind is fractured, the network of thoughts are split, the full self can't find a direct pathway home to center. It can't decide which consciousness train to get on. And it was clear more people would become mentally and consciously fractured in the future. But there was hope. This is a new and returned architecture, a whole new geometric structure. Some will be caught in a labyrinth. Others will find direct pathways with different frequencies based on their consciousness. Like stations all on the same radio, just at different frequencies. There are highly encoded beings. New architecture over cities, places, and in beings. Structure. BE, then it comes. Oneness and unity with ancestors. *Empower* the New Earth/Gaia and what it represents. Empower those thoughts no matter what is going on around you. BE there, then it comes. The *wave* will be taking others to a false matrix. It's through their eyes," they said.

People were consciously or unconsciously going to continue to let the veils be pulled over their eyes and minds. There was nothing anyone could do about others' choices. There will be cities where people are infected. Cities are where infection lives the most. There will be other people and beings who will walk around just to infect. "Not about forgiving but shaking free from the virus. It's not repairable, but she (Earth) is already lifted," they said.

"How can I help?" I asked.

"Tell them to go home; come home to Earth. There are enough that already lift her frequency. The children will all be together soon in the physical. There is light at the end of the tunnel. It doesn't matter where you are. It's not about running and hiding. There will be us who affect those around us in a positive light. New architecture to reinforce. Going home, through the heart space. This is what you're here to do. Collective SHIFT codes. Slow down. Clear the body, mind, and spirit. Heal, accept, forgive, love. New patterns. BE. Hold light (accretion)," they said.

"We are the SHIFT. We are the Bridge. We are the Grid. Empower and envision what is needed through the song. Don't get distracted with what comes; stay on mission."

At this point, I saw a vision of large hands motioning. They were moving in a swiping motion like someone was swiping something clean off its hands. Then, I could feel exactly what it meant. God is going to show its hand and wipe the slate clean. It's the same process as before/after death. I was having a vision of floating like a baby in surrender. It felt deep and yet peaceful. The Majesty, the universe will show you who and what is King so that you're not/we're not attached to this physical reality. Yes, it is real. The preparation helps us crawl then walk. We're getting ready to open an entirely new existence.

"There is a spiritual war happening in the shadows. There are Mother Arc codes, Transitional Hubs, and Gateways," my guides said in finality.

I've fought for the Light for a very long time throughout lifetimes. Spiritually, I could see and feel there were other warriors coming in now to help a new Army of Light. I told myself, it's ok to retire, every warrior has their time. I felt like I was being escorted from the battlefield, and I thought to myself, "Where do all the good soldiers go? Where do they rest? Where is their home?" I could immediately hear my higher self.

"All warriors get ready for war," it said. "The war of the future will be a spiritual one, not a physical one. It's time to make a choice. Have to make a choice."

I had to look at what I was choosing to leap towards. I found myself stuck between two worlds which felt like a purgatory. I wondered about the future.

My higher self replied, "Money won't matter then. If you don't prepare, listen to the warning, you will pay. You will survive, but lucky. Must have courage. With this spiritual war, it is why St. Michael has appeared, to lead God's army against evil. It's a spiritual war because it takes place in higher dimensions. One side/group wants humans as slaves, to feed off energy, fear, and

Earth's natural resources. The other side/groups want us to be love, free, and to evolve. It's the macro to the micro. Be humble. Get rid of ego, it's not about you. Veils are lifting; everyone will see what rulers have done. People will be up in arms. Depending on where you are is what you will see, manifest, experience. Have to take a leap. Listen, follow vision. Scared, but don't let fear bind you. Be the voice, be the bridge. Out of time."

The warning made me feel anxious. Would I change if there wasn't any danger? I didn't know if I would change if I knew things were going to be ok. I kept feeling like there's not enough time to get things done. I had to refocus my thoughts.

My higher self continued, "Don't spread yourself thin in thought. Can take people to different places in the woods for ceremonies. Show them the safe places. Receivers and keepers of Information. Can be anywhere in spirit."

Soul Braiding

By this time, I'd made a very important connection when it came to my guides. After years of questioning, I knew my guides were all different aspects of me in different timelines, coexisting at the same time. Something began to happen in the spiritual realms where all versions of myself began to spin and twist. A soul braid began to take place. And I knew and felt deep within that all parts of myself were merging. It felt like a relief, like something that was meant to happen that I wasn't even aware of.

XII
WORKING SPIRITUAL TOOLS

We can only gather so much in one lifetime. But a mentor once told me as he had learned from his predecessor, that there is a universal collective consciousness.

It is, "The-Spirit-That-Moves-Through-All-Things."

This consciousness field is an energy field that can be tapped into by any person with the right dedication simply by asking, "What is the collective feeling?"

What if we used our conscious awareness to tap into the collective to download information quicker or use our energy and the energy of the ley lines to positively affect the rest of the world? The truth is, we can. Most are just unaware of these possibilities.

Working with Patients

In early 2022, I decided to take another healing course with a new teacher to expand my training. The course specifically worked on etheric or quantum healing that can be done physically or remotely. I never thought remote healing could be as powerful as it is, but it works. In the class we would work on each other and eventually have the option to work on others. We learned specific healing codes and pre-programming codes to help facilitate release and healing in the physical and spiritual body. I loved every part of it, and most of the exercises made complete sense to me. The biggest lessons were staying out of your own way as a facilitator as you received messages about a client. We learned about empowering the codes to make them more powerful, which is something I had learned before. And lastly, it was about trusting your own intuition - especially if you were working from your heart in trying to help someone.

After a week-long intensive, we were allowed to work with other clients, but we had to work on the first 20 clients for free. We would then send in our results to the healing school's trainers to make sure the work was correct, which made me feel really good because I could have my work confirmed or get advice. It also felt good that the school was being accountable with follow-up for their future facilitators and not just allowing people to fend for themselves. I respected that. I took a few more weeks to tie this new information into what I had already learned over the past decade. And when I felt ready, I quickly started to get a visual *ping* of who I knew that might need help. It's like the names filed in.

The first person I worked with was a very close friend of mine who was like a younger brother to me. He actually came to me in a dream and looked to me for help. The dream was strange. I saw him wrapped up and bound in a sexual encounter and he wasn't enjoying it. It was like he was bound by this person somehow, not just in the act, but also by an energetic cord attached between them. Whoever he was attached to had a very dark energy within him.

I called my friend the next day and just started talking to him. A few minutes in, I asked if I could share the dream I had about him. He said, "Sure."

I went into further detail telling him I could see a darkness behind the man that he was in sexual relations with. It felt like there were others involved, other men who were also bound to this man. I asked my friend if he was involved in something. And he began crying over the phone. The dream was spot on, and we both knew it. I felt bad because he was like a little brother to me, and it was a vulnerable conversation to have. I told him about the class and the work I was doing. He laughed and said, "Of course you are, Seth. I just didn't think my situation would come through." I told him I felt his spirit ask for help in the dream. And he told me deep down he needed the help. I asked him if I could look into it deeper, and he agreed.

We had a session and I used my vision and began to see the scene unfold before me. I spoke to him as I saw it. I told him it felt like there were drugs involved and that this is how this man kept others tied to him. The drugs were a gateway for crazy sex parties. My friend told me that there were a couple other men that were the ring leaders, and the men bound to them didn't know how to get out. They were all hooked. I asked if I could do some work on him, and he agreed. The minute I began to look deeper I knew his health and his life were at risk.

The first thing I decided was necessary was a breaking of "contracts." It was a recited phrase the client repeats to break all contracts, physical and spiritual, from any attachments. It was a way for the conscious mind and the higher self to make a free will declaration to break free of "unseen" or "unknown" agreements that may have been made unconsciously. My friend told me it was going to be hard to really break away as these people were also involved in the entertainment industry, which was already a small circle. I told him that breaking the contracts and no further engagement would allow the relationships to eventually disappear. He had to lay low for a while. He was so nervous. I could hear the fear in his voice, unsure if he would be able to break away from this community, the drugs, the sex, the parties. I was nervous for him because I could see how deep and dark the main people were and how strong their attachments to other people were. It seemed like the world he was in was dark, endless, and easy to fall back into. I prayed for and shielded him and took extra measures to make sure nothing was attached because I didn't want to think of the worst-case scenario. Luckily, he had a strong will. And eventually, after a few weeks he got out of the loop.

After many years of tapping into energy and especially after working with different clients I started to get clearer on how thoughts, experiences, trauma, or past life karma can create or bring in dark energy.

Demons

Demons are lower vibrational energies or entities that can seed and grow from traumas, experiences, and even repeated negative thought forms. They can even be passed down through a family bloodline. Some demons are lost or trapped souls. Others can be collective beliefs that grow into a larger entity. Some demons are so old they can be summoned and revitalized over thousands of years, just like angels. Both angels and demons operate on different frequencies on the light spectrum, and some can exist beyond time. Most demons have what I like to call, "flavors." These flavors can be anger, resentment, drinking alcohol, addictions, porn, trauma, distraction, confusion, isolation, self-doubt, etc. Depending on what the issue is, it can create an opening in a person's body and/or auric field for a demon to grow in or slip into. This is where scanning your critical edge and aura comes into play. Demons can also come through sexual partners. A person may be completely unaware that their kinks and habits are actually a demonic energy feeding through them. It's gross and I've seen it. But it's more common than you think, especially with porn imprinting and programming.

Demons also like to fester in certain areas that have never been energetically cleared like bars, clubs, certain households, and places of dark worship. These places become portals for these energies. They also like to harvest energy at concerts. If the music is a lower vibration, the musicians or artist can knowingly or unknowingly open up a portal for demonic entities to siphon the energy of the concert goers. This has been seen and felt by some concert goers more recently and it's very real. This is why shielding as a spiritual and energetic practice is important.

Demons also love violence. Portals can open in locations of war. They feed off the death and bloodshed. Wars that go on for extended periods of time can actually be blood sacrifice and create inversions in that specific geographic location. That inversion goes into the Earth grid which sends out a program of death and fear which continues to feed the false matrix overlay. What is different now is that these programs can and are slowly being stopped energetically by spiritual individuals and angelic forces.

How does a person defeat a demon? **The three main ways are to fight, surrender/starve, or heal.** You can fight a demon spiritually, but you must always remember rule number one: **Never get cocky in a spiritual battle.** There are tools which I will share a little later. A person can also get help from shamans and priests, many of whom have dedicated their lives to helping others, including exorcism. It has been happening in this realm since humanity has existed, and each culture has its own process.

Another way to defeat a demon is to surrender to it for the time being, or to starve it over time. A person may not have all the information about where it came from or how to defeat it, but they can ignore it, the same way they can ignore a misbehaving pet or a child having a temper tantrum. If the person knows the demon's flavor, they can starve it from what it needs to survive. Sometimes, if the thought forms or trauma are healed over time, the demon has less energy and strength and eventually can be dissolved or healed.

Another way to defeat a demon is to face it head on and begin to heal and clear it with unconditional love - no matter how long it takes. Sometimes demons are ideas and thought forms that take control of the person. Demons can't stand to be around love or light. It's they're worst enemy. Overall, I look at demons as beings or energies that lost their connection to Source. Over time, the entity has a chance to evolve its energy into the light spectrum until it, too, is healed. But remember, **Yeshua was so powerful in his light body and faith in God, that demons would bow at his feet. If we believe in the sacred and esoteric teachings and we have God in our hearts, we know we can do what Yeshua and his disciples did.**

Demon of Distraction

I remembered my first mentor speaking about the demon of distraction. Distractions can simply be distractions. But if they get out of control, thoughts and distractions can be spiritual infiltration or escapism. There will be things—thought forms, beliefs, even other people or entities—that will distract you from your path. They become demonic if they pull you from your day-to-day wellbeing. Distraction and self-doubt are two of the biggest demons a person will face on their journey to living their vision. And with technology added to our daily lives, the demons of distraction and self-doubt lead the way with leashes on people's minds.

As I view this world as a free-will experience, I can see there is technology that has been created that advertently and inadvertently creates distractions, which over time can create energetic openings in people and eventually the collective. Unfortunately, other malevolent energies can enter through these openings, meaning the technology can become connected as gateways to a darker or inorganic side of things. In different visions I have seen that there are unseen energetic threads or tentacles that can come through the phone and computers, some of which are connected to AI and darker entities. I have seen how technology and the artificial intelligence behind it can actually change the genetics and spiritual geometry in a human being who is overusing it. If a person remains too distracted for extended periods of time, they can become detached from themselves and lack compassion or many qualities that are natural to being human. It's harder for them to stay connected to Source, and they end up needing or thinking they need the system to survive. They will actually say they can't live without it.

Technological distractions can pull and even trap the consciousness into a false matrix. The human attention span is becoming shorter and shorter- some say as fleeting as three seconds. Traveling thought to thought without being able to settle on one feeling or emotion, the whole collective is experiencing attention deficit disorder and people are becoming more confused, depressed, and lost. Even science has proved that social media is making it worse. The eyes are the window to the soul, and the thieves have come in through the open windows to methodically suck people of their energy, leaving them feeling empty and depleted, and slowly robbing them of their souls. Yuck.

The demons of distraction and self-doubt are real, and awareness about what distracts us could allow us to excavate them from our daily lives. That was my lesson, to eradicate the distractions and self-doubt again. The medicine was about bringing people from their erratic minds home to their hearts.

Angels

Angels have a very light and loving frequency. More than likely, they will not look like the angels you've seen from scripture. However, if you do see an angel that looks to you like Saint Gabriel or Saint Michael, it could be them. Your mind is only associating with memory in order to make the connection so you know who you're communicating with. Most times, angels may look like wisps of light, or they may look like light clouds. They can vary in color too.

I ask my angels to clearly communicate to me. I pray for them to show me my path, show me where I am needed, and to show me my power and my medicine. I ask for peace, clarity, and love within.

They shared something very important with me: "Angels of Light cannot be touched. Service to All is higher vibrationally and allows one to exit the matrix. The vampires are vibrating with frustration because their plan is failing. Nothing is working. We are the creators, architects outside of the matrix," they said.

A person must use their discernment when first trying to communicate with their angels, or when certain energies start coming around. Many false beings of light try to cloak themselves and trick a person into being guided in the wrong direction. This is why it's important to discern energies. Your true angels have a certain peaceful feeling to them. If you're in your heart space they come in signs, synchronicities, or light forms at first. They will come gently over time so as not to scare you. They may not fully enter your field, based on your fear. Angels are here to guide you and want the highest good for all beings. It's very simple. If you ask for help from God and from your angels, help will come. It may not always be at the time you want. But if you do your best to keep your heart open and your actions true, they will appear.

Getting Grounded

As I continued to work with more clients, it fascinated me that most of them had not been outside in nature for long periods of time. They were going through things emotionally or spiritually, and when I suggested going outside to take a walk or sitting next to a tree, most of their initial anxiety began to clear or at least got them out of their head. They would always immediately say they felt better, even if it was cold. And I would say, "Yeah, Earth is the jam!" We get our energy from the Earth, and we start to get discombobulated when we lose that connection. Connecting and grounding with the Earth is important physically, emotionally, and spiritually.

Another thing I like to tell clients is to stay ten toes down. In your spiritual pursuit, you will find that by going "in" you will also travel "out." Traveling in any sense of the word is awesome. You may find yourself traveling to different dimensions, timelines, etc. However, I've learned this pursuit can leave one very lofty or spacey. **Having spiritual experiences or doing spiritual work is exciting, but we have to stay grounded here on Earth. This is where we are needed and where we are meant to live life.** Being in the astrals too long could also lead to escapism. Earth is always home, and she has many lessons that keep things in perspective. When I start to get a little lofty, I usually hike, go camping, or work some primitive skills. These things will literally bring you back to Earth and appreciate what she has always generously provided.

Reprogram / Clearing Old Imprints

I realized that what most people – society as a whole – needed was a major purge. There is so much gunk inside of us it feels like everyone needs a mushroom or MDMA journey. I say it jokingly, and maybe it's just a hopeful wish. But ultimately, we as a species have a lot of imprints and programming to clear. Imprints and programs are thought forms, ideas, and beliefs that are instilled since birth. Imprints and programs come from family, friends, the neighbors and countries we grew up in. It continues in religion, education, and media. It is why people dress and talk the same from the same areas. It is why certain families want their children to become doctors, farmers, or athletes. These imprints of ideas, beliefs, and expectations are repeated over and over again until they become an established program in the mind or in the environment.

A person can go to a different environment and see the programs of that area being lived in real time. They can become imprinted and reprogrammed with new ideas and/or beliefs. But when they return to their home environment, those new ideas and beliefs will be met with the old programs and either revert to their original programming or conflict. This is why families argue when a new program (i.e., beliefs and ideas) is introduced. The program is established only if they continuously repeat the imprints.

Programming usually starts with what our immediate family has taught us. No one is born a racist, or enters greedy, hateful, or deceitful. Maybe there are a few exceptions. These ways of being are learned patterns. And when a person evolves, family imprints are usually the first things we discover we need to change. These family imprints can be the most annoying and sometimes the hardest to remove. They don't resonate with us the way they did before. Our partnership and relationship programs are imprinted through seeing our family dynamics, society, and the relationships we've already experienced. Partnerships should develop on a case-by-case basis depending on what fulfills the partners. As long as there is mutual consent, all options and lifestyles should be open. Partners in these relationships should also have the flexibility and room to grow. Evolution can be accelerated when both partners are willing to grow individually and together. That's what relationships are meant for, in most cases.

We also have karmic programs and imprints from past lives. These karmic imprints can come up in ceremony, meditation, or past life regression. Removing them is usually done working with a therapist, shaman or healer. It can be done on your own if you have the spiritual foundation and experience or have been trained. Some of these imprints can be war programs, trauma, slavery, fear of persecution, you name it. Through the journey of healing, we have the opportunity to heal these imprints and programs in this lifetime. That allows those imprints to no longer affect us in this lifetime or in the future. At the least, it loosens the power these imprints and programs once had on us or our family.

Clients would ask me how to begin clearing these unwanted programs. Awareness always was, and still is the first step. Once you see the programming, you can't deny it. If you notice an uncanny fear and you don't know why, it might be related to a past life trauma. If you notice you like to fight or you have an internal rage that you can't understand, more than likely it could be past life war programming that you need to heal in this lifetime. Either way, these fears, emotions, and tendencies are something to look into. You can ask yourself simple questions.

"Where did this all begin? Was this from my current life trauma? Or a past life? Please show me."

Answers tend to come by asking the right questions in a sacred manner. A question is like a prayer to the universe. By universal law, the answer has to appear. The answer, however, can come in its own time. Which means a person must be still in their heart and mind and consistent and patient to receive the answers. The answers can come in many ways, including visions, feelings, or in dreams. However, if an answer doesn't feel right, or it's convoluted, it's probably not the right one. This work takes a lot of diligence. It's as though the universe or God is seeing if you're patient and humble enough to receive the answers. Either way, the answers are always inside of you.

Awareness Tools

On the topic of self-healing and finding internal awareness and balance, I thought it would be best to add some basic tools for anyone that wants to reference them later. My first mentor always said, "Know thy enemy." And as I said before, his golden rule when dealing with other energies in the spiritual: **RULE #1: Never get cocky in a spiritual battle.**

He always told his students as it was taught to him, "**Awareness is the most important physical skill. Awareness is also the most important spiritual skill.**" Awareness allows us to know how we truly feel once we get through the layers of emotion and thought. It allows us to find our baseline. It also allows us to follow the baseline and flow of nature—what a typical day is like for the birds, the animals, and even the weather. With consistent observation and awareness that also comes from stillness within, we will know when the subtlest energy is off in the environment. Awareness also allows us to know what the baseline is at any moment in the collective or in a group environment. Anything that sticks out will feel like a peak or a spike from the natural baseline. Going into meditation in different environments and really working the skill of silence has changed the level of awareness in me. We all have awareness, and we all have intuition, but it can be dialed in to be a precise tool in the physical and the spiritual realms. However, like all things, your awareness can weaken if not used like a muscle.

Critical Edge Exercise

This exercise I also learned from my first mentor, and I still practice and use it to this day. The critical edge is the space around you at arm's length, including above and below you. It's the closest boundary to your body, the most personal and intimate. Everyone has felt their critical edge. It's the feeling when someone gets too close to you, and it feels like they've crossed your personal space. That is your critical edge. Also within your critical edge are your own energies or energies that may be affecting you, your auric field. This is where you may notice shadow work or any energy on or around you that doesn't belong. This is also the space where you can feel other energies in your field. It's your responsibility to keep your field clear.

How to feel your critical edge: Start to imagine that sphere around you at arm's length, even above and below you. As you go about your day, feel into it. See what it feels like when someone passes by you. If you're sitting in nature, feel what might be just below your feet on the Earth. Does it feel like soil or rock is beneath you? Do you potentially feel water flowing underneath? Imagine expanding or contracting that sphere around you. Using your imagination is the fun part. Even if you can't see it, feel it. This is a major foundation of energy work. Eventually, you will build up the sensitivity of feeling your critical edge. You might feel as though you're about to step on something, and you may look down and see a piece of glass. You may have an object fly at you that you will feel first and automatically dodge it. This exercise can be practiced by yourself or with a partner. If you have a partner, stand 20 feet apart. Close your eyes and turn your back to your partner. Have your partner slowly walk toward you with either happiness, seething anger, or no intent at all. Your partner should never tell you what they're feeling before they start. As they walk toward you from the back while holding their intention – raise your arm above your head when you think they are in your critical edge. Do this exercise three times with a different intent each time. See what results you get and how the intent changes things. This is a great exercise in learning about awareness, intent, and your critical edge.

Threshold Exercise

Next is the threshold that extends at or past your critical edge. It is also like a sphere, but I also view it as a larger field. If you are in your home, your threshold may extend no further than the room you are in. However, with consistent work it can extend throughout the house to know when someone is walking from one room to the next, even if they're on a different floor. You can even extend your threshold sphere outside of your home to know when the mailman is entering your property without even seeing them. This work is real. In fact, the hunters of native tribes used this technique to know when an animal was within their threshold or even to sense when an enemy was approaching and from how far. But something to note. I would first practice this at home. Or if you're outside, do this in privacy. In some cases, your threshold or critical edge can be felt by others, especially animals.

The Threshold exercise will be similar to feeling into your critical edge. But you can push the threshold further. Think of your critical edge as your personal sphere. Think of your threshold as your radar screen or larger sphere/ field outside of your critical edge. Again, as you go about your day, feel into it. See what it feels like when someone passes by you. If you're sitting in nature, feel what might be deeper below your feet on the Earth or further up in the sky. Imagine expanding or contracting that sphere around you. As you are in different environments, see what is different. Sometimes you can "see" a person in the apartment below you. Or sometimes you can "feel" or "see" a hawk in the tree in your backyard.

You can use this exercise to learn the technique. But if you "see" into someone else's space, slowly back out. We cannot invade someone else's privacy without consent. It goes against moral law, and you don't know if that person has other protective beings or ancestors that can "see" you as well. Some protective beings or ancestors of a person may retaliate, as they are there to protect that person. But if you are doing the exercise for learning purposes, those beings will feel the intent and then ask you to leave.

Discerning Outside Energies

All of these exercises are to become aware of your own energy, which allows you to also become more aware of external energies. A person knows when they feel "off." Sometimes it's just a crappy interaction. Other times, it could be something else like spiritual residue from another person. Scan yourself and use discernment. Be aware of entities you speak to, and don't let your eyes deceive you. As I've said before, some beings like trickery and mask themselves as light beings. You need to understand how to discern energies, vibrations, and mannerisms as much as possible when speaking to an entity, even ones you work with. You will know if you're speaking to something Light or angelic by how it feels. But also, don't let your own fear get in the way. It is also a practice. If you want to know how to interact with a being you haven't felt before, do the following:

Ask them to show their true selves at least three times.

Next, ask them to speak their real name at least three times. You will know if it is truly them.

Then, ask them what they want. Be patient in getting the response. If something isn't clear, ask the energy to be clear. Discernment can sometimes be tricky. It can be confusing or create self-doubt. This is why you have to slow down and use it as training.

Working with Light

A quick note: it's important to create a sacred space within your home. It is a place you can empower to make it easier to drop into meditation, angelic and ancestral communication, and the like. When you dedicate a small space, even a small altar, it becomes easier to "drop into" our spiritual work. View it as your mini temple.

As we move forward in our awareness, it's important to rebuild and empower your Light body. In your Light body, you can heal many things within yourself, others, and in nature. In one specific meditation I was told by my guides to work on my Light body.

They said to me, "Feel, feel, feel! Hold the light, feel from the heart. Just by being in your presence, they will feel healing. Not trying to change them, just show them love/light and let it be, and know it is done. Leaving them with love they never felt before and with light to see."

You can empower your light body by imagining white light building into a sphere within your heart. It's the light that is always inside of you. I believe it is the original God spark or God light. Build this sphere and empower it in your imagination each time you exhale with your breath. As you feel the sphere ready to expand, allow it to grow into a larger sphere in your body each time you inhale. Once the sphere is in its next larger form, empower it again until you feel it's ready to expand again. Do not rush the process. Each breath fills the sphere with more light. As you practice this exercise more consistently, you will be able to take your empowered light sphere from your body to your critical edge and even to your threshold. But I would also suggest shielding and cloaking your light sphere anytime you're doing intentional energy work, even at home or in your sacred space.

The Christ Light can also develop from working the light body. We all have light within us, but in order for the Christ Light to activate within the heart space a person must be devoted. From our inner light all types of healing can take place. We can heal in person or remotely. We can transfer the light energy by sending orbs of light that can be used to send out positive energy, protection, guiding energy, clarity, healing, you name it. You're only limited by your imagination. These orbs must be empowered over time. The Christ Light can also remove tumors, parasites, entities, and implants. There is no limitation.

We bring light to the darkness. The darkness does not always want to be exposed, and it likes to hide. But a shaman or even a being of Light simply sheds light, wakes people up, and allows what needs to come up. They are only there to hold space, protect, and be a catalyst for the awakening. In my opinion, not all healers or shamans are meant to heal everyone. If a person's higher self does not give consent, healing too soon may take away the lesson they need to learn. It could even remove karmic debt that a person must experience. It's very tricky sometimes, but there is a lot of listening that needs to take place. It's not about what the healer or shaman wants. It's about what's needed or guided by God or the person's higher self. If you are in your heart space and operating with the Light within you, everything tends to find its healing, eventually.

Entity Removal

There were times I felt inconsistent in working with my guides, but I always felt them available in the background. They said most people don't meet or council with their guides. They show up as consistent as a person does, just like any relationship. They are willing to continue to teach as much as the student shows up.

They were going to show me more about entity removal than what I had previously known.

I decided I needed music in my meditation and began to play my drum. There was a force field of white light that began to build where I sat in the spiritual field. I could still see my guides. I saw a door to the lower right in the ceremony space, meant for entities to exit through. My guides showed me a client to work on. I could see it was a girl in a ceremony space who had an entity inside of her.

I asked, "Am I there to extract something from this girl?"

They replied, "The entity won't always jump out easily. Sometimes it will want to stay or try and hurt the possessed on the way out. Must be careful. It may tempt you into a fight. Stay calm and rebuke it. Rebuke is to remove. Must demand the entity leave the body. Can call upon Jesus Christ and the Christ Light. The entity can exit through the door."

I worked on the girl in spirit and began removing the entity. It was nasty, and it didn't want to come out. I used some tools I had, and after about ten minutes was able to get it out. I still don't always understand who these people who need help are in these spiritual realms. The only thing that feels true is that people pray, and others are there to help them. It's an act of faith.

I share these stories as information from experience. I believe in the power of healing and faith. I also believe that new healers should tread lightly in the practice of entity removal from others. Practicing on oneself is one thing. But practicing on others needs to be a complete devotion to the craft. I've seen clients who've worked with other healers and never had the entity properly removed. In some cases, the root cause of the dark entity or entry point was never addressed, and the person's field was left open, causing more problems down the road.

Time to Sit Down

I needed to slow down. I had worked with thirty people throughout the summer, and the work was intense. I learned so much working with my first batch of clients. I realized I was meant for this type of work, and I liked helping people. But by the last three sessions I wasn't as clear in my vision. Some of my own visualizations were coming through, but the messages were confusing or didn't make sense. I realized this type of work called for a type of stamina I didn't have yet. I found myself depleted after two or three sessions. It was a new lesson I needed to learn in order to find ways to regroup my energy after each session. So I decided to stop until I became clear. I also knew from prior training that stepping back is also good medicine for practitioners and their clients. It is not about us; it's about the people we are helping. If a person is not clear, I honestly believe it could cause more damage to a client. So, removing ego and taking care of oneself is extremely important.

I was also getting tired from working on the land. I was still struggling to get help on my land, as it was hard coordinating people's schedules. When I wasn't physically active, I was active in meditation in the spiritual realms. Things were shifting so rapidly, and I was barely finishing what was already in front of me. I found myself working on something intensely for a day, a week, or even a month at a time, then completely dropping it, only to come back later confused about where I had left off. I was tired of doing everything on my own. It wasn't fun to create all of it and have no one to share it with. I had guilt for not becoming exactly who I thought I was going to become. I moved to the mountains to master myself, only to feel like I was the furthest from actually achieving that. I still had some addictions, I still had frustration, and I was still inconsistent in a lot of areas of my life. I hit a wall. I needed something. I took on too much at once and thought I could do it all…I couldn't.

Who I really was, compared to what I really wanted to become, was not the same person. As much as I wanted to, I hadn't turned into the shamanic healer I wanted to be. I felt guilty because I wanted to answer to God. I knew I was still somehow answering the call I felt in my heart. And I had to accept that life is overwhelming sometimes. But I still held a lot of self-judgment. I still felt impatient, wanting to control the outcome, inconsistent, and distracted. That's all I saw. Feeling so frustrated after creating an off-grid cabin sucked out the excitement I expected to feel. What was this teaching me?

Two things became apparent. One, I needed to stop being so hard on myself. And the other answer came quickly and easily from one of my favorite movies, *Into the Wild*. "Happiness is best when shared." When I looked at the bigger picture, I could see that I had finished my dream of building an off-grid cabin. I started this book, and I was helping others. Even though things didn't turn out completely how I had imagined or in the timing I wanted, they were coming into creation and completion. Most importantly, I was learning, healing, and my heart was in the right place. I had learned acceptance and the real lesson that no one knows everything. There are times when we are high in our spiritual evolution and times when we are in the valley. Which is why it's always important to remind ourselves to remain humble and have gratitude. Yes, I had life-changing experiences and special spiritual gifts, but it didn't separate me from everyone else. I knew, the minute we point to other people as though they don't know any better is the minute, we've lost ourselves. And even though I didn't find or become *everything* I wanted; I did become everything I needed.

After a lot of reflection, I realized I had seen the shamans I worked with also live regular lives in regular homes. They would do their work during the week, teach or run ceremonies, and go home to their family. It was a mix of both. I felt such relief when I finally put two and two together.

Later that summer I had a soul brother come to the land to do a vision quest. The first day we caught up, and I showed him a little bit of the land. The second day he found and prepared the site where he would do the vision quest. He quested for four days and nights. I would periodically check near his site where he would leave stones to let me know he was ok. On the fifth day he came out from his journey. He stayed for a couple more days to reintegrate as I finished more projects on the land. I kept getting a feeling I needed to quest as well, but I wasn't quite sure.

A week later, my friend was gone, and I got the urge to do my own vision quest. I tried to tap in and listen to see if it was time for me to quest. The feedback I felt was 50/50 on whether or not it was the right time. I had time to take a break from projects, so I decided to do it. My intention was to clear all mental debris and overthinking. I wanted to feel the sacred silence and hold it within. But that's not necessarily what happened. As I was walking towards where my site would be, I heard, "Acceptance."

I set up my tarp and took a tent as well. A tent is not recommended for quests because you're a little more cut off from your environment, but I took it just in case. From the beginning, it felt like I was rushing to get to silence. My mind was racing the entire time. I was looking for answers instead of enjoying the quest. By night time, I was exhausted from overthinking. I slept the entire next day. When I finally came out of it, I didn't feel good. I didn't like what was happening or what I was about to discover. I slept some more and by the next morning I was done, and I packed up to end my quest. I felt bad, but I remembered my mentors telling me to not feel guilty, that time in a vision quest is still a quest. And after that thirty-six-hour period I realized what I had to accept—that my ADHD was real, and it affected me. I had to finally accept that my thoughts and the amount of thoughts and feelings I get are different from most people. I had to accept that mental silence is hard for me, really hard, especially if I'm out of meditative practice. I had to accept that I could no longer deny that I had an issue that allows me to create great ideas but always has me bouncing from one thing to the next. I was able to go this long in life being able to balance things. But without the hyper focus of performing every night, it was difficult to focus my energy without the structure.

Even though I didn't finish the quest, I took the following few days to do absolutely nothing. It allowed me more time to catch the nuances of my mind. I even calculated the time it took me to go from one thought to the next thought, which was shorter than three seconds. This was hard to accept. And when the things I wanted to do in life were completed, I always looked for a next goal or life experience. At that moment, I decided to look at all perspectives on where I currently was in life instead of always being so hard on myself. The lesson was about acceptance. And I realized that as I was nearing the end of a ten-year vision and commitment to myself and others to have an off-grid cabin, I'd kept my word as a man and as a friend, and I was determined to finish. But then what? For the first time in my life, I didn't know what was next. The lesson moved from acceptance to surrender. I didn't know what I would be doing or who I would become. I didn't even care to know. It made me feel nervous and also free at the same time.

Deeper Still – Personal Healing

Life became more lonely. I still wasn't seeing a lot of people, nor did I have too many people to talk to as it was still the middle of the pandemic. Over time, I had to pay attention to escapism. I realized I was making up scenarios in my head where I was famous- a famous basketball or football player, rapper, musician, you name it. It had been going on for quite a while before I realized the effects. My mind imagining fame repeatedly was creating distortions. The desire to feel love from an audience and have attention was what my mind needed. It is what I had known most of my life. But in my heart, all I really needed was self-love and community.

I knew when I stepped away from the entertainment industry that I was going to a place where there was no applause. I didn't want it, and I didn't need it. I wanted to know who I was and what I was about beyond my career. In healing this, I felt as though I found what I was looking for within myself and within the universe. I knew I was letting go of what I'd always been known for, and even though most of my peers didn't even know what I did anymore, I knew I was on my path. But I had to work in silence for years and be comfortable with that.

I knew I was meant to speak and continue helping others. But when I continued to speak by putting out videos, it felt as though friends and family were confused. It made sense they were confused since they were not having these experiences, and I was usually very private. It was also as if the information I was sharing was coming out of left field. But to me I had been silently gathering the information and sharing from my heart. When people close to me pulled away, it hurt and brought on more loneliness. I was trying my best to be a vessel for God. The intention was not to tell people how to live their lives, only share what they maybe could not see and to help in their evolution and planetary evolution. Some people loved it. Others got scared, as if I'd lost it. From that, a deeper fear was revealed, the fear of not being loved. I knew I was being tested spiritually. At this point, I knew I was in a cocoon and that everything I was experiencing as I continued on my path was going to make sense and fall into place, eventually.

Pick Up The Pieces

After many months, something major began shifting. I could hear myself and my guides again.

"Work from the pre-matter space. There are templates there. Be patient, architect. Operate from your highest self," they said.

"How does the highest self-operate?" I asked

"From love, leadership, patience, faith, listening, empathy, guidance, knowing, acceptance. All the things you already know."

"What is happening? What is all of this teaching us? What is it showing me?"

"Babylon is falling," they replied.

"What should we do as humans?"

"Are you afraid?"

"Sometimes I'm afraid,"

But then I felt something come over me. My inner fire burned, and I felt another part of me awaken.

"Destroy that fear. Fear is the portal through which they feed. It is a sickness. It is the dis-ease. Let Babylon burn to the ground. Let it burn in its fiery flames. Let it burn the illusions that have been masquerading in front of your eyes your entire life and lifetimes. Let it burn to ashes. The programming, the fear, the anger, hate, envy, jealousy, and greed. Because what do we do when we fall? We rise."

I asked them, "What is all this human suffering and psychological warfare showing us? Is it a reflection? Is it a cycle repeating to feed off of the energetic fears of the planet?"

"It all happens again and again. This is a free-will planet. There are eight billion human co-creators here at once, each with their own needs and desires. The truth is, we don't control any of it. We can only do our best, help others, and enjoy the journey. That's it," they replied.

"How do we free the bodies, minds, and consciousness of the planet?"

"Ceremony and prayer," they answered simply.

All of these questions were leading me to the truth. But the truth of what? What am I looking for?

My guides asked me, "What brings you pain?"

"Not knowing what's next because I'm not in control,"

"How can loneliness build you up?".

I thought for a moment. "Appreciation."

They continued. "What do you do for self-love?"

"Stretch, meditate, light some candles," I said, giving a somewhat surface answer.

"What else can you do for self-love?"

"Appreciate how far I've come. Appreciate that I listen, I watch, learn, and grow. I give my word, and I honor it. I get things done. So I guess overall, thoughts of self-appreciation,"

"Good. Slow down, again,"

Then I felt a familiar feeling in my entire body. I knew that change was coming again.

My guides said, "We're moving you out of here to focus." Then they told me that where I currently lived was not home. "It is ok for now. But it will all make sense soon." I was shocked. I wasn't ready to accept that the land and home I had been working on the last three years was not my home. It was made with love, sweat, and tears. But I had to surrender.

They said, "Why did you think it would be anything else?" They meant, why did I think it wouldn't be hard work? Then, I laughed. I understood. It was time to come out of the woods. What good is a monk being by themselves in the woods to the people? "What is coming to you is for you and through you. It is a school. Same information, just coded and decoded for you, by you, and through you. It comes in packets of threes. It is the same information that has always been there, hidden. It is time now. Remember who you are. Love yourself, first. Self-appreciation for what you know, and what you do not yet know. It's coming. We are waiting with you. We are not done," they said, and I heard them laughing. They continued. "We were waiting for you to be done (with the home). Now, it's time to move on. This was not for you. Took longer, extra. But you did it right. Now, it's Mission. Only mission. Follow your heart. And see where it leads you again."

I took the rest of fall to finish up everything that needed to be done with the home. I knew it was time to go, and I found tenants to rent my home so I could go back to California. It was the only place I felt called to. I packed a few suitcases for LA and put the belongings from my house into my garage. It was time to move on.

Return to Society For Real This Time

By late fall, I was back in LA. But I did not feel settled. Although I had been to LA the previous three winters, I had mostly kept to myself or with a few friends. I was still mostly in a spiritual container because of the pandemic. The return to live in LA felt different – something was happening in the collective. It felt like I had left, then come back into society, yet nothing was the same; the whole world was inverted. Being in the mountains, as beautiful as it is, is nothing without sharing the happiness. But when I returned, the biggest question in my heart was, "Where did all my friends go?" I felt that no one had time to listen and that I couldn't fully share with people. It felt like I was on a time limit when I spoke with people. I saw a few friends, but most didn't want to make time for our friendship. This broke my heart. I felt like I was on an island. I realized that I woke up with nothing to look forward to and no one to share anything with. Everyone was in a time of transition and had put the future on hold. All I wanted was hugs, intimacy, and friendship.

The pandemic changed everything. I understood that everyone was tired and had their life to live, but it completely shifted the collective consciousness and the energy field of people and the planet. I knew people were trying to feel good again. But interactions with others felt like a movie, as though people were still trying to prop up "the show," as if the whole world hadn't changed. But I could see the truth in their eyes, the disbelief and confusion. Most people felt lost, desensitized, or in denial.

Breathe Reset

I had to reset myself emotionally and spiritually to stay in my own baseline. When I tuned deeper into the collective again, I could see in my vision that most people were consciously quarantined on the planet as they were physically. Yet there were a few others that were consciously and physically free from the quarantine. The physical quarantine was a microcosm to what was happening spiritually. From the macro level, I could see two timelines happening at once and I recognized this was a window of opportunity where souls' consciousness could evolve.

It seemed that negative beings were a part of a plan to keep humans under a frequency net to harvest their energies. But those negative beings were now being stopped and having to face some form of judgment. I saw forces of Light that were present and there was a guardianship happening on the planet. Something in the Earth body was "online." It was the Guardians, the angels protecting the planet.

My guides were coming in again.

"You have a big task ahead of you. One you need to pull and bring into focus. We pulled you out for a reason, remember? Yes. It's coming soon. Hold fast. Clear your mind. Ask for vision. It may not be the one you want or expect. But it will be your path, your vision. It takes time. Clarity. It is a place. Your recovery phase. Slow down. Gathering."

I was taking a lot of notes over the next few months. I was exhausted from all the information. My brain function was changing. I was letting go again. It felt like I was in a purging phase of the old, but at a deeper level this time. Everything I had been looking for—truth, magic, purpose—I had found. But I always seemed to return to a place of, "now what?" It was as though I recalibrated to being in a place of "found," the feeling that I was in the right place. It's always a little different than I expected. It's a little less dreamy, not perfect, but special and spectacular.

The found space within creates less desire, less need for more. The place of fulfillment is like the end of the crescendo. There are less waves and more stillness. Stillness is the key. And I must be able to let go of searching. After speaking to a close friend about all my journeys and what it might all add up to, she told me something that changed my heart.

She said, "I get it…this world doesn't make sense to you. You've been looking for New Landtopia where none of this shit is happening. You're blazing a trail to show the rest of us how to get out of here and get to places you've found."

She was right. It was that simple. And immediately after our phone call, I had a vision.

New Landtopia

There is a split between two worlds. One world is the old world of thought and limited consciousness. The other world is the new world is free from a mental and spiritual prison and brings unlimited possibilities in consciousness awareness. The split is the doorway. Everyone is so busy watching the reality show of life and wanting to be the main characters, yet they don't realize they're part of the show. The characters in the show try to keep it alive because it seems so real to them. But they will play forever not knowing they're in a show until they start knocking on doors, floors, and ceilings and asking, "Who is the creator?"

Who is the creator? Everyone is. But there is a reality outside of this one. Others have made it. They left the show, and they went home. Some of us are ushers to the other world(s). These worlds are collectively called New Landtopia. Realms and realities of organic consciousness and harmony.

I opened my eyes for a minute to drink some water. I looked over and saw two books on the TV stand in the home I was staying at. *How Things Work*, and *How The Universe Works*. It was confirmation. The creators of the show are using an intelligent computer to program the minds of characters to keep their world existing. The show can only continue if characters play; it's the only way it works. If the characters stop playing, the game idles. The creators want power and energy. The characters playing the game give the creators power and energy. When the characters start asking for the creators and looking for the truth, the creators shake the world up like a snow globe. They make characters turn on each other; they make the mice confused. They reprogram the game or experiment to make sure the mice fight for the same piece of cheese. If the characters wake each other up, the show is over and the game has limited players. But there will always be new players who want to enter the game, and some who will never leave. It is their choice to stay in the illusion. But by the time they look up, a lot of people will be gone. They will have left reality.

When someone new arrives to a world in New Landtopia, integration is slow. For some it is difficult to adjust to a world that is peaceful and true because the reality show they left behind was all that they knew. But they knew in their hearts it was a dream. The same rules do not apply in New Landtopia. People are not fighting for their lives. They are not fighting each other for the same piece of cheese. They do not need cheese. Life is similar to how people used to live; needs are met, people are kind and well mannered, and they live and let live because they are in their hearts without an overlay of mind control. But how do we know New Landtopia is a real place and not another show or level to the game? We don't. But we know we're home when we're in our hearts.

After this vision I was instructed to help people get free in their day-to-day lives so they were no longer led by stress and fear. That way, when the world gets shaken up in the future, they can hold firm and stay grounded.

"When their minds are free, show them the door. Help them get their mind power back to use that power to find New Landtopia and simultaneously create it. It comes in words, it comes in images, and it comes in sound. Use the medicine. Use the codes. You have them," my guides said.

I have to admit this show on Earth is the wildest shit I've ever seen. Most people are lying to themselves and each other. Everyone is trying to hold up the show, but their smiles are see-through. "Be in this world, but not of it," is a saying that still holds true. And what mattered now was that the sacred was meant to be shared. It was the doorway to New Landtopia and original timelines.

HEALING THE MASCULINE

Peace Be the Journey

After so much consciousness expansion, my feet needed to touch the ground again. I needed to go to Ohio to take care of my father. He had recently retired and just purchased a new home. But within two months of retirement, he found out he had cancer and was going to need chemotherapy. I would help him for a couple weeks at a time, then fly back home. Luckily, after a few months and a lot of unexpected weight loss my father went into remission and was getting better. He was planning trips to places he wanted to visit and friends he wanted to see. For me, I was just happy he was ok.

By the end of 2021, the cancer came back. This time, it was lymphoma, and it was in his lungs. I went home again for a few months, as he could not take care of himself. He stopped eating again and had lost more weight. My father, who weighed around 250 pounds my whole life, now weighed around 162 pounds. He didn't want to try any alternative healing routes, so there wasn't much I could do except take him to chemotherapy. I feel that the chemo is ultimately what destroyed his body and emotional stamina. I know it works for some people, but chemotherapy is not a one size fits all therapy. The doctors don't speak of diet, alternatives, anything. And the centers where people get their chemo feel like cattle ranches. It's the only way I can explain it. It looks like they treat patients the same way they treat big industry farm animals with crappy food and tubes of chemicals being pumped through them. It was hard to watch.

My sister took over as caretaker and eventually had to take my father back to the hospital. I drove to LA to rent an apartment for the winter. I needed a break from caretaking, building, and everything else. I was tired. But by early spring, I knew I was going to have to go back home. I knew he wasn't doing well; I could feel it. He now weighed 150 pounds and didn't have the strength to get to the bathroom. I waited as long as I could for doctors to tell my sister and I what was going to happen. But he was already on a breathing tube and dialysis. My sister called me and told me to wait before coming back to Ohio. But I knew I needed to go home.

I caught an overnight flight and saw him in the hospital the same morning. He was sleeping and not really responsive. By then his doctors was able to take out his breathing tube, only needing to supply him with oxygen. She told us his organs were not going to hold up for long and that we would need to make a decision to keep him going or take him off the oxygen. I told her that we needed to try and wake him up so *he* could decide. She wanted to allow him to rest, but something in my gut told me we needed to try and wake him up. I feel that every person, every soul, should get to decide when it's their time to go, if possible, especially my father. I knew he would have wanted that decision. I immediately shook him awake. His eyes opened slightly, and he was confused as to what was going on. I told him he needed to stay awake, and he did. My sister ran to get the doctors, who came back into the room. As they told my father the diagnosis, I could see him calculate in his mind what was happening. Then, in a low and raspy voice he said, "I'm screwed." He sort of raised his eyebrows like saying, "Ok."

I knew he had decided. My sister and I were able to speak to him briefly before he fell asleep again. We told him we loved him. He looked us both in the eyes intently and with little voice left, whispered, "I love you too,' to each of us. Within a minute or so, he quickly fell back to sleep. We decided to let him rest that night and went home.

The next morning as my sister and I were waking up to make our way back to the hospital, the doctor called her cell phone. My father passed away early that morning. My sister and I decided to go anyway to gather his last belongings. When we arrived, the nurse said we could see the body. I initially didn't want to see him. I didn't want to see the shell of the man that carried my father. He was already gone. But the hallway we walked into was in a different part of the building and I accidentally passed a room with a large window. He was there in a room; the curtain wasn't even closed. I was ready to cuss out the nurses for not closing the window curtains. But I stopped in my tracks and started crying. I walked back into the hallway past my sister. She decided to go in and see him, but I couldn't. I just cried in the hallway.

After a few minutes, I decided to go into the room and join her. He wasn't in pain anymore. I knew he needed to leave his body, but I still missed him. I didn't stay long. I didn't need to. We gathered the last of his things and drove home in silence. I didn't cry after that; I was numb. I only wanted to take care of what needed to be done at his home. It was the easiest way for me to process.

I stayed home for another week or so helping pack up his things and put the house up for sale. We knew he wanted to be cremated and didn't plan on having a service. But I decided to have a last-minute life celebration for my father for our friends and family. We were just out of the pandemic, and I felt like I owed his friends and the people who knew him a chance to mourn and celebrate him. I gathered as many photos as I could find to make a timeline of his life. Most of my local family made it, including some of his old friends. My sister didn't stay; she was exhausted after weeks of helping him and didn't want to see anyone. I understood. But celebrating his life felt good. Life needs closure. Not just for the person that has passed on, but for others to remember the good times. It's a reminder to live life the way you want to.

Soon after, I went back to LA for three more months. I continued to process what I could with my father. A loved one passing always puts life into perspective. What do we work so hard for? All the stress of work, raising children, and paying bills—is it all worth it? It was a reminder that we take nothing with us. And what we leave behind is up to us. Leaving a home for your children gives them an advantage in some aspects. Money and assets could help the next generation if managed properly. But *who* we raise and *how* we help them grow is really one of the few things that lives beyond us. My family wasn't wealthy, but we had what we needed. I had to forgive my father and come to peace within myself. He did the best he could with the knowledge and experiences he had. He was far from perfect, but he raised me to be a great man. My sister and I are what he left behind to be the next part of the evolution. He and my mother created a foundation that pushed us to fly. Sometimes when I came back down from my experiences, I was a little weirder, I'll admit. But I was always a lot more expanded and experienced. Is that not a life mission? To raise your kids to fly further and expand farther than you could?

It made me think about what I wanted to leave behind. I could continue to live and experience life for myself, but I wanted to create something that would help other people, even when I passed onto the next realm. I had been getting signs for the past year to create a school, but I wasn't sure what I would be teaching. I just knew it had to do with spirituality and primitive skills. In order to find out more I had to finish this book. Somehow it would help me organize my thoughts and experiences, and put it all into perspective. From the onset, I needed to write this all from my heart and put it down. I had no expectations for it. I wasn't writing for money. I want it to reach people by the millions. I want it to touch people and for them to trust themselves, their experiences, and to go live the life they want to live. And to trust God.

Healing the Masculine

One of the many other reasons I decided to leave society in 2018 was to have time to focus on healing my divine masculine. I always knew I was a good man. But I knew I wasn't operating from my highest self as a man. For example, when I was younger, I always had a thirst. I didn't want to settle in a relationship. I always wanted more of something, even if it was just in my mind. Looking at myself honestly, I felt like it was time to step up and that I had a lot of healing to do. Men as a whole have a lot of healing to do. This came from an accumulation of years of paying attention to and learning from the women in my life; from the women in my family, my female friends, and the women I had dated. But these lessons took years to integrate and understand.

I asked my higher self, "What needs healed?"

"The father figure: Need to heal ego, or let it go. Need to heal masculine energy," it said.

When my father became sick with cancer and died a year later, I noticed a lot of anger came through my body and spirit. And I had to look deeper. Overall, my father was a great father. But, like everyone, he had issues, and they had been passed down to me. I personally saw a lot of escapism growing up; people wanting their own space. When my parents got home, everyone went to their own rooms. We rarely ate meals together. A lot of these memories didn't come up until I was in my thirties and noticed issues in my own relationships. I knew I had a fear of commitment that came from always wanting my space and freedom. Maybe I didn't see enough intimacy? When I felt a partner was getting too close emotionally, I would push them away.

Accomplishments = Affection

I recognized that, as a child, affection mostly came in the form of my accomplishments – whether in sports or the arts. Don't get me wrong, I received a lot of love as a child. But I noticed that when I made others proud, I received a more intense form of love. I subconsciously programmed those accomplishments equaled affection. And most times in my life, I pushed away real affection to stay focused on accomplishments. It was a fear of commitment, and it wasn't working anymore. I didn't want to push away potential love anymore.

Fear of Commitment

Most of my life I was not ready for a relationship, and it showed. I did have long-term relationships when I was completely in love with the woman I was dating. But I would become overwhelmed by the thought that the relationship would be forever and that I couldn't provide the idea or reality of "forever." And as a young adult – traveling and performing – I knew I wasn't ready to settle in a relationship. I was afraid I would change too much, and I didn't want to hurt anyone. I was right in some ways. I changed so much in short periods of time; I don't know if some of my relationships would have grown with me. But ultimately, I was afraid to lose my freedom. The idea of being with one person for the rest of my life led me to question whether monogamy was natural, or even right for me.

This came from my parents getting divorced later in life, and I knew it. I think some people get sick of their partners, and they want to escape. It is a feeling I think is completely understandable, especially with kids. Like most families, I knew my parents had grown apart, and the relationship was not healthy for either of them. I knew early on as a kid that people change. This led to me avoiding and being emotionally detached from some of my partners, which eventually caught up to me in life. But as an adult, I didn't want to escape from someone when I needed to process my thoughts or feelings anymore. The only way I could heal this was to no longer run away from myself or my partner and always face feelings head on. If the love is real or still holding the relationship together, both parties should face the issues. If the issue is dealt with correctly, the problem can be just a moment or be healed over time like all things.

I asked my higher self, "When my wife is living with me, what can I do in order not to escape or be resistant, or short-tempered? What can I do to keep the love alive?"

"Create spaces; spaces within the home," it said.

Love Patterns

I continued going deeper through more meditations.

I heard my higher self say, "Old sex patterns; related to lack of love, past."

I wanted to change that, and it took more presence to find the roots of these issues. I realized I grew up looking at women from a physical and lustful perspective. I remember around four years old stealing *Playboy* magazines from my dad's closet. In all honesty, the pictures allowed me to find beauty in different types of women. But it definitely translated into early sexual desires and the desires to want to experience different women, which continued into adulthood. As I worked through healing this, it was difficult knowing how much lust was programmed from an early age. It was even more difficult knowing if it was a natural desire.

When I looked at nature, I realized that most animal species, over 90 percent of mammals, have different partners. They mate and move on. This was confusing. How much of my desire was natural and how much was programmed? It felt like it was a bit of both. When the world doesn't make sense, I look to nature or the universe. Deep down I feel that the desire to have different partners is completely natural. And some couples do expand beyond their relationship if it's right for them. But I also know you can't touch God in a relationship without a deep personal, emotional, and spiritual connection. Building in these ways has to be the focus for a healthy relationship. As a man, I realized there is a divine need for monogamy in relationships in the times that we are in. Both sides need the vulnerability and safety of opening up and the security of knowing their partner is devoted to them. Both men and women need to heal together, pray together, grow emotionally and spiritually together. We need healthy love patterns and prototypes of divine love.

When I observed the bigger picture, I realized that oversexualizing women is rampant in most cultures and has been for centuries, if not longer. It's dangerous for men, as it can create a perception that a woman is separate from her body or lacks real emotions. If men – or anyone – continues in this perception, they can develop an appetite for desiring others solely in a sexual way. They, too, have a separation from their heart. If the appetite isn't recognized, it will create a potential long-term trap and they will be "thirsty" forever. I had seen men who had a lot of sexual partners and were completely unsatisfied after a while, if not depressed. Sexual or non-committed relationships will only last so long for anyone. After a while, the heart needs real connection, and that is what I needed in my life again. The trap of lust was a trap on all sides. Men with this cultural programming may never notice their perception was tainted like mine. Women with this cultural programming may fall into the trap by matching the over-sexualized archetype and never really attract a partner who matches their heart. Both sides have veils over their eyes.

As an older man, I had too many female friends and women in my life who didn't have men they could feel safe with or confide in without sexual attention. The consensus was how rare "good men" are. This bothered me because I knew I could be better, and men as a whole *had* to be better. I kept looking at what I was imprinting on a daily basis. "Do I actually want this, or is this old programming? Is it love? Does this thought bring me to the man I want to be? Are the thoughts of higher frequency?" I ran questions like these as much as I could to filter for thoughts and ideas I wanted to work on.

A few years earlier I had worked with a woman who taught me about a sexual energy cleanse. In short, it's a self-clearing process where you take a salt bath with essences, give thanks to your past partners, and at the same time remove all energetic ties and chords. The clearing worked. I was grateful for the relationships I had had in the past. hose connections were special, but I wanted to become the highest version of myself. I wanted to be clear of the appetites and old programs I had within me. But as it goes, the healing always takes place in layers and over a period of time. The next layer of healing was for myself and for my future partner. I wanted to be fulfilled in a committed relationship and to set an example.

Survival Mode

Throughout the process of healing the masculine, more anger emerged. I noticed my continual need to always be "doing something," which is something I saw my father do. It was hard for him to sit still. I realized he was in survival mode. But I had to ask myself, "Why?"

I would visualize his life from a child, to an adult, to the time I was born. And I realized he was always a provider; he was always giving. In fact, it was hard for him to receive gifts or praise. I found the same for myself as I got older. My father was the oldest of nine children. Always the caretaker, he probably missed out on having the childhood one would want, in order to look after his brothers and sisters. No wonder he couldn't sit still. I looked at what that could have been like for the family with all those kids and not a lot of income. In short, you make do with what you have. But I think growing up that way subconsciously put him in survival mode. This was the beginning of a healing I didn't realize I needed. And more anger emerged.

My father always had to be right, he always had to have control, and his ego pushed most people away. Neither my sister, my mother, nor I had much say in matters. And sometimes, that's okay because a man is the head of the household. However, sometimes he just wanted to be controlling. I never could define it as a kid, but I could feel it. It always pissed me off, and it's why I don't like being told what to do. I asked my higher self how I could heal this.

"Work and define truth. Making peace with the past. Look at father's true self, not his shadow self," it said.

As I continued to look deeper into my father's true self, I would see his shadow before I saw the other side of the coin. Yes, he was a know-it-all, and it drove me and my family crazy sometimes. But as I continued to observe, he was that way because he had to have the answers from an early age, having been a caretaker for his younger brothers and sisters. And once my sister and I came into the world, the need to have the answers, or seeming like a person who had the answers, drove him more into that personality trait. The need to have answers and solutions may also be the same reason he was always in survival mode.

I also recognized my father as a father to many of my friends. He was always guiding them, offering them advice or a place to stay at our house. He would buy football cleats if a friend didn't have them. He would always go to my cousins' football and basketball games to support them. He was a father to many. The same side of the coin was wanting to give and help because that was his love language.

Even after he passed away from this realm, I was still in communication with him spiritually. I heard his soul say, "What about me?" And from the observer standpoint, I immediately understood and felt it. I realized the know-it-all trait was because my father just wanted to be seen. He learned the trait of "needing to be needed," having to always put others before himself. With an outpouring of giving, he just wanted to be appreciated. And I had to let it be, all of the good and not so good. The shadow aspects weren't necessarily going to change, but I could understand and have compassion for them. In hindsight, I had to give him the utmost respect. I couldn't have walked in his shoes; being a black man in a world that is against black men, a black man in a bi-racial relationship in a time where it wasn't socially acceptable, dealing with one good kid (my sister), and another hyperactive kid (me), just trying to get by while supporting his family and community.

Lesson learned? **Don't judge another man whose shoes you are not ready to fill.**

I remembered sometimes asking my dad if he was "ok." He would always tell me, "Everything is fine," even if it wasn't. Men create a thick skin in ways I think can be beneficial in order to have tenacity throughout life. At the same time, thick skin is harmful to the heart. There is pent-up energy from not being able to express that leads to stress and heart problems. I started to see why so many men had to keep their feelings to themselves. If men are expected to be providers, they don't necessarily have time to fully acknowledge their feelings or begin to heal what they're feeling. The expectation is real, and it never lets up, especially with children. Most men are not really provided space in their lives to access and talk about their feelings. There was a new balance that was needed; healed men who were still willing to fulfill their duties as a man.

How Do We Heal This?

In the last fourteen years on my journey, I noticed that men were rarely in healing circles or at ceremonies I was attending. And there weren't many men to talk to about healing or spirituality in a grounded way. I also noticed that most men weren't operating from their heart. We had been led down a road of conquest and war that was fruitless or fulfilling a material life that left most men unsatisfied. There weren't many examples for men of positive and balanced leadership as there had been in other decades. So, the sacred question entered was, "How do we heal this?"

Again, the answer was in creating time to process these feelings. One of my mentors had an exercise accessing the Temple of Self simply by asking, "How am I feeling?" In practicing this teaching over the past decade, I can return to inner stillness and view things differently and have more compassion for myself, my process, and others. I wish more men, including my father, had taken the time to access their hearts. Maybe the world would be a safer place.

Relationships

I knew it was time to do some more heart clearing for myself. In meditation, I found myself in the mountains. I saw a cave and walked in. It was dark at first. I realized the cave represented my fear. I sat there in the dark and let it surround me. Suddenly, I went through all my relationships. I realized I had not been in love for years. I had shut down my heart in certain ways because it was easier emotionally. What was it about the women that I did love when I knew I didn't want anyone else? The obvious answer was that love happened when I wasn't looking. I also realized those partners felt like "home." And we both seemed to have similar beliefs and were working towards similar goals. As I continued to sit in this cave, I felt deeper. True love felt like music. It was warm. It was a feeling of the pressure being off and being our true selves.

I heard my higher self say, "People have come into your life for a reason. Love is God, love is growth. All the women in your life have been wanting to give you love. You have not wanted to receive it because of the pursuit of money or because you kept looking over your shoulder for something better. You haven't taken a chance on love. It's time."

There were women who had changed me into a better way of being. I won't go too deep into the relationships out of respect. I will only share what I learned through them. My first love was my everything. Though we were young, we had so much love for each other. Even our families knew it. The love felt natural, like we had done it before, and it just made sense. A big factor for us was the fact that we went to church together. There was a spiritual aspect to the relationship that was important to both of us, and I was in love with the spiritual woman she was. But eventually, college and moving out of state led us to go our separate ways.

I had to learn how to communicate with my second love. Talking and communicating are two different things. Talking is saying your part. Communication is openly listening as well as speaking. And I realized I had to understand how I felt and how the other person felt in order to listen and speak effectively. That love taught me patience, communication, and to pay attention to what a partner needs.

Another woman had extreme intellect and spiritual knowledge. She raised my vibration through spiritual growth, and we were a match in many ways. But I realized she had a lot of unrealized ego which brought up anger in me because it reminded me of my father. It was the first time I had seen so much ego in a woman, and it was a turn off for me. I also knew I had my own issues to work on. I was a workaholic at the time. I let work consume me, and I wasn't present as a partner. It didn't allow me the mental or energetic space to share with her.

I had to release a lot of guilt about the last woman I had a heart connection with because I wasn't ready to be in a relationship. But I learned about embodying joy from her. Every day, I was trying to make spiritual or career progress and it seemed like every day she just had a smile on her face. She was pure joy, so much so that it was confusing. It showed me a way of being I had never seen before. I was good at slowing down and finding stillness and meditation, but her way of joy and being was something I had yet to embody. I heard my higher self-come in.

"The 'stars in your eyes' love is not the right one. It will be a little more reserved in the beginning. Live through your heart. All things must change, eventually. Go with the flow. Be thankful. Love."

Towards the end of the meditation, I chose to be grateful for all that I had learned from them. I was grateful to see all the beauty in them, but I had to release them and let go of the heart chords attached. I had to release all of it. And when I did, the cave became green in color and filled with life, and I was in the center. The love I know I have to give is like a sacred jewel. I needed to unlock it myself through more self-love. I knew I was ready to share it, and I was waiting to hand over the jewel. I also knew at that moment that my future partner would know the code. I was waiting for her and trusted she was coming. I made a mantra, "I will know when I see her. I will know when I see her. I will know when I see her. She will know when she sees me."

Masculine / Feminine Separation

I continued to look at myself and also observe the separation of love between men and women and it didn't seem natural. As I viewed the collective and all the people I had known and met, there weren't many examples of love left in relationships. It didn't seem as though many couples were still in love or at least 60 percent truly happy or satisfied. I knew many people were dealing with their own traumas and programming. But what happened to us? This separation started to feel like a larger program.

Men want sex, attention, and love. And women want safety, security, and love. I will say, some of these needs may be as natural as humanity itself. Most men are not ready to be in a relationship until they're ready. They have to feel safe to be themselves while giving up other pursuits. And they subconsciously need the feeling of unconditional love, the way they needed it from their mother. But women feel similarly. They need to feel safe and secure while not being worried about other pursuits. They subconsciously need the unconditional love they needed from their father. Both sides want similar things. So which side sets the tone? In my personal opinion men need to set the tone of safety and security. That is the natural way of being for any male in nature. Once that is provided, a female can open up into her true self and become the nurturer that the male needs. But in modern society, both sides are looking for red flags to escape and ultimately protect themselves. And trauma or past unsuccessful relationships will not create a strong foundation. What both sides *want*, they must first *provide*.

On the physical plane there is a lot of debate about what works for both men and women. There is also programming between men and women that must be looked at deeply. Some women don't want to depend on men, or simply want to have their own careers. Some say it puts them more in their masculine energy. I'm not here to debate either side because I'm not a woman and I think everyone should decide what they want to do in life. But it changed the programming of a stay-at-home mother, which to me, is fine. Some men actually took the stay-at-home parent role and are completely happy with it. The question is, what if men don't want the traditional role of being provider? Do they even have a choice? In relationships where the male is still expected to provide everything, are the women still prepared to follow the traditional program of taking care of the home? I don't have answers to all of these questions, but I do recognize there are a lot of old paradigms that may need to shift per relationship needs. And ultimately, I know there is a larger aspect at play.

I did a lot of meditations on this separation and looked back to past life remembrances – I could see the collective turmoil throughout different lifetimes. During more spiritually enlightened eras, when societies knew they were cosmic citizens and had contact with other beings outside our planet, there was a general sense of togetherness. The separation began when outside negative forces began infiltrating and dividing the masculine from the feminine. These same negative forces took lands, natural resources, and declared wars on different planets. They had complete disregard for anything sacred—the planet, the women on it, or any feminine principles. They didn't see a "use" for the feminine other than procreation. This infiltration happened on the physical plane over thousands of years. And the men who were defenders of the land were separated from their families because of these wars on Earth within the galaxy. There were female defenders, too. But the same process of disregard for the feminine while waging war and stealing sacred lands has continued in most races on this planet. This patriarchal tyranny is something that was programmed into humanity. It is not who we are. But the programs continue until we recognize them and flush them out.

One of the most destructive tactics is to divide natural ways of being. In most indigenous cultures, men revered the woman as a divine essence. We revered the divine feminine essence in the Earth and higher forms of Earth, Gaia. She always provided all our needs, and Father God, Sky, the masculine, always guided us. It took both energies. The feminine was revered for being nurturing, graceful, and divine with intuition. In our original ways of being, we lived from the heart, and both the feminine and the masculine energies were appreciated as two sides of the same being. This is not some romanticized ideology; it was felt. I remember it.

This separation continued over a long period of time. Women, just like the Earth, were stripped of their voice and their essence. You can actually see the proof in our collective history as programmed men continued to claim other lands that were not theirs, destroying entire races of people in doing so, and brainwashing their own race in their pursuit. These programmed men became disconnected from their heart, the feminine side. And as they became further disconnected from themselves they got lost to a darkness of divide and conquer.

Again, this is some backstory to what I observed and remembered. Both men and women were healing war wounds they didn't understand they had. On the physical plane, both sides were healing from outdated programming or family trauma. But it was time now for everyone to take responsibility for their own healing and healing in their relationships. I continued working on this area of healing, which was about applying all that I'd learned from all of my relationships in order to prepare for my future partner. For me, a healthy partnership became my priority in life. I knew if I was going to meet a partner, I had to not only have myself together financially, but I also needed to heal these programs or as many as I could. I had to re-evaluate what I was magnetising to me. I needed to be clear on what I was emitting within myself and to others in order to be able to attract the partner that was right for me. I needed to understand what I valued in a relationship. I knew spiritual growth, happiness, love, truth, acceptance, good communication, and fun were top priorities. And I also valued patience and allowing people to be their true unique selves. I valued a queen, who embodied grace, beauty, caring, self-discovery, knowledge, and compassion. I valued someone who liked to see and do new things. I felt my higher self say, "You will choose when the heart knows it's right."

In my being, I knew this was the wake-up call for Divine masculine to move into union with the Divine feminine within himself and within his relationships no matter the sexual preference. He must shift from lower energy frequencies to match the Divine feminine vibration. As men, we must learn how to love ourselves every day. We must have the willingness to go back into past relationships and admit our faults and lack of awareness. I personally didn't know how to love the way I do now. And because I didn't know how to love, I may have hurt others. But I, as well as everyone else, had to find the ways we loved well. **Self-love is not destroying ourselves or others for our past experiences. Real self-love is correcting what doesn't feel good while embracing our highest qualities.** It was time to move on in love with myself and all things.

Her

After a few years, I felt my future partner on my radar screen. I didn't know who she was, but I could feel her, and I knew she was coming. I remember seeing in a vision years prior that when I met her, I must open up my heart and envelop her in the love energy and make the first kiss on her third eye. I knew that the love would be on a different plane, and the realization and feeling that it would be on a different plane was interesting to me. But I didn't necessarily know what it meant.

Then, a friend whom I had met in Mt Shasta six years prior was living back in Los Angeles. We decided to catch up and spent a few months hanging out periodically. We had a lot of respect for each other, but didn't really know each other personally. We spent some time together for a few months. On my birthday, I remember grabbing this specific friend's hand to have her walk in front of me and I felt a spark in our hands. In my right hand I felt nothing coming from the woman I was dating. "Shit." I had never felt that before. Soon after I moved on from the woman I was dating, not because I was ready to get into a new relationship, but because the same energy between us just wasn't there. Also, my friend was in a relationship with a woman and wasn't interested in men.

Weeks later we met up for lunch near the beach. During lunch I shared a crystal with her. We hugged at lunch, and I felt an energy in my heart start to flower. Low and behold, she had placed the crystal between us during the hug. I only saw it when we pulled away.

"What in the world just happened?" I asked.

She just smiled. It was like we'd opened up a heart portal.

We walked to the beach holding hands as friends, holding the crystal between our hands. I really saw this woman as a friend. Yet, something had shifted. Holding hands with her again now, I felt the same energy. My attraction for her was different. I could feel the corrected spiritual architecture in her aura. I had never felt that in someone else before. She was a student of the Sacred Rose. I could feel the true divine feminine embodiment was within her. When we made it to the beach, we felt a mutual call to bury the crystal and the energy into the sand somewhere. We found a spot, buried the crystal, and stayed to watch the sunset. Our hearts were open. Not in a way of sexual attraction, but an attraction, nonetheless. We knew it but had no intentions of moving forward with it. She had a partner, and I respected that completely. And an attraction more than a friendship didn't feel present for either of us.

A few months later, she told me she was ending her two-year relationship. Before I could catch my words, I blurted out, "I want to be with you." I was shocked. She was shocked. I said it without controlling it—the words just jumped from my mouth. Uh-oh… this was going to be different. To start, she hadn't been with a man since high school nor had any interest in doing so. She had trauma with men early in life and told me this was the first time she felt safe with a man. It made me feel like the work I was doing on myself was showing. If she was my reflection, I must be doing something right. But she wasn't sure if she was ready just yet and might have wanted to date other people. I told her it was ok, because I knew she needed the time to decide. But I told her that I wouldn't wait for long and that she would probably be wasting her time with other people. I didn't mean it to be cocky, but I just knew.

A week later, she decided she wanted to try with me, and we began dating. I told her I simply wanted to walk with her on this journey in life. I wanted to walk together on this spiritual path. That is what I felt, and it was very simple.

But intimacy was much slower. I was nervous and very much in my head to make sure she was comfortable and felt safe. It made me think about the way I had gone about things with women before. I usually didn't take things so slow, and I had to grow up as a man and approach things differently, especially with someone I cared about as a friend. This approach was a different foundation, it felt stronger. We had each gone through our own layers and levels of self-healing. And we were both willing to let go in ways we didn't expect. Most of the intimacy initially came from doing yoga together and stretching. I would place my hands on her hips and hold the stretch. I could feel the energy start to build in her and eventually she would start to cry. I realized there was pain and trauma stuck in her left hip. I could feel the energy brewing underneath my hand. I would breathe and just send light and love to her hips. She would cry harder. I would ask if I should continue holding the stretch and she'd say, "Yes."

I had to listen to my heart and to her heart about what she needed. I told her she was safe now. And she cried even harder. This happened on two different occasions. Afterwards, we would just lay there for almost an hour. She didn't know there was trauma still stored there, but we worked through it. I was learning a new way of developing a relationship with a woman. She was learning to let go with a man. I felt honored to learn from her and to be with her.

There is something special when a person is in union with themselves. Levels of healing can happen in ways that are hard to describe. It's as though lifetimes of healing happen. Both people recognize the weight or trauma of their partner is not their own. Some weight can be lifted when talking things through with a partner, however. I know now that I cannot heal everyone's scars, nor can they heal mine. But when we find someone, we love, we help take the weight off each other's shoulders. Telepathy between partners happens quicker. And different perspectives are accepted easier. I felt grateful for that. I had been wanting my queen but knew I had to find and heal my king self.

Heirogamic Union

Within weeks the divine union template was becoming a theme with us. Because I could feel and sometimes see the divine coding in my partner, I realized not all queens are divinely coded with the right architecture. And not all kings are divinely coded either. I discovered the coding is a God spark within them that creates an architecture where they operate from Divine Will as opposed to personal will. And this was an important discovery to see how I was operating myself. Only a king could see a queen's template. And it became clear my partner and I had reasons to grow together. We would get mutual messages simultaneously. We received the beginning guidance on a meditation for men and women to bring in divine union templates for them. It was all about sacred internal architecture coming from God Source.

For weeks I began to see King Arthur and Guinevere in my vision sitting at a round table. I knew there were other couples around the table, but I could not fully see them. I didn't understand what was happening, but I knew it meant something was developing. I had to be patient. I had learned enough to know this was an introduction, and I had to trust it. I started to question why divine relationships were hard to find in the real world. I had so many questions, as usual. And after being on this spiritual journey for a while I realized a lot of questions can go unanswered for a period of time. But I knew I would get a mission direction from my higher self and the answers would come. And not long after, the direction came.

I felt the call to work with men in their healing and spiritual journey. I had looked around at a few other men's groups. There weren't many to find initially, but one group seemed to be doing great work. I tried to reach out to this group multiple times throughout the year to offer my services, even for their young men's group – but I never got a response. After a while it felt like a sign that I was supposed to start my own. I also realized the pricing for these men's groups or retreats seemed too expensive. Even though I believe energy exchange is important and that people should invest in themselves, the modern economy was not allowing a lot of people to get the help they needed. I needed to create something affordable where more men on their spiritual journey could get help and talk with others similar to them. I continued to research other men's groups with large followings, but it felt like they were touching on pain points in men in order to get them to sign up:

"Wife cheating on you? Can't get a girlfriend? Do people bully you? Sign up for our course!"

It felt like it was bringing people together through trauma, and that didn't resonate with me. Maybe they do great work, and I'm sure they help a lot of men. But I felt into it, and it didn't feel personal, nor did it feel like it had any spiritual architecture in it. I stopped my research and kept returning to meditation and prayer. I asked for the highest divine masculine codes. King Arthur and Guinevere came back to me in my vision.

He showed me his sword, and she gave me a rose and smiled. The divine masculine and the divine feminine, the sword and the rose. Arthur's armor looked like it was made of gold and silver with huge gemstones all over it. Guinevere looked like she was floating when she walked. She felt like pure love and the definition of grace. They had a hierogamic union – a sacred marriage. They had a divine mission and the corrected codes within them. And it felt like their essence had been revitalized.

In another meditation, I saw a masked Egyptian man wearing black and gold. He looked like a pharaoh or king. I thought it was a version of me. In his right hand he held the crook and in his left hand, the flail. I had to research what the tools meant. The crook was only held by kings and pharaohs. The flail brought fertility. I asked his name, but couldn't quite make it out. He told me Nefertiti was his wife, and I discovered he was Akhenaton. Another divine union pairs. These two kings were going to help me. Somehow, I knew the queens were going to as well, but that would come later. I had some training with them and needed extra focus. They showed me a few codes that would be necessary to begin my training. I realized **great teachers give few lessons, as a student only needs a few tools to work effectively**.

MISSION WORK

Remember

I got another tap on my shoulders from my guides.

"Do you know who you are?" they said.

"Yes." Then, I was led into a meditation, and I was taken through the temples of healing with St. John the Baptist.

"The people need healing," he said. "We are one. Upgrades. Genetic rehabilitation. Let it go. It's ego. Let it go. What do you desire?" he asked.

"Love and finding home. But what is happening? What is needed of me?" I answered.

"You chose the path, remember?"

"Yes. I know,"

My guides surrounded me and continued. "Christ consciousness. We've been calling you. This is what you've been waiting for. Get your head out of the clouds. Ground. The task is at hand."

The time had come. The task was at hand to begin my mission

work. So, I began organizing my knowledge. My guides told me I would be building a school that is multi-dimensional in form. It was my task to build this school. It was about corrected angelic coding. The more the year went on, the more I realized this mission was about correcting DNA templates in humans and getting the planet back to its original divine coding. It was also about hierogamic union templating, where we have a balance of masculine and feminine energies within us, our partnerships, and a balance within the planet.

Spiritual Team

Later in the summer, I found a woman online whose videos resonated with me. I remembered her spiritually, and I was able to schedule a healing session with her. Weeks before, I was having visions of her and her son. I wasn't sure if he was actually her son, but in my vision, he was always looking over her shoulder to check and see if I was who I was. I had remembered them from past lives. I had worked with them before somehow. During my session with them, I remembered her immediately. We had definitely worked together before in past lives.

After the session I asked her about the vision and if she had a son. She brought someone on screen who was not her blood son, but her cosmic son. As soon as I saw him, I knew he was the kid looking for me. He was twenty-one and spiritually gifted. It felt like I'd found a part of my family. The three of us and the rest of her team connected all summer. By fall, she wanted to test my spiritual skills and gifts in her client sessions to bring on more healing facilitators to her team. I shared with her that I had worked with clients two years before but had decided to take a break because I had doubts about my abilities. But in these sessions, I would be working with the young man who was also spiritually gifted. I worked on three clients throughout the week while she "viewed" the session. It felt better working with someone else in the quantum healing space to double-check each other's work. I was shocked by how good the team was. They were shocked at how good I was. And after the third client, she gave me clearance to work with her team. It was another sign I was on my right path.

Angel Christ Michael

Angel Christ Michael began showing himself and appeared in my vision. For years, I always had a baseball-sized card of him in my car and a statue of him in my bedroom. I didn't understand my connection to him, but now, he was fully present and said he was going to teach me. His energy is huge. Angel Christ Michael showed me how he is the hand of God; his army is the fingers of that hand that cast out darkness. We were focusing on spiritual defense and demonic removal. They were the beginning teachings he gave me. And I was told to share the information with others. I pray that it helps.

Angel Christ Michael Protections

The most important note Angel Christ Michael gave me and for anyone called to use these techniques is to "STAY DISCIPLINED."

<u>Shielding</u>: Michael showed me his metal shield and sword. Most people recognize him for the sword and shield. He showed me; a sword is for protection, but it also means yielding power. A shield also represents protection, but it also means honor. Most people get a shield before they get a sword. And that is *if* they ever get a sword. They have to learn honor first—honoring the self, others, all beings, and all forms of existence, including the waters, fire, earth, air, and ether. Protecting others can be physical, spiritual,

or both.

Most people need to shield energetically. Shielding energetically protects against energetic residue from others. Just shaking someone's hand or the touch of another person's hand on your shoulder or body can release unwanted energetic residue. Shielding also helps against people who put curses on others. Sometimes these curses or hexes are intentional. But what I've also found is that most people are unaware they are putting curses on others, by simply yelling at them, thinking bad thoughts, talking negatively towards the person, or simply judging them with a negative eye. It is the same reason you have seen people wear the evil eye necklaces or bracelets to yield off these unwanted energies. Energetic shielding can protect others in the physical and spiritual, as well as the Earth.

Prayer is a major form of shielding. And that prayer can be empowered by visualization and consistency. A person should create a color for their shield. Try to use a white shield first. Imagine it as a sphere completely surrounding your body, eight inches above your head and below your feet. You can also create a shield for your home, your car, and even when you sleep at night. Like all things, empower your sphere with passion! You can use prayers you already know. "Yea though I walk through the valley of the shadow of death, I will fear no evil, for the Lord is with me, the rod and thy staff they comfort me." -Psalm 23:4

Another important step as you shield is to add a cloak overlay. You don't want your shield to be seen by others. There are different types of cloaks—3D, invisibility, and anything left up to the imagination. A 3D cloak is good for your day-to-day shielding. An invisibility cloak is good to practice if you are ever in moments of danger in the physical or the spiritual realm. The invisibility cloak should be practiced consistently – yet used sparingly in public, as a person could disappear from view and actually draw more attention.

Shielding and cloaking are best for highly populated areas like cities, airports, concerts, amusement parks, etc. Imagine that all the people who walk around cities or airports are leaving an energetic trail behind them, similar to car exhaust or airplane chemical trails. If a majority of these people are leaving behind a negative energetic trail as you pass through, it only makes sense you would be passing through a negatively charged area or energy field. In other environments such as concerts, the energy given off from the crowd could be siphoned. There have been numerous reports over the last decade of people feeling like their energy was being siphoned at concerts, the concert goers feeling drained and out of balance. That is because some concerts are dark ceremonies that capture enormous amounts of energy.

Most importantly, there are others who train in the dark arts and are very aware of energy. Some of these dark artists can throw energetic weapons towards others to harm them, track them, or feed off them energetically. These could be energetic darts, hooks, chains, and the like. These weapons can have cords attached to them and be connected to the person or entity. Some people have so many cords they are puppets to their master, knowingly or unknowingly. I've also seen a lot of energetic cords come from sexual partners where the sexual energy is being used by one partner, whether they consciously know it or not.

With all of this information it is important for the reader not to become paranoid. This is only to develop more awareness. Which is why these tools have been around for centuries. And they are meant to be practiced and empowered. It's important to know how to use your spiritual tools to prevent unwanted energy or if a person happens to come under spiritual attack.

Strike: A strike is used in a spiritual altercation. A person can spiritually strike with a tool or by sending out intentional energy. For example, an energy sphere can be sent to freeze the opponent, or to blast the opponent away. An energy sphere filled with love or healing light can be empowered and sent as a strike as well. Remember, demons can't stand in the energy of love. You can also send a strike that repels the negative energy and returns it back to the sender. Any strike must be empowered by practicing it. The number of different types of strikes a person can create is up to them. All of us can move and shift energy, it is our birthright.

An energetic strike can also be felt in the physical. It is the same as using "the force." If a person sends out love or healing to a person, the receiver may all of a sudden feel better or protected. It starts in the spiritual, but can be felt in the physical. The types of shields and strikes created and used are only limited by a person's imagination. Less is more. And empowerment and practice are key.

Remove/Heal:

Remove and Heal is a prayer used if you want to remove an entity from yourself or your home. It must be spoken at least three times and with conviction.

"In the name of God,
In the name of the Holy Father,
In the name of the Holy Mother,
In the name of all the Angels of Light,
In the name of Angel Christ-Michael,
I command you to be removed and banned from this person/place."

Speaking Truth:

Speaking truth cuts through the veils of illusion/lies. It can help heal mentally, emotionally, and spiritually. It is the real way of casting spells for good or breaking spells for freedom and sovereignty. Speaking the truth is connecting to the sword (power) and shield (honor/protection) to help others. But not all are meant to speak. Angel Christ Michael made it clear for me to be aware of my own energies. And at the same time to trust myself. A person must be aware of the entities they speak to. Angel Christ Michael said, "Do not let your eyes deceive you." A person needs to know themselves, scan themselves, and have good spiritual hygiene. They need to know the vibrations and mannerism of the beings and team they work with. It's all about knowing the true energy signatures. Speaking the truth and commanding other beings or entities to do the same will cut through the illusion and trickery.

There is more to know with spiritual tactics. But not all is meant to be shared here. These are the foundations to help people on a base level. These tools may seem uncommon to most people. But they are meant for the few that were looking for them. Most people will use shields and prayer once they realize spiritual targeting and attacks are real. That is why the tools are here for reference.

True Kings

In continuing with the story, I began to see dragons and feeling King Arthur and Queen Guiniveire in my vision. I had seen dragons before, but it seemed as though King Arthur and Queen Guiniveire were shapeshifting from dragon form to human form in my vision. I heard, "Kings. The Round Tables." What does it mean?

I heard, "The true kings must return to their thrones. The kings must enter the simulation. Women need them now, more than ever. You're going to have to get over it, whatever it is. You're going to have to step into the true architecture or be left behind. Our sisters, mothers, nieces, daughters, need us. Ignite, embody, and walk the Earth. It's time!"

This was interesting. I knew it was going to lead to something. I just wasn't sure what it was.

Throughout the remainder of the year, I continued to write this book and work with clients in healing sessions. I still didn't feel called to perform anymore. And by this time, I had organized all the spiritual experiences I had had and the tools and exercises I had learned throughout the years. I knew it was time to focus on the school that needed to be built. God immediately told me it would be called True Kings Academy. It would be an online school to help men heal and step into their divine blueprint.

Throughout the entire building process, I was working spiritually with King Arthur and King Akhenaton on how to build the men's academy. They gave me the structure of the course, showing that it would be held up by four pillars—Protect, Provide, Heal, and Lead. The foundation and higher connection was God. The men were going to finally sit in their thrones, which were located in the heart. The throne is a spiritual architecture. Once seated on the throne that is within the heart, a man can get direct correspondence from God on how to lead. There are other divine masculine men who sit at their thrones, who consult and pass down sacred information. Of course, the divine feminine eventually comes into play, as a king is not a king without a queen and vice versa. But the men need counsel and guidance from each other first before joining with the divine feminine.

Each side must understand and master their own practices before joining together physically or alchemically.

Creating the coursework for the academy came fast. And as I was creating it, the woman I worked with said in passing that she wanted to have a course for the male clients. I told her I was already working on it, so she gave me the go ahead to lead the first course and promoted it to her following. I realized the doors couldn't open without the blessing of a goddess. It takes a goddess or priestess' blessing for some spiritual endeavors to manifest into reality. So, it began. I had six men for the first sixteen-week course. I brought on her spiritual son and a gentleman that was a little older than me to have three different generations of men present. For sixteen weeks, we worked through the course and quickly created a bond. For the men, it was a safe space and a mentorship where spiritual and life questions could finally be answered. For me, I had no doubt I was in the right seat. It had been twelve-plus years of dedication for this arrival, and I had spiritual and physical guidance throughout the entire process.

I was at another part of my vision. And I knew writing this book would be for anyone who had questions on their own spiritual journey. Stories are meant to be shared to spark curiosity or to pass down wisdom for others. So where do we go from here?

XV
WHERE DO WE GO FROM HERE

Returning to the True Self

If anyone is willing to take time to develop themselves spiritually, they will inevitably "wake up" to the true state of the world and the illusions of society. They will eventually find balance and a closer relationship with nature and their true self. The true self that is led from the heart and not ego. This awakening process has its ups and downs. But that is also the ebb and flow of life. These ups and downs are what many call the "Dark Night of the Soul," when a person's belief systems begin to crumble and their foundation of programming falls beneath them. This process may take months or years to work through, but everyone can get through it.

On the other side of the Dark Night of the Soul is truth, wisdom, and new eyes. This person will begin to become temporarily enlightened and they will want to tell everyone about their experiences. I feel it's best for people to keep these realizations and visions to themselves for the first few years if possible. In the eagerness for others to wake up, the newly awakened want to give their all in helping the collective because their hearts are open. When they find other people may not be responsive, they will unintentionally "other" them. And everyone should be careful not to become judgmental of others. If a newly awakened person speaks as "all-knowing," they will eventually become humbled through some experience or being corrected by an elder. A great shaman once told me, a person should never share their big vision, that is personal to them. Only some visions are meant to be shared.

But I completely understand this part of the awakening process – a person wants everyone to be "awake." It's the heart's desire for everyone to "get it." But it takes time to realize how long humanity has been in darkness. A collective awakening does happen in certain eras, when many people all over the world receive collective insights, downloads, and prophecies within the same few years. The reality is that humans wake up separately and at their own timing. This can't be forced, and no one should try to rush someone else's timing or experience. Everyone arrives in their divine timing.

Steps to Remembering

"Free your mind. Empty your cup."

We are higher dimensional beings who have returned to this planet to heal our karmic past, wake up out of the false matrix, evolve into higher states of consciousness, and help humanity and the Earth to ascend. Humanity fell from a higher dimensional plane called Gaia, then Tara, and into lower dimensional Earth after many spiritual wars with different factions of negative aliens. These are some of the same wars spoken about in ancient religious texts. DNA digressed, cosmic ancestral memory was wiped throughout lifetimes, and souls and soul groups were either harvested or severely fractured. Humanity was placed under a frequency net that keeps them in a lower vibration for energetic harvesting. The DNA digressions in bloodlines and memory wipes disconnected spiritual templates within the human body and the Earth. It's similar to missing very important hardware and software for your energetic system.

The aim for humanity is to heal individually and collectively in order to heal the species and the planet and to remember we are all One. We are all connected to the planet and God Source. Even though our beliefs may differ, they are all roots to the same tree, the Tree of Life, the true twelve-grid tree. All paths lead to One. The Light is operating differently now, which is why things will continue to evolve, and the war will not go on forever. The fight is not a fight anymore; it's a letting go. That is where we are right now.

If you don't know why you're here on Earth at this time or you're seeking your ancient origins or past lives, it's good to begin asking sacred questions to your higher self or God. It's best to communicate through the heart. Speak your prayers and meditate to remove interference of the mind or trickster energy in the field. You can begin with these examples of sacred questions to help you or if you've had a bit of confusion on what questions to ask.

"I returned to Earth. Where did I come from? Please, show me."

"I am here on Earth. What is needed of me? Please, show me clearly."

Also, be patient in receiving, as some answers don't come right away for many reasons. You could still be asking from the mind, or it may not be your time for the information. Stay consistent. You can ask your benevolent ancestors to come through, your higher self, or God. But in asking for information from your ancestors or angels, ask them to come one at a time so you can begin to build a relationship with them. I also always suggest lighting a candle and preparing offerings—water, flowers, cornmeal, tobacco, etc. You can also ask what they like specifically. Some like candy, so get them some candy. It may or may not make sense to you, but an offering is showing up in thanksgiving. It's an energy exchange.

Pay attention to the signs. Using your heart as the eternal compass, follow the breadcrumbs of signs and symbols that lead you further on our journey towards enlightenment, atonement, and evolution. As we pick up the internal and external signs and symbols allow yourself time to digest the new information, just as you would in school. If you take in too much spiritual information or try too hard to understand, you will burn out. If you try to receive all the downloads and upgrades you want so badly in the time YOU want…your physical body would literally explode. There is so much light and plasma in some downloads and the information is meant to be revealed over time. It's in you but it won't completely click until certain phase locks release in your physical, emotional, or spiritual body. So, my impatient friends who are stuck on the idea of time, sit with it. Allow yourself to BE uncomfortable with it. Know it. Because in time it will become a part of your unconscious competence. You will just KNOW.

Another sacred prayer you can put out to your higher self is:

"God or Higher Self, please reconnect my DNA to its highest original blueprint. I choose to be in Oneness and on my highest ascended timeline. Help me bring it forth. Thank you."

Steps to Healing

Here are more sacred questions you can ask yourself over time.

"I want to return to and live from the heart. What is in my way?"

"Where do I need to grow?"

Sacred questions for purpose:

"What do I prepare for?"

"How am I needed?"

"What is my soul mission? My vision?"

Remember to unplug from Babylon. Cry and dance and sing through all your pain and joy, it's only a clearing. Forgive yourself and others. Do not judge. Empower your Light every day. BE quiet. BE still. Higher vibrational consciousness evolves in the heart by slowing down. It develops through love and knowing there is Oneness in all things. Higher timelines are real and eventually it will feel more and more like you're in this world but not of it.

Expressing ourselves is an essential part of healing. When we talk to a professional, a friend, or someone close to us and they listen with full intent, healing begins immediately. But we cannot just be selfish in always talking or dumping our thoughts and feelings on others. A lot of healing also comes from truly listening intently to others and holding space. Listening without interruption allows the listener to find a new perspective which could lead to a different approach. This new perspective should only be offered if the person is willing to receive the information. A new perspective or new approach tends to lead to healing.

Other main principles that lead toward healing are simple:

Eating healthily or steps towards eating healthily. I've noticed when I eat less, I'm also lighter. My guides have told me many times to eat fruits and vegetables because they contain Light energy from the sun. Our light bodies need Light.

Moving Energy—most people need to move their bodies to move energy, especially when doing spiritual work. Tai Chi, qigong, yoga, or light exercise is huge in terms of healing. It helps move stagnant energy in the body. I have had many clients where I can see their energy is stuck because they need to move. Simple light jumping or bouncing is amazing to break up energy in the physical and spiritual bodies. Shake that booty!

Using the Voice—humming, singing, or chakra toning. We don't use our voice much beyond talking. We used to sing and shout, whether in ceremony or in play. Let it go!

Meditation—Just quieting the mind. Meditation or sitting in a sit spot does take practice, especially when it comes to initially quieting the mind. I sometimes think, "Still the pond, still the mind." Or I'll focus my breath and repeat the prayer, "Peace, be still, and know that I Am God." What I've realized is that slowing the breath allows our body's pulsation rate to slow down. When our body's pulsation rate slows down, our spiritual body's pulsation rate can speed up, leading us to our higher selves, higher frequencies and higher dimensions. But it's important to find and be stillness first with no objective, no thought, and no emotion.

Breath Work—Everything begins and ends with the breath. God created all of the universes through "the breath." We inhale 50 percent of the time and exhale 50 percent of the time. It is a lesson in duality; we need both. An average person normally doesn't breathe deeply enough or get enough oxygen to their brain. Whether rapid or slow breathing, a person should take their time with this. I even suggest that some people may want to work with a professional, especially when practicing shamanic breathing.

Psychedelics—A lot of people in certain cultures and spiritual communities have used plant derived psychedelics as part of their practice for thousands of years. It's clear I've done my fair share of journeying with different types of plant medicine. But as a healing tool, I only say it should be used in a ceremony or an intentional way. Any psychedelic can have negative effects if used in the wrong way or used too often. But most psychedelics offer some of the most beautiful journeys a person could ever experience. For anyone who has worked with psychedelics or is considering it, I would suggest there always needs to be an intent in working with the medicines.

You can ask simple questions like:

"Please show me what I cannot see." Or...

"Please show me how to heal _____ within me." Or...

"I ask to receive my magic/mission/special skill. Teach me like you taught the masters."

I also suggest bringing an offering of some sort before your journey. If you don't have anything, simply say, "Thank you," to the medicine. Respect the ceremony. And remember, the medicine is there as a catalyst. At some point, you shouldn't need it.

Psilocybin mushrooms are also magic depending on where they are sourced. It has become such a huge industry that it may have changed the resonance within the medicine. I feel as though they reach different planes of existence and experience compared to other medicines. But they can be very good in tuning into the Earth frequencies on a deeper level. I also suggest working with a professional shaman or space holder and using this medicine in ceremony.

Ayahuasca—Mama Ayahuasca is a beautiful and master teacher. It has been used for ceremonies for centuries and is very powerful. Again, as with most ceremonies, it depends on the shaman's self-preparation and intention in alchemizing the medicine. I have journeyed with the medicine many times and I believe Ayahuasca specifically should only be administered by shamans or people who have a history with the medicine. Remember, the medicine is not necessarily dangerous. What makes the experience dangerous are the "pop-up" shamans, those not from ancient lineages who are harvesting, preparing, or administering the medicine without the proper training. There are also dark shamans who work black magic, and it is up to the participant to do their research on the Ayahuascaro. The medicine of Mama Aya has also turned into a bit of an industry. In my last journey with Mama Ayahuasca she showed me she was going to lash back at those that were abusing her medicine. She knows she is being used for profit. It felt like a microcosm of what is happening to Earth Mother.

Lastly, I've seen plenty of people who want to experience plants who are not well prepared. They come with the "just heal me" attitude, which is very lazy. We can't heal if we don't first try to heal ourselves. People can have "bad trips." But the nature of the plant is not to "trip." It is meant to journey within oneself if he or she is actually ready. A person will know it is their time to work with the medicine once they know internally they are being called by the plant. Being called is very very important, yet most people don't know how to listen. Mama Ayahuasca, for example, is a grandmother plant that can bring much wisdom and healing. Those who come into ceremony not respecting her or the journey will definitely feel her wrath. But those who listen and are open in their hearts will purge what they need only to find that she is there to help them release their old paradigm and find the beauty in themselves and all things. This is not to deter anyone. These are only things to pay attention to. Whatever medicine or ceremony you decide to participate in, always remember to follow your heart, no matter what. If the medicine is for you, the "call" will be clear, and you will know it in your gut. Certain things are meant for certain people, and I only suggest to follow your heart.

Where Do We Go From Here

As I've come to grow older and somewhat wiser, I've concluded that realities on this planet and even realms beyond our veil are much more complicated and fascinating than I could have ever imagined. The possibilities are truly infinite! One of many truths I've learned is that the only way to meet our future is to evolve consciously from our present moment. Happiness, peace, and internal freedom is a daily attunement. It's what we tune into that dictates how we feel. The current consciousness ascension is all about healing ourselves to remove old programs and beliefs, connecting to our ancestral and star lineages to activate our DNA, helping us remember who we truly are and to embody original timelines of peace, harmony, and balance. We are galactic beings with the opportunity to become cosmic citizens again within the larger intergalactic society. And there are many star races on the Earth, within the Earth, within our solar system, and outside our solar system who are helping us. They are waiting for us to return to this remembrance.

We have the choice to wake up from the dream. There are many people who choose to live close to the Earth, who choose to open their hearts and heal and who choose to evolve. We're one of the few generations with technological advances, yet we lack a connection to our natural environment, resulting in poor mental, emotional, and spiritual health. Those who awaken to their higher potential eventually emerge into higher energy timelines. Some can remain in higher consciousness and timelines. Most people fluctuate back and forth between realms. But as more people remember their connection to the planet and cosmic history, the truth will also ripple to others and help in their evolution as well as the Earth's evolution.

I believe because I remember. And I only share a critical choice point to those who will listen and feel this in their hearts. We get to choose, because this time is a very special time. The Ancients always knew this time period of galactic spiritual evolution was coming again. Throughout time they have been waiting for this 26,556-year cycle to end and begin again. And that is exactly where we are as a humanity, in a time of complete transition into a Golden Age. As we rebirth, we will see destruction, but we must continue to have faith and live from our heart, even with the fire around us. It is the purifier, a way for all beings, including the Earth, to truly phoenix. As we shed our old selves, the Earth is shedding her "old" self and releasing herself from the negative frequency net that has kept her from giving and receiving the energies she's used to. We need to stand up for her – Earth Mother –in her divinity.

For people who are struggling, if they were to ask me, "What's it all for?" I would say the choice is up to them. Humankind has been asking themselves the same question for ages. The great spiritual leaders always showed us that if we can reconnect to ourselves and reconnect with Source, things become clear. It doesn't mean that situations are always solved. It just means they will be clearer. Christ taught us to resurrect from our old ways and to rise above the ways of the world. He did not judge or separate himself from the world. He placed himself in it. Christ is not returning as man; Christ consciousness is returning *within* humankind. The true Christ or Krist energy has returned as an energy of pure loving Source to those with open hearts, pure intent, and with willingness to live beyond the self, as service to others will benefit all. This Christos consciousness has always taught the same lesson—that we are all one. It is unity consciousness based on The Law of One. We can all walk this path with peace, which I believe everyone would agree is priceless.

We both individually and collectively choose what path we want to take—a service to self or service to others. This idea felt like separate paths to me for a long time. Even though they can be different paths, I don't think these choice points always need to be completely separate. I think we can have abundance while helping others on their path. I'm completely aware that the extreme service to self is what drives and destroys society and the planet in the form of greed. But not all people are meant to directly serve others; we can help our local communities and whomever else we meet on the path while taking care of ourselves. Historically, it's always been a few in each generation who are meant to take the path of the medicine people, prophets, and spiritual healers. So, each of us gets to decide which frequency we want to operate from and which timeline we choose. The decision is happening now at this very moment on a day to day. To those who can hear, this is a final call. The Earth is ascending and there is angelic help.

"Your reality is what you choose to create."

What Have I Learned on This Earth?

If you were to walk to the "Gates of Heaven" and you had to look at your life and the trail you left behind, what would you see? What would the reflection in the mirror look like? Did you help anyone? Did you touch a life beyond your own? We have the opportunity now to reflect. I don't remember where I heard this quote, but someone once said, "It's about falling in love with the problems you want to solve in the world." For me, love is the foundation. Self-love naturally transmits acceptance of self and others. If the whole world had love, there wouldn't be as many problems. There would be less judgment, division, and less destruction. We could return to respecting all beings on this planet. I pray that every person will know love; that they will feel love with every fiber of their being.

I've learned the fight is not a fight; it's a letting go. We are breaking free and rebirthing from an old and dark paradigm. If more people unplug from the matrix, if we simply say "no" in our mind, heart, and consciousness, we can no longer be used or manipulated. If we don't play the game, who do they have to fight? Eventually, all evil implodes on itself.

Empowering the Future

I dream of a world run by clean and free energy and where everything produced can be safely and equally returned to the Earth. I dream that people won't need jobs just to survive and that they can do what they like and be fairly compensated. A world where all beings are free from all mental, monetary, and physical slavery, and where greed no longer exists. I dream of this planet being a place of peace, where no person worries about their day-to-day safety, where wars are unnecessary, and everyone agrees there is enough to share. I dream of having direct relationships with other beings, traveling to other planets and galaxies, and learning from other benevolent races. A time when humans can become part of the galactic society again. I pray these dreams continue to become a reality.

Exercise

Take a moment and imagine a world you want to live in. Close your eyes and go there. See it with your mind's eye. See the colors. Maybe Buddha is doing the moonwalk on cotton candy rainbow clouds. Maybe the people you see aren't necessarily people. Maybe they're trees that walk and talk. Maybe you're riding a Pegasus with golden hair. Maybe your best friend is a sixteen-foot blue-haired teddy bear that has a great sense of humor. In this place, YOU can be anything. You can speak any language. Maybe you don't even use words at all. But in this world, you are fully accepted and fully loved. Everyone is One. Go there.

Now, let's say you're immersed in this world that is amazing and beautiful, a place of no time. And let's say you hear there is another world called Earth. But in this world, people were slaves to others, and they didn't even realize it. They are being forced to do things against their will, and many are being tortured or killed. What would you do? And again, the choice is yours. Would you chill out and enjoy your heaven? A place of beauty and no time? Or would you look into this place called Earth to see what's going on? You could look away, continuing to enjoy your life as normal with no judgment. But let's say you choose to do something to help these other little creatures break free. How would you do it? And why would you do it?

Would you fly them up to your world of heaven? Would you watch and observe for a while to make sure you didn't impede their planetary and universal laws? Would you put them on a spaceship and whisk them away to wherever their hearts desired? What would you do? Put yourself there now. But this time transport yourself into the body that is now doing this exercise. Oh, hello there, friend. There you are. Do you see now?

So the questions remain:

What have you learned in your time on planet Earth?
What will you do to help others and the planet?
What would you like the world to know?
What gifts would you like to leave in the future?

Plant your seeds deep, family. Stand, or sit, or be still. Grow your roots so deep that when you rise, you can't be plucked. Grow so strong the winds cannot move you; they can only make you dance. Enjoy the soils for now. Enjoy the darkness for now. Grab all the minerals and nutrients you can. As we grow, we rise. That is why we are here. That is why we are strong. Because we are the ancestors of a new generation. It's about acceptance and passing the torch of White Light. That is why we have faith. Keepers of the Light, unite! I love you.

• *311*

www.ingramcontent.com/pod-product-compliance
Lightning Source LLC
Chambersburg PA
CBHW070944160426
43194CB00030B/1430